FRENCH ENTRÉE 6

BOULOGNE

Pays d'Opale and Picardy

FRENCH ENTRÉE 6

BOULOGNE

Pays d'Opale and Picardy

Patricia Fenn

Quiller Press

Other French Entrée guides:

French Entrée 5 Brittany
French Entrée 8 The Loire
French Entrée 9 Normandy Encore
French Entrée 10 South of France
French Entrée 11 Paris
French Entrée 13 Provence

First published 1987 by Quiller Press Ltd
46 Lillie Road, London SW6 1TN
Updated and reprinted 1990, 1993

Line drawings: Ken Howard
Area maps: Paul Emra
Cover: Tim Jaques

ISBN 0 907621 83 X

Printed and bound by Firmin-Didot (France)
Groupe Hérissey - N° d'impression : 23777

Contents

Notes on using the book and an appeal

1 The area maps are to help the reader to find the place he wishes to visit on his own map. Each place is given a reference on the relevant area map, but they are not designed to replace a good touring map.
2 o.o.s. stands for 'out of season'. Other abbreviations such as f for francs are standard.
3 L, M or S in the margin stand for Luxury, Simple and Medium.
4 H stands for Hotel and R for Restaurant and C for Chambres d'hôtes in combination with 3 above, ie (H)S, (R)L etc.
5 The ➛ symbol means the establishment fulfils exceptionally well at least one of the author's criteria of comfort, welcome and cuisine (see also pages 8-9).
6 Credit cards: 'A' = Access, 'AE' = American Express, 'V' = Visa, 'DC' = Diners Club, and 'EC' is Eurocard.
7 Ⓜ means market days
8 The figures above the addresses. eg 62000, are the postal codes, which should be used in all correspondence.

Author's appeal

In order to keep 'French Entrée' up to date I need all the latest information I can get on establishments listed in the guide. If you have any comments on these or any other details that might supplement my own researching I should be most grateful if you would pass them on.

Please include the name and address of establishment, date and duration of visit. Also please state if you will allow your name to be used.

Patricia Fenn,
c/o Quiller Press
46 Lillie Road
London SW6 1TN

Foreword by Bill Moses,
Hoverspeed's Managing Director

The privilege of being asked to write the foreword to a gastronomic guide about the Boulogne, Côte d'Opale and Picardy region comes at a time of particular significance as we are now the only ferry operator providing a cross Channel route to Boulogne.

This company has enjoyed a long association with Boulogne, operating hovercraft services as Hoverspeed from 1981 and previously as SeaSpeed since the late 1960s. Our coveted relationship moved into the future in 1991 with the introduction of the world's largest and first ever car-carrying catamaran SeaCat onto the cross Channel routes operating from Dover to Boulogne.

In 1992 Hoverspeed introduced a SeaCat onto the Folkestone–Boulogne route, realising the exclusive advantages of these two ports and their popularity amongst ferry passengers, particularly for the day trip market.

For the many passengers who visit France for a day or longer, Boulogne and the Côte d'Opale conjure up an immediate atmosphere of a real taste of France, more than any other port, town or region.

Our customers are familiar with the quality provided by Hoverspeed and this guide will help to discover the delights of a region with so much to offer and within easy reach of the town of Boulogne.

Hoverspeed's fast cross Channel services can bring you closer to the chic resort of Le Touquet, the mediaeval town of Montreuil, sandy beaches of Hardelot and Berck, picturesque valleys of the Course and Canche, Edwardian Wimereux, the artistic delights of Desvres, the forests of Hesdin and the battlefields of Agincourt.

It is a pleasure to introduce our customers to the culture and gastronomy of a unique region of Picardy.

Bon Appétit

Author's Preface to Third Edition

There can be no area of France where more changes have taken place in the last few years than that of the North. New autoroutes have brought hidden villages into prominence and made backwaters of towns through which the old routes used to thunder. The imminence of the Channel Tunnel hangs over the whole area, the effects of which are uncertain, but bound to be enormous. P&O have pulled out of Boulogne and the town will now have to find a new identity beyond its port.

Hotels and restaurants have had to adapt to changing needs. For some it will all mean new prosperity, new opportunities; for others the changes have not been kind and they have given up the struggle. In this area, more than any other, the British market is of prime importance and the future prospects of many a French family depend on its whims. It is certain that many more GB cars will arrive in the Pas de Calais in the next few years, but will they stay, or will the new easy exits encourage them to hasten south?

I believe that the joys of the short break in France will become a regular feature in the experience of ever larger numbers and that it will be more than ever important to look for good value and interesting situations. I forecast the rise and rise of the chambre d'hôte, representing outstanding value and the chance to meet the locals; I am convinced that the hotels and restaurants that adapt to the new conditons will offer even better value; I hope that by the time I come to write a new book on the North of France there will be many more treats to describe. Meanwhile, please remember that this guide has not been re-written – only updated to fill the gap.

Please keep writing to tell me what you have discovered and help me make future Entrées more valuable to you.

Please address correspondence to Quiller Press Ltd., 46 Lillie Rd., London, SW6 1TN. I promise to acknowledge all letters eventually, but please be patient.

Patricia Fenn

Entrée to the 'Entrées'

One of the most welcome comments on the French Entrée series has been that they are a good read. I take it as a compliment that a friend keeps his in the lavatory. I know by now that some 'regulars' will be buying FE6 even if they have no immediate prospect of going to Picardy, and they, who have heard it all before, might well skip this resumé of the raison d'être for the books, and get on to the nitty gritty.

The idea is to cover one region of the vast country that is France at a time, in considerable depth, at a price cheap enough to make the building up of an increasingly comprehensive library possible. Unlike most guides, which generally concentrate on a little of a lot, FE offers a lot about a lot of little areas, so that if one option fails – if one desirable hotel/restaurant is too far, too expensive, too full, closed – another is readily available.

Most important is that the reader should have enough information to make up his own mind as to what is right for him. Symbols are fine but they're not going to wise you up about the hidden extras, like a drunken patron or the disco blaring all night. For this kind of background briefing it is absolutely essential that the experience should have been sampled and described first hand. Then you decide. You may well like the idea of a booze-up with the boss or somewhere to rave-up with the little number you met on the boat.

The arrows (see p.17 for a list) are the ideals, worth arranging a holiday around, tested and verified. But it's no use suggesting only these paragons; there are many times when second-best is far, far better than none at all. So other ideas, with suitable reservations, have been included to offer a choice, and one or two warnings away as well as towards. Value for money in all categories has been the prime consideration.

Throughout the range, though prices are creeping up and the exchange rate deteriorating, you can expect a lower bill than at home. It will be interesting to see what effect the de-blocking of prices will have. Some say that profiteering is inevitable, others that free competition will be good news for the customers. We shall see.

Time was when you could hardly go wrong in France – the

welcome was warm, the food wholesome and cheap, wherever. Sadly that's no longer the case – the freezer has arrived, short cuts are common, children no longer wish to follow their parents in running a hotel or restaurant. I personally particularly deplore the vanishing veg – tinned are common, frites a cop-out, even when the market stalls are brimming. So that's all the more justification for a good guide. Old readers will know that this will be a subjective guide, with all the faults and strengths that implies. Its author's prejudices will be obvious – however much she may live to regret it, she would choose an individual, preferably family-run, establishment with all its unpredictability, to a sure-fire chain hotel, with reliable plastic-cube bedroom. Part of the justification for this tunnel vision is that any fool can track down the latter without help, and be pretty sure what to expect, without pages of description. The only exceptions are where a stop looks desirable and there is no more colourful alternative, or where readers have been particularly enthusiastic about one of the despised species.

Readers' letters have been, as always, a fund of practical up-to-the-minute information. Although my boast is that I have personally inspected every entry in the book at least once in 1986, my experiences might have been atypical. Look at the Hotel Univers at Arras to see what I mean. A steady trickle of year-round reports is the only sure way to check on what's what. That said, I still reserve the right pigheadedly to differ, and reading between my lines is not only allowable but desirable. Please keep writing, particularly as a large part of the area covered in FE6 is new territory and I need feed-back. I promise to answer all letters personally, somehow, sometime.

Categories

French Entrées are not designed for one income group. My theory is that we all have need of different kinds of bed and board on different occasions (even the poor have birthdays, even the rich lose their credit cards). So the categories, 'L' for Luxury, 'M' for Medium and 'S' for Simple, are designed to suit some of the people some of the time:

'L' will meet only exacting standards. Not only must the hotel be comfortable, it must be special in some way – its building, its service, its furnishing, its site, its food. Look at the Château de Montreuil (p.113) for a good example.

Anything above 500f a night for a double room would come into the L category and quite a few below. When you consider this is the equivalent of £30 a head, you will realise that luxury hotels will be available in France to readers who could never consider their equal at home.

I would expect recommended 'L' restaurants to cook exceptional food and serve it in elegant surroundings. The chef should be able to add a touch of genius to mere professional competence. Here are the places to judge the *nouvelle cuisine*. If the limited choice on the lowest menu happens to appeal, you'll get a bargain, often cheaper than at humbler establishments, and cooked with the same flair as the à la carte extravagances. These menus are often only for lunch and rarely at weekends. Otherwise expect to pay upwards of 200f in this category.

The best **'M'** hotels are comfortable and pleasant, well equipped and, by virtue of being mainly family-run, assure a warm welcome. Essentially bourgeois and proud of it.

The food in this category should be good enough for *demi-pension* to be acceptable. This is where the modest stars can be found – the *chef-patrons* who lack only the long professional training to equal the big names. Their ingredients, though more modest, should be just as fresh and preferably local; their dishes, though less elaborate, should show some individuality and no short cuts. The price range is roughly from 200-500f for a double room with bath, or around 150f without, and from 90-200f for a meal.

When judging the **'S'** group, bear in mind that there is nothing quite like them at home. At under £10 a head for a bed and £5 for three courses, certain allowances should be made. (The cheapest hotel in the book, the Hôtel de la Gare at La Chapelle aux Pots, see p.85, charges 96f for a room and 52f for a meal.) For this you should expect undoubted cleanliness, hot water in bedroom, washbasin and shared bathroom, but not powerful light bulbs, thick piled carpet, fleecy towels and free packets of bath oil, nor even soap. Above all, the welcome is important in these modest, invariably family-run establishments. Here is where you are most likely to get to know the patron and the locals. You'll get atmosphere even if you have to forget some of your back-home standards.

I get more excited letters about 'S' establishments than for any other. And I can understand the thrill of the chase for a bargain. However, a bad meal is never a bargain and it is all too easy to end up with a waste. Don't even think of asking the *patron-chef* to come up with something too *recherché* for his limited talents. Stick to the simplest dishes on the menu and if he buys honestly and freezes nothing, you're on to a winner.

HOVERSPEED SEACAT FROM FOLKESTONE – THE ONLY ROUTE TO BOULOGNE

Hoverspeed introduced a SeaCat on to the Folkestone – Boulogne route in April '92 and is now the only cross-channel operator for what has always been a popular motorist and foot passenger route. They operate up to 6 sailings daily on the Folkestone–Boulogne route with a crossing time of just 55 minutes.

The SeaCat Folkestone–Boulogne service provides both the cross channel link for London–Paris–London rail services, where passengers benefit from the quick transfer arrangements from ship to shore at both ports, and also the link for the prestigious Orient Express.

SeaCat is the largest catamaran ever built and the first to carry cars, with a capacity for 80 vehicles and 450 passengers.

Features include panoramic views from the central and side lounge cabin areas. Every passenger has an aircraft style seat. There is a separate lounge bar at the stern of the craft and an outside deck area. Forward there is an observation deck with views through to the bridge. Duty Free shops, mother and baby room and vodafone facilities are also on board features.

Markets

We Brits go to France to sleep cheaply, eat well and to shop. The markets are more than just a utility – they are part and parcel of the French scene, and everyone loves them. Take your time strolling round the colour and hubbub, and experience the pleasure of buying from someone who knows and cares about his wares. The man selling you a kitchen knife will be an expert on knives and will want to know what you need it for; the cheesemonger will choose for you a cheese ready for eating today or in a couple of days' time, back home. Trust them. Choose for yourself the ripest peach, the perfect tomato and buy as little as you need and no more, so that you can buy fresh again tomorrow. Stock up on herbs and spices, pulses and dried fruits, soap scented with natural oils, honey from local bees, slices of farmers' wives' terrines – every village a veritable Fortnums on market day. The day of the market in the nearest town is listed in most entries.

Closing Times

The markets, like the rest of the town, snap shut abruptly for lunch. I regularly get caught out by not shopping early enough; if it's going to be a picnic lunch, the decision has to be made in good time. From 12 p.m. to 2.30, and sometimes 3, not a cat stirs. At the other end of the day it's a joy to find shops open until 7 p.m. Mondays tend to be almost as dead as Sundays and it's likely to prove a grave disappointment to allocate that as a shopping day.

It does not pay to be casual about the weekly closure (*fermeture hebdomadaire*) of the restaurants. It is an excellent idea to ensure that not every restaurant in the same town is closed at the same time, but do check before you venture. Thwarted tastebuds are guaranteed if you make a special journey only to find the smug little notice on the door. 'Sun. p.m. and Mon' are the most common and often it will take a good deal of perseverance to find a possibility open then.

Booking

Sunday lunch is the Meal of the Week, when several generations settle down together to enjoy an orgy of eating, drinking, conversation and baby-worship that can well last till teatime. You should certainly book then and on fête days. Make tactical plans and lie low, or it could be a crêpe and a bed in the car. French public holidays are as follows: New Year's Day; Easter Sunday and Monday; Labour Day, 1 May; VE Day, 8 May; Ascension Day; Whit Sunday and Monday; France's National Day, 14 July; The Assumption, 15 August; All Saints' Day, 1 November; Armistice Day, 11 November; Christmas Day.

If you wish to book ahead and do not speak French, try and find someone who does to make a preliminary telephone call. If necessary, write in English and let them sort it out but make sure when you get the confirmatory letter that you understand what you've booked. Many hotels nowadays will ask for a deposit. My method is to send them an English cheque; they then either subtract the equivalent from the bill or return the cheque.

Make good use of the local tourist bureaux, where you will find English spoken. Let them do the booking for you if you have problems. This is the place to pick up maps and brochures.

Maps and Guides

Good maps are essential and I must stress that those in the front of this book are intended only as an indication of where to find the entries. In addition to the relevant Michelin maps I counsel the purchase of the green Michelin guides, *Flandres, Artois and Picardie* and *Environs de Paris*, both unfortunately only available in French.

The red Michelin, apart from all its other virtues, has useful town maps. It's a bit slow to spot a newcomer though, unlike its rival Gault-Millau, also now in English, though I prefer the French version. This gives more specific detail but has less comprehensive coverage and is strongly biased in favour of *la nouvelle cuisine* (its authors did invent the label in the first place); it is useless for the really basic hotels and restaurants.

Logis de France do a good guide to their hotels, obtainable at the French Government Tourist Bureau at 178 Piccadilly. This is the place to go for general advice, free maps and brochures and details of the admirable gîtes system, which provides simple self-catering accommodation in farmhouses and cottages. We have stayed in gîtes all over France and found them invariably reliable and cheap, and often more comfortable and interesting than hotels, but you have to be quick off the mark to book the best in peak season.

The rise of the *chambre d'hôte* is a phenomenon I particularly welcome. They fit in perfectly to most of my requirements of having character, being family-run, and offering good value for money, but because these are not professionals, the need for vetting is even more important. I found that when they are good they are very, very good and that when they are bad they are excessively horrid. Several are such stars that I could easily have made them Hotels of the Year.

Wine

Restaurant wine is a common hiccup in more ways than one. The prices are meant to be controlled like those of the menus but somehow they creep up to ridiculous mark-ups. It is not uncommon to find the bottle of plonk that costs 6f in the supermarket on the menu for six times that amount. The patron's local reputation stands or falls by his house wine, so at least try the 'réserve de la maison', 'choix du patron', though these are more likely to be red than white. Travelling alone, I often want just a glass of wine, and this is maddeningly difficult to achieve. Wine bars may have arrived in Paris but certainly not elsewhere in France. I am very pleased that we persuaded Jancis Robinson and John Doxat to write the wine and other drink sections this year, see p. 163, and they can offer some good advice here.

Breakfasts

A sore point. The best will serve buttery croissants, hot fresh bread, home-made preserves, a slab of the slightly salted butter favoured in the area, lots of strong coffee and fresh hot milk, with fresh orange juice if you're lucky. The worst – and at a price of between 150 and 400f this is an outrage – will be stale bread, a foil-wrapped butter pat, plastic jam, a cup of weak coffee and cold sterilized milk. Synthetic orange juice can add another 10f to the bill. If you land in a hotel like this, get out of bed and go to the café next door.

Bread

Everyone loves French bread but débutantes to France may not realise how much it varies. Look for the *boulangerie* with the longest queue and buy your *baguette* or *pain* there. Ignore the plastic-wrapped hypermarket specimens – you'd buy better French loaves back home. It all goes stale very quickly, so unless you can get it in a freezer promptly its not worth stocking up, however delicious the freshly-baked specimens might be.

Similarly croissants can be very nasty from an inferior *patisserie*. 'Au beurre' are the richest and best, but cost a bit more.

Speciality bread shops selling dozens of different varieties of bread are a new breed in France, and still only to be found in big towns. I like the brown variety with hazelnuts embedded, but generally the traditional crusty white is too good to forgo.

Take with You

Soap (only the grander hotels supply it) and a decent towel if you're heading for the S group and can't stand the handkerchief-sized baldies. If self-catering, take tea, orange juice, breakfast cereals, biscuits, Marmite, marmalade – all either expensive, or difficult to locate, or horrible.

Bring Home

Beer is a Best Buy and the allowance is so liberal that you can let it reach the parts of the car that other purchases fail to reach, i.e. load up. Coffee is much cheaper; cheeses are an obvious choice if the pong is socially acceptable. If, like me, you have a weakness for *crème fraîche* and resent paying double at home, you can rely on it staying fresh for a week, so long as it's not confined to a hot car. I buy fresh fish if I see a boat coming in while I'm homeward bound, and early expensive vegetables like asparagus, artichokes, mange-touts and the wonderful fat flavoursome tomatoes. Electric goods, le Creuset pans and glassware are often cheaper. The notes on pp. 165 and 168 will help choose the best bargain of all – the wine – now in vastly greater quantities.

Tipping

Lots of readers used to the outstretched British hand worry about this. Needlessly – 's.t.c.' should mean what it says – all service and taxes included. The only exception perhaps is to leave the small change in the saucer at a bar.

Changing Money

Everyone has their pet method, from going round all the banks to get a few centimes advantage, to playing it the easy and very expensive way of getting the hotel to do it. It depends on how much is involved and how keen a dealer you are as to how much trouble it's worth. I change mine on the boat, where I have always found the rate to be very fair. If you get caught outside booking hours, the *bureaux de change* stay open late.

Telephoning

Most of the public telephones in France actually work. You put your 1f piece in the slot and watch it roll down for starters, then as many more pieces as you estimate you will need. If it's too much, out it all comes at the conclusion of conversation.

To dial UK from France: 19, wait for tone, 44, then STD code minus 0, then number.

Inter-departmental: Province to Province: Dial just 8 figures (eg 21.33.92.92)
Province to Paris: Dial 16, then 1, then 4 followed by 7 figures (eg 1 6/1/4X XX XX XX)
Paris to Province: Dial 16, then the 8 figures
Please note that all numbers you refer to should be 8 figures only [eg. 21.86.80.48 not (21) 86.80.48].

To dial France from U.K: 010, pause, 33, 8-figure code.
Emergencies: Fire 18; Police 17; Operator 13; Directory Enquiries 12.

Writing

Do use post codes (given next to map reference) before each town when writing, ie. 62200 Boulogne-sur-Mer or 80301 Picquigny.

Arrows

These are the hotels and restaurants that have consistently pleased readers for the following reasons:

Amiens *Le Prieuré* (HR)M Prime position, historic building, good value
Hôtel de l'Univers (H)M-L Extremely comfortable central hotel
Les Marrissons (R)L Good value haute cuisine in an attractive setting
Le Saladin (R)S Good cheap lunch stop
Anserville *Madame Coubriche* (Ch d'h). Comfortable and cheap.
Arras *La Faisanderie* (R)M-L Superb food
Attin *Auberge du Bon Accueil* (R)S No. 1 choice for good value family restaurant with interesting cooking
Aubin St. Vaast *Madame Vezilier* (Ch. d'h).Comfortable cheap rooms
Boulogne *La Liègeoise* (R)M-L Luxury cooking at reasonable prices
Bar Hamiot (R)S Boulogne institution
Le Fats Domino (R)M-S Good value
Chez Jules (R)M-S Cheerful, bustling, good food
Bournonville *Auberge du Moulin* (R)S Outstanding value
Chépy Auberge Picarde (R)S Unusually good cooking for the area
Cucq *Chex Claudine* (R)M Reliably good value
Douriez *Madame Graux* (Ch d'h.) Comfortable, cheap, attractive setting
Inxent . *Le Relais Equestre* (H)S Budget accomodation on the river Course
Lumbres *Le Moulin de Mombreux* (R)L Haute cuisine in attractive setting

Montreuil *Le Château de Montreuil* (HR)L No.l choice for luxury accomodation and outstanding cooking
La Grenouillère (HR)L Best cooking in North of France?
Onglevert *Maison de la Houve* (Ch.d'h). No. 1 choice b. and b. in North of France
Pont de Briques *Hostellerie de la Rivière* (H)M(R)L. High quality cooking and inexpensive accommodation near Boulogne
Le Touquet *Le Café des Arts* (R)M Interesting cooking at affordable prices

New Arrows.

These are the restaurants and hotels that have emerged as outstandlng value since the last guide was published:

Auchy-les Hesdin *Auberge le Monastère* (HR)M. Good value, friendly owner.
Hesdin *Café Jules.* (R)S Really French, really cheap
Preures *Auberge de Preures* (R)S New owners, best value in district
Wierre-Effroy *Ferme-Auberge de la Raterie* (HR)S Wonderful rural atmosphere
Wimille *Relais de la Brocante* (R)L Best cooking in Boulogne vicinity.

Boulogne, the 'Pays d'Opale', Picardy, Somme

Coast to Capital

They call the Nationale Un *La route des Anglais,* because it is always full of English intent on belting down the 243 km from coast to capital with as little reference as possible to maps and scenery on the way.

If the drivers have to stop *en route* it's usually by *force majeure.* They find the nearest bed and grumble about the traffic noise. 'Dreary journey,' they say. 'Thank God that's over.' Pity.

As the N.1. slices neatly through the middle of the area covered by this book, no suggestion for meal or bed is more than a short detour from it. Many are worth more than a necessity one-night stand.

As in the other *French Entrées,* I urge you to make full use of local maps (Michelin 236 covers the North, 237 the area nearer Paris) and to leave the artery of the red Nationale to follow some of the narrow veins of the yellow or white roads that lead off it. I guarantee unforeseen pleasure.

The region undoubtedly merits a visit in its own right, not just as a transit camp, and perhaps an overnight stay might be the introduction to a subsequent weekend or longer. After all, hardly anywhere is more than a two-hour drive from the port, and look at the variety on offer.

Rewards come early. Just inland from Boulogne is the little known region of the Boulonnais, dotted with rounded hills, forests, rivers, manor houses, ancient mellow farms. Try taking the D233, following the little river Wimereux, and see if you can any longer doubt the picturesque rusticity of this area so near the tourist beat. Follow any of the rivers in fact, the Course, the Canche, the Authie, the Ternoise, the Somme, the Oise, and you find villages, villagers and scenery very different from those popularly associated with the North.

The coast can offer similar contrasts, from the rocks and spectacular cliffs of my northern limit at Cap Gris Nez, along the opal coast, via the busy port and shopping centre of Boulogne, through the vast sand dunes around Hardelot, where the tide disappears into the horizon, to the sophisticated glitter of Le Touquet, down to the unique Marquenterre bird sanctuary, on to the wide estuary of the Somme with its huge skies, and the two charmers, Le Crotoy and, particularly, St. Valéry, on either side.

Inland, favourite towns, all ideal for winter breaks, are the ramparted Montreuil, Picardy's historic capital Amiens with its intriguing watery surroundings, fascinating and unique Arras, royal Senlis, all with arrowed restaurants and hotels that add up to a good reason for leaving home.

This battlefield of Europe bears many scars and memorials as lasting witness to its tribulations. Its rich and inoffensive farming land is where yeomen archers lined up, where horses were caparisoned for battle, where trenches were cut, where marching boots churned up the mud, where tanks rumbled, where treaties were signed, and where the victims of the conflicts fell, body upon body. It's such a short drive and such a long time between Crecy and the Somme.

There is no other region that can rival the gothic churches and châteaux of Picardy. In villages, cities, crossroads, throughout the countryside you can trace the development of gothic art, from the first pointed arch (at Morienval) to the final expression of the flamboyant. The cathedrals of Senlis, Amiens, Beauvais, the abbeys of St. Germer-de-Fly and St. Riquier are individual history lessons of the conception of the religious architecture of the times; some, like Amiens, constructed with such industry that a young craftsman might have lived to see its completion; some like St. Riquier, whose building was interrupted by war, and St. Germer, with additions and reconstructions that explain, as no schoolteacher could, how fashions changed in the intervals.

In the southernmost limit of this book, where Picardy merges into the Ile de France and less than 50 km from Paris, lies the incomparable Chantilly, whose château and stables, together with the enchanting neighbouring Senlis, alone would merit an excursion to this region. The eastern boundary is the autoroute, mercifully diverting much heavy traffic from the old N.1.

Gastronomy in the north tends towards the hearty and the traditional rather than to the delicate and *nouvelle*, but that is not to say there are not some sophisticated high-fliers, and seven Michelin stars, along with the simple village inns.

Ingredients are prime. The northern seafood is unbeatable, vegetables from the dark rich soil supply much of the rest of France, the lamb gain flavour and plumpness on the salt marshes, crisp apples and pears are the basis for many a 'tarte maison', chestnuts and game thrive in the forests. Thick warming soups, like the soupe des hortillons made from cauliflowers, carrots, artichokes, leaks, are staple; frogs from the *étangs* surrender their legs, their fellow eels end up in pâté. Amiens' pâté de canard en croute has been made there since the 17th century; Abbeville and Montreuil use woodcock for their speciality terrine; entrails from the fat black pigs go into the andouilles from Arras.

With all those rivers there is no shortage of fresh water fish, and many a little inn has wisely based its reputation on serving a trout straight from stream to pan. Carp and pike, as well as eel, feature on many of the *menus régionaux* which are commendably beginning to re-appear.

Ficelle picarde is probably the best-known and ubiquitous regional dish – pancakes layered with ham in bechamel sauce, with mushrooms, cheese or whatever.

Cheeses from the north owe little to subtlety. Not for the faint-hearted are the Boulette d'Avesnes, the Maroilles, the Dauphin, but do try them, discreetly.

Northern chill induces a fondness for a sweet, and every town has its full complement of *chocolatiers* and *pâtisseries*. Crunchy tuiles d'amandes are worth bringing home from Amiens, buttery croissants are the best anywhere.

No wine is produced in the area, but plenty of cider and beer, and wine is often replaced in cooking, so that coq au vin becomes coq à la bière. Houblons (baby hop shoots) are tender delicacies certainly not to be missed for the short period they appear on enterprising menus.

Good News

Boulogne now has a good central brasserie once again. Chez Jules in the Place Dalton has been completely re-vamped by the Leuleu family, formerly of Le Manoir at Hesdin l'Abbé, and can now be heartily recommended for a first or last taste of French food for families, parties, or anyone else for that matter.

At Pont de Briques Pierre Martin has upgraded eight rooms, which at around 300f, are now worthy of the standard of cooking in his dining room. This has always been a favourite place to stay – indeed there is none other in the immediate Boulogne area where you can fall straight into bed after a superb meal and now there should be no hesitation as to where to book a gastronomic weekend.

A recent meal at the Relais de la Brocante at Wimille was a strong indication that an arrow is long overdue here. Local residents confirm that this was not a one-off and that the standard is consistently high.

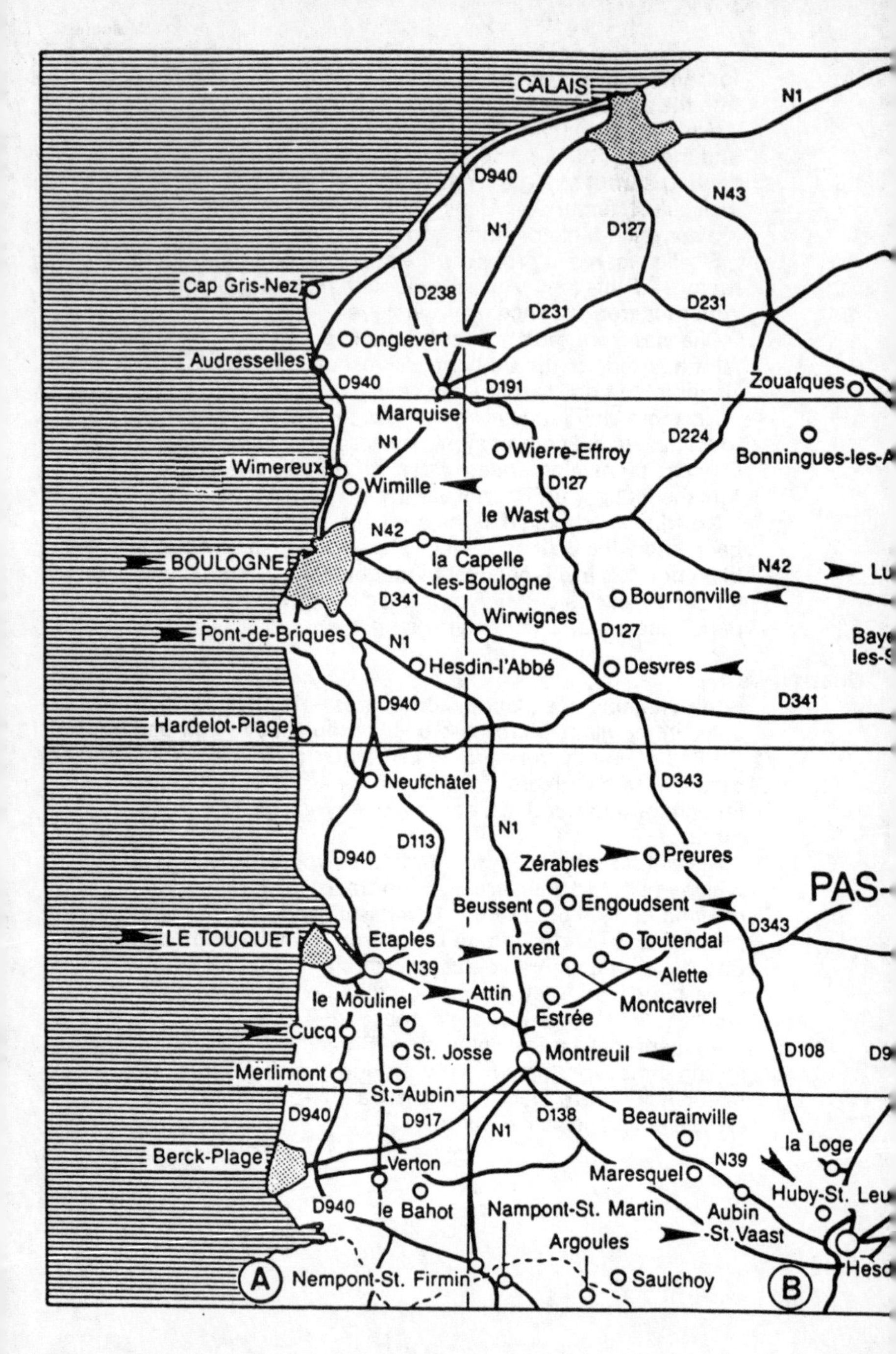

CALAIS
N1
D940
N43
N1
D127
Cap Gris-Nez
D238
D231
D231
Onglevert
Audresselles
D940
D191
Zouafques
Marquise
N1
Wierre-Effroy
D224
Bonningues-les-A
Wimereux
D127
Wimille
le Wast
N42
BOULOGNE
la Capelle
-les-Boulogne
N42
Lu
D341
Bournonville
Wirwignes
Pont-de-Briques
D127
N1
Bay
les-
Hesdin-l'Abbé
Desvres
D940
D341
Hardelot-Plage
Neufchâtel
D343
N1
D113
D940
Preures
Zérables
PAS-
Beussent
Engoudsent
LE TOUQUET
Etaples
D343
Inxent
Toutendal
N39
Alette
Attin
le Moulinel
Montcavrel
Estrée
Cucq
St. Josse
Montreuil
D108
Merlimont
St. Aubin
D940
D917
D138
Beaurainville
N1
la Loge
Berck-Plage
Verton
N39
Maresquel
Huby-St. Leu
le Bahot
Aubin
D940
Nampont-St. Martin
-St. Vaast
Argoules
A
Nempont-St. Firmin
Saulchoy
B
Hesd

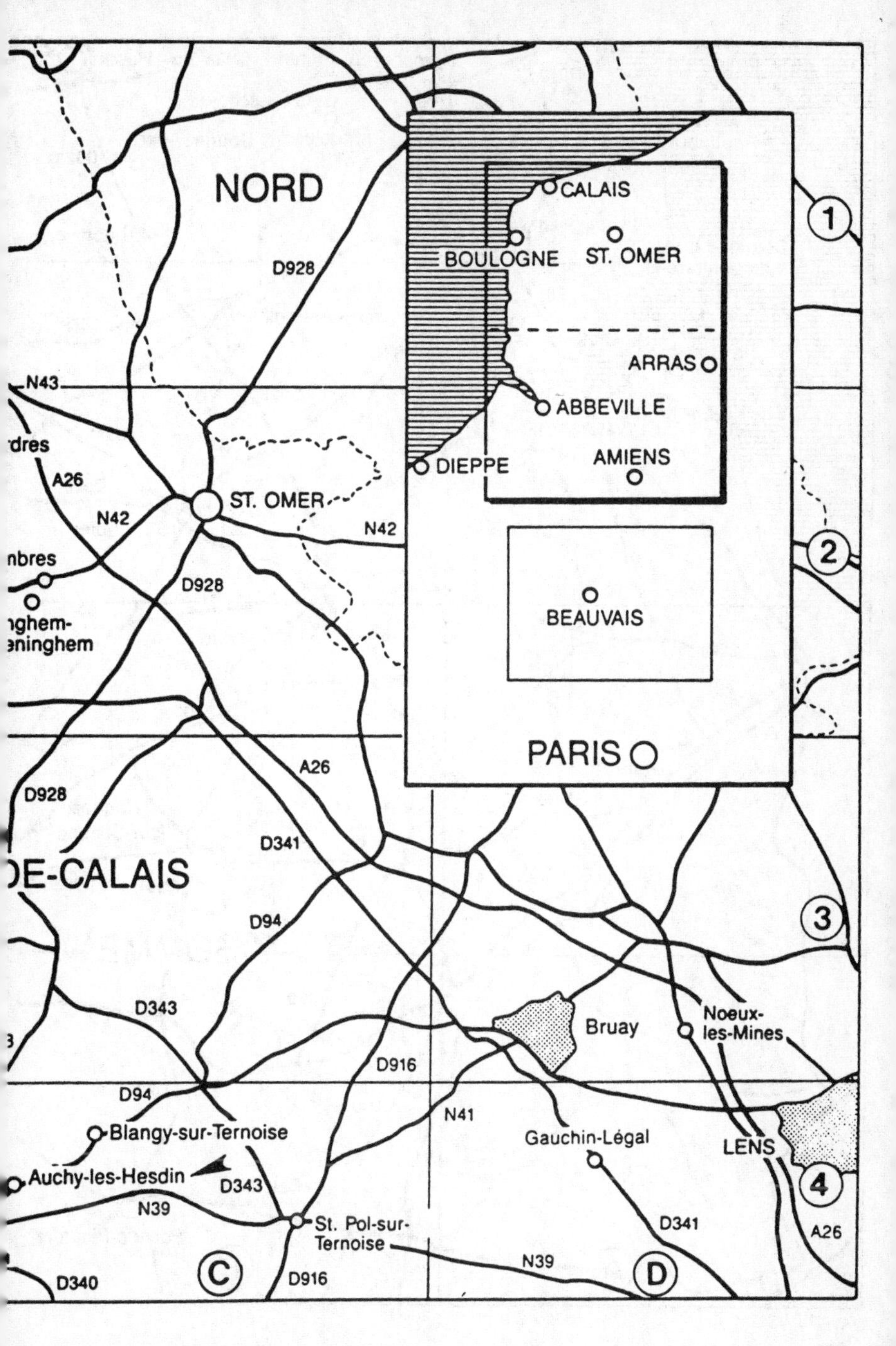
NORD
CALAIS
BOULOGNE
ST. OMER
D928
ARRAS
ABBEVILLE
DIEPPE
AMIENS
N43
rdres
A26
ST. OMER
N42
N42
nbres
D928
ghem-
eninghem
BEAUVAIS
PARIS
A26
D928
D341
DE-CALAIS
D94
D343
Bruay
Noeux-
les-Mines
D916
D94
N41
Blangy-sur-Ternoise
Gauchin-Légal
LENS
Auchy-les-Hesdin
D343
N39
St. Pol-sur-
Ternoise
D341
A26
N39
C
D
D340
D916
1
2
3
4

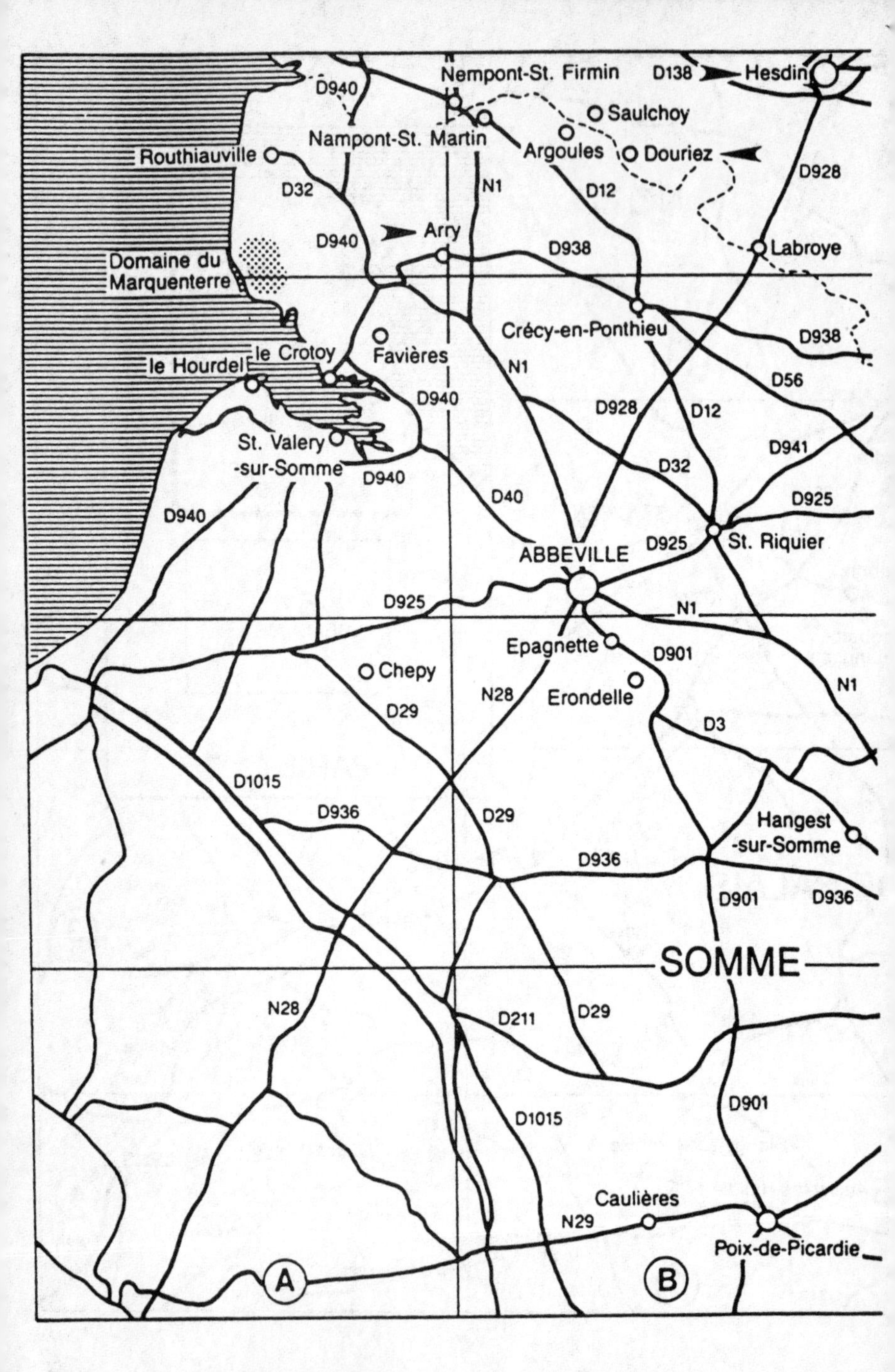
Nempont-St. Firmin
D138
Hesdin
D940
Saulchoy
Nampont-St. Martin
Argoules
Douriez
Routhiauville
D32
N1
D12
D928
D940
Arry
D938
Labroye
Domaine du Marquenterre
Crécy-en-Ponthieu
D938
le Hourdel
le Crotoy
Favières
N1
D56
D940
D928
D12
St. Valery -sur-Somme
D941
D940
D32
D40
D925
D940
ABBEVILLE
D925
St. Riquier
D925
N1
Epagnette
D901
Chepy
Erondelle
N1
N28
D29
D3
D1015
D936
D29
Hangest -sur-Somme
D936
D901
D936
SOMME
N28
D211
D29
D1015
D901
Caulières
N29
Poix-de-Picardie
A
B

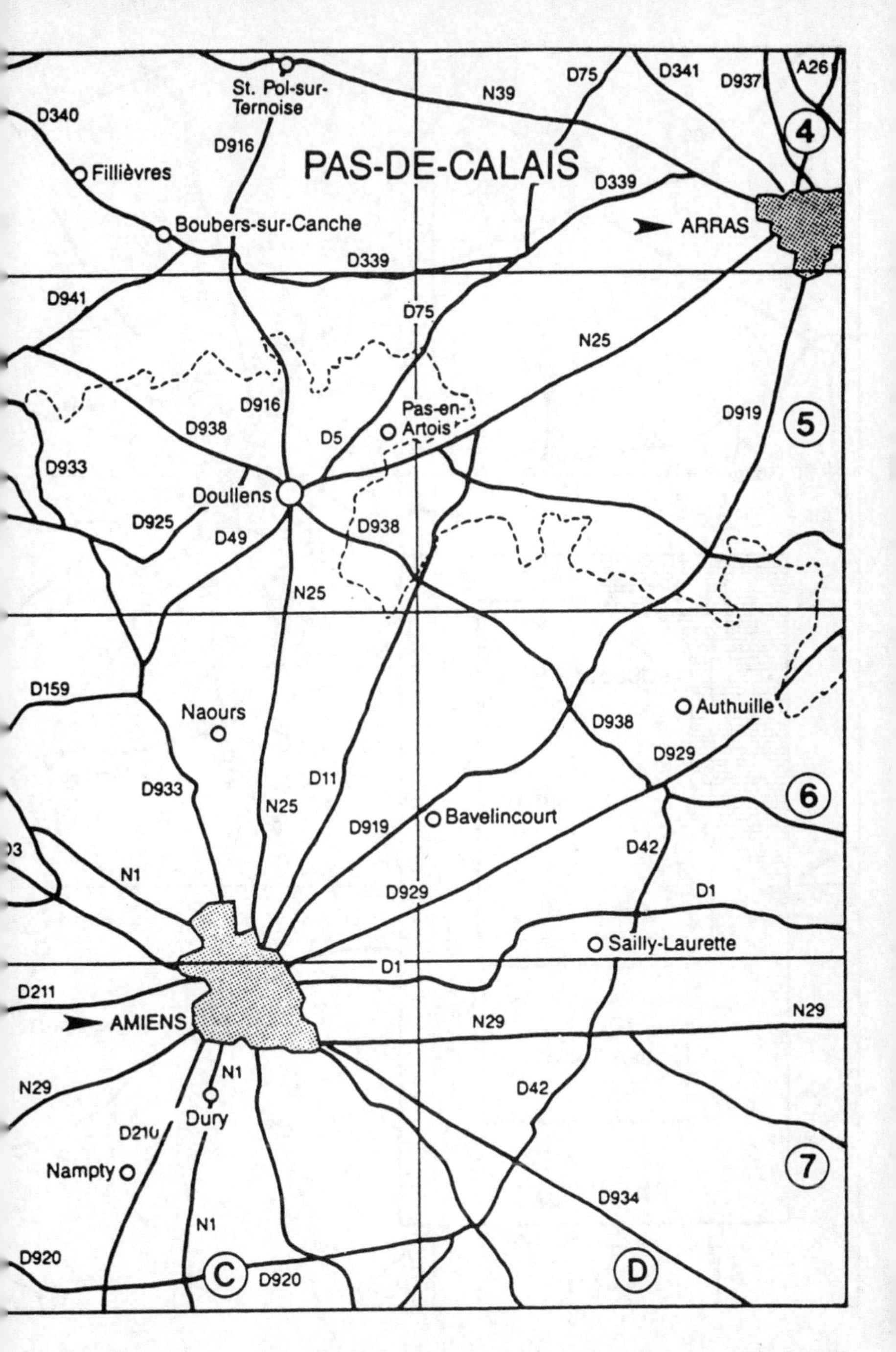
PAS-DE-CALAIS
St. Pol-sur-Ternoise
D340
D916
Fillièvres
Boubers-sur-Canche
D339
D941
N39
D75
D341
D937
A26
4
ARRAS
D75
N25
D916
D938
D5
Pas-en-Artois
D919
5
D933
Doullens
D925
D49
D938
N25
D159
Naours
Authuille
D938
D929
D933
D11
N25
D919
Bavelincourt
6
D42
N1
D929
D1
Sailly-Laurette
D1
D211
AMIENS
N29
N29
N29
N1
Dury
D210
D42
Nampty
7
D934
N1
D920
C
D920
D

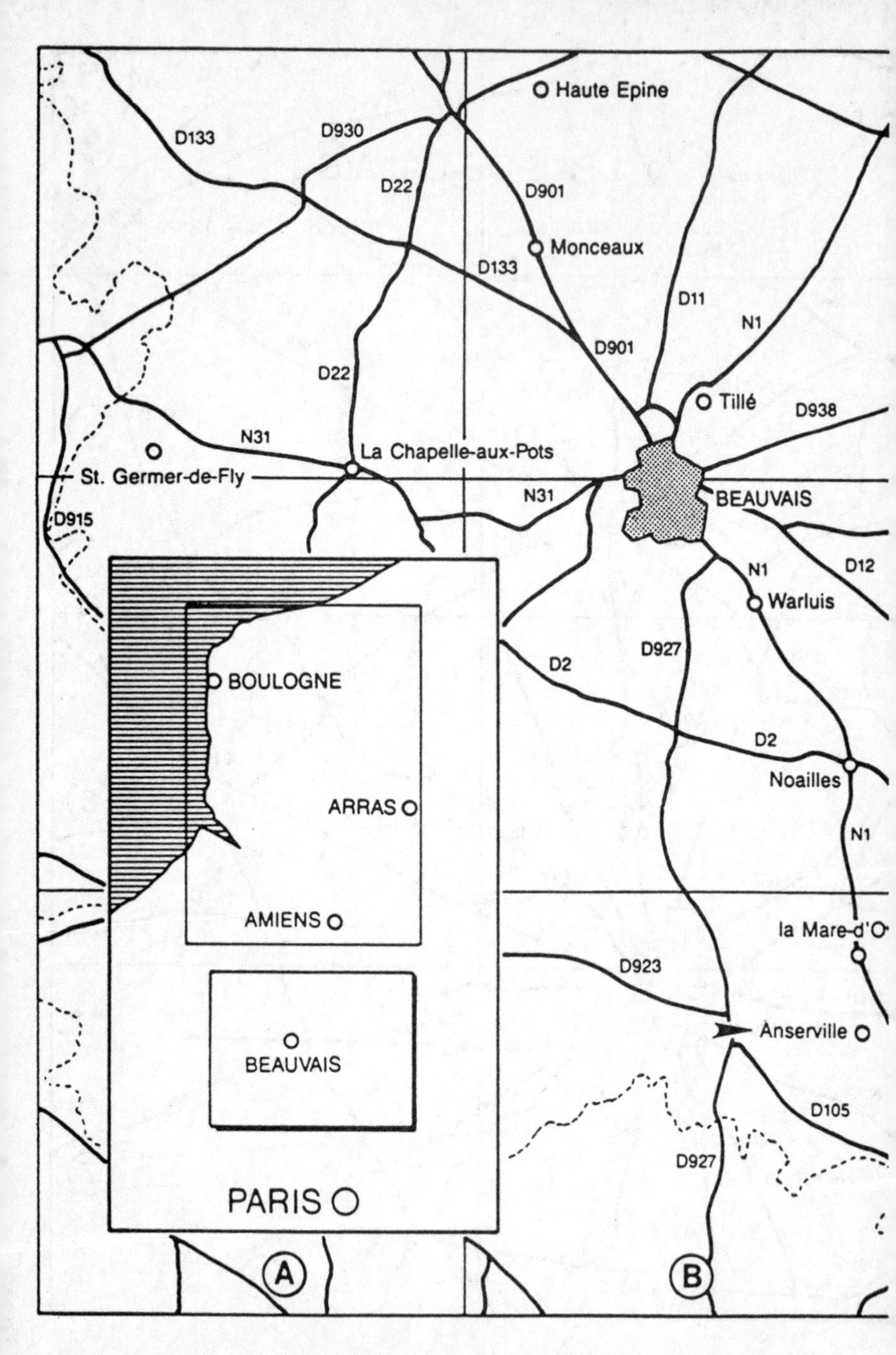
Haute Epine
D133
D930
D22
D901
Monceaux
D133
D11
N1
D901
D22
Tillé
D938
N31
La Chapelle-aux-Pots
St. Germer-de-Fly
N31
BEAUVAIS
D915
N1
D12
Warluis
BOULOGNE
D927
D2
D2
Noailles
ARRAS
N1
AMIENS
la Mare-d'O
D923
Anserville
BEAUVAIS
D105
D927
PARIS
A
B

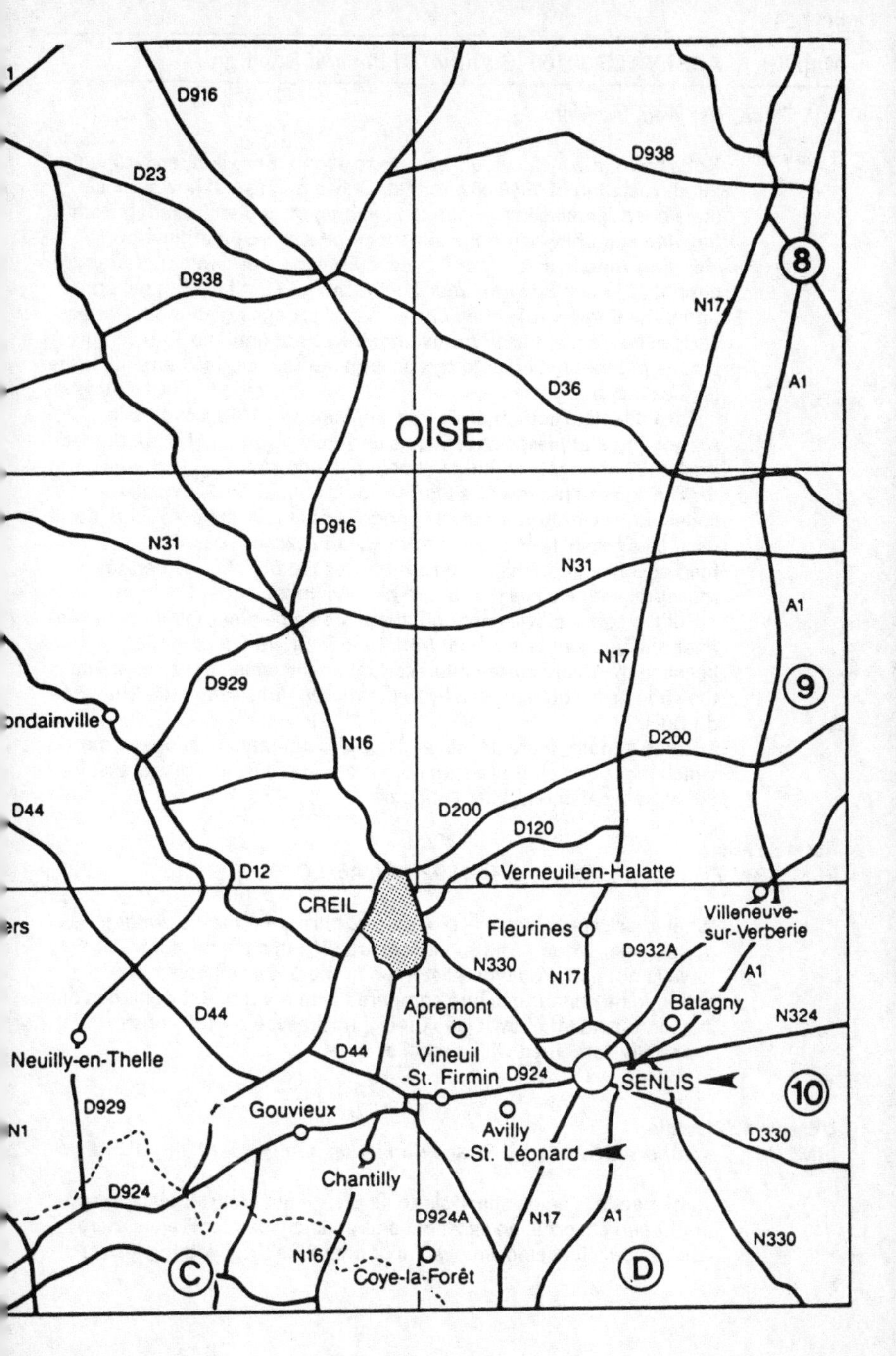
D916
D938
D23
8
D938
N17
A1
D36
OISE
D916
N31
N31
A1
N17
D929
9
ondainville
N16
D200
D44
D200
D120
D12
Verneuil-en-Halatte
CREIL
Villeneuve-sur-Verberie
ers
Fleurines
D932A
N330
N17
A1
Apremont
Balagny
N324
D44
Neuilly-en-Thelle
D44
Vineuil-St. Firmin
D924
SENLIS
10
D929
Gouvieux
Avilly-St. Léonard
D330
N1
Chantilly
D924
D924A
N17
A1
N330
N16
C
Coye-la-Forêt
D

Map 5B **ABBEVILLE** 80100 (Somme) 81 km s of Boulogne

Thurs., last Wed. in month

Not a town in which I would choose to spend more than an odd night - the devastation of 1940 saw to that. Only a glimpse of how it must have been remains in the isolated building of character, dating from the 16th century when Abbeville was a prosperous maritime port, shipping wine, wool, salt and dyes to England. For two hundred years after 1272, when Edward I married Eleanor of Castile, it flourished under the English rule, the rich valley soil producing abundant wheat and waide – a plant used for dyeing. It was not until the 18th century that its prosperity began to recede with the sea and the demand for its textiles faded.

The collegiate church of St. Vulfran, begun in 1488, covered in scaffolding and plastic sheeting, is currently a sorry sight, but the red-brick folly of Bagatelle, hidden behind an unpromising brick wall on the outskirts of the town, is worth a look; built in 1752, it contains a collection of furniture from the periods of Louis XV and XVI and is still used as a family home. Open from 1/7-1/9, except Tues. The mediaeval belfry in the town now houses the Boucher de Perthes museum, with a collection of pre-historic finds.

But the town is lively enough, there are some pleasant spots by the river and you can take a boat from here to St. Valéry or, better, because the river is more interesting than the canal, to Amiens. And the shops are good, especially in the rue St. Vulfran and the Chaussée-du-Bois.

What is more, there are several good restaurants to choose from, which makes an en route stop here more than just an evil necessity. For a practical one-nighter I suggest:

Hôtel de France
(H)M *19 pl. Pilori 22.24.00.42 Closed 15/12-15/1 AE, DC, EC, V*

What it lacks in character - big, boring, plastic – it makes up for in good value. A double with bath costs 250f, which in the centre of a town is not bad. You won't list it top of the pops and don't think of eating in its restaurants but, compared with my not-so-bright idea of staying outside the town (see Crécy), this makes a lot of sense, especially combined with a meal at:

L'Escale en Picardie
(RM) *15 r. Teinturiers 22.24.21.51 Closed Sun.; Mon.p.m. 3/9-5/10 AE, DC, EC, V*

Just opened is an ancillary bistro, le Bistrot des Huîtres, all light and bright and cheerful, an excellent and unusual idea for France. Here you can take just a dozen oysters or other shellfish, with a glass of wine, which makes a lot of sense if an afternoon's driving and/or gourmand evening meal is envisaged

But the restaurant itself is a treat too. It also centres on fish, cooked by Gerard Perron in both traditional and more modern ways. Interesting ideas like profiteroles stuffed with smoked salmon in a chaud-froid sauce, spiked with chives, and a soufflé of red mullet mingle with standard poached fish, always perfectly fresh from the Channel or Rungis, served with beurre blanc. A delectable tarte Tatin (traditional) is served with a purée of quinces (modern). Menus at 135-245f.

Auberge de la Corne

(R)M *145 32 Chaussée-du-Bois 22.24.06.34 Closed Sun. p.m.; Mon., 1/3-15/3 and 1/7-15/7 (but it was closed when I was there in August!)*

Stick to the menu here unless prices like 280f for the same quality on the carte don't frighten you. For 95f or perhaps the next price up at 145f you get a very good deal indeed, with a chance to try Yves Lematelot's cooking of lamb from the salt marshes, fish from Hourdel, interesting offal dishes. Coming from Normandy, he knows how to make good use of prime ingredients, cooked simply, as in turbot with girolles or sole cooked in a paper case, wrapped in sorrel. There are three dining rooms, small intimate and beamed, currently in the course of redecoration.

Au Châteaubriand

(R)M *1 pl. Hôtel de Ville 22.24.08.23 Closed Sun. p.m.; Mon.; 8/7-31/7 EC, V*

Don't be put off with the brash sign or its position in an arch straddling the Chaussée du Bois. Inside is a comfortable restaurant with an excellent value 75f menu. There are others, but there is no need to pay more when this one offers such a good variety. Not the same atmosphere as the other more exalted choices, but a good choice nevertheless.

Buffet de France

(R)M *pl. de la Gare 22.24.04.26 Closed Wed. p.m. o.o.s.*

A fine example of that essentially gallic breed – the good station restaurant. Usefully open most of the time, when other Abbeville restaurants are useless, it offers a range of prices and possibilities. You can in fact eat for the same price in the restaurant as in the brasserie, and pay no more than 80f. Otherwise it's 105, 140, 180. M. Bigot likes to use local ingredients for his cuisine de terroir, enlivened with rich sauces. Not a curled-up sandwich in sight.

Map 7C **AMIENS** 80000 (Somme) 100 km from Boulogne

(M) ***Pl. des Halles:*** *Thurs., Sat.;* ***Pl. Parmentier:*** *Tues., Thurs., Sat.; r.* ***Florimond:*** *Wed., Fri., Sat.*

Ancient and historic capital of Picardy, home of the largest, most magnificent Gothic cathedral in France, set in a unique watery landscape, well endowed with good hotels, restaurants, smart shops - there is no way Amiens should be ignored.

But strange cities are especially intimidating to foreign drivers. Their sprawling suburbs, frantic traffic one-way confusions, hidden directions, all add up to the kind of stress that holidays are meant to avoid. My tip is to make straight for the cathedral. These are always well-signposted, invariably in the heart of the most interesting section of the city, usually with a quiet precinct in which to stop for a moment, find the map and get orientated.

This system certainly works well in Amiens, always provided you can tear yourself away from that staggeringly beautiful cathedral, miraculously spared from the holocausts, and save its delights for more relaxed moments. (If you elect to stay at the Prieuré hotel (see p.34), you needn't worry any further about parking elsewhere.)

From this vantage point all becomes clear. What had seemed an impassable tangle resolves itself into one main road, with all the recommended hotels and restaurants within walking distance.

The venerable city of Amiens, bisected by the Somme, suffered dreadfully in both World Wars and lost 60% of its old buildings in the conflicts; its ancient ramparts have given way to busy ring roads. But it is still an interesting and animated centre economically, intellectually (university seat) and artistically. An exciting new development is in progress in the crumbling quarter of St. Leu, just across the river from the cathedral, where every Saturday morning the flat bottomed punts, loaded with vegetables from the hortillonages, tie up alongside at the Place Parmentier to sell their wares. (On the second Sunday in the month there's a flea market here.) The mediaeval houses had degenerated into slums, the minor canals were clogged, until this ambitious and extensive restoration scheme got under way. Already, even with many of the cobbled streets impassable, blocked with rubble and bulldozers, canals drained of all but tin cans and garbage, and some of the picturesque cottages reduced to propped-up façades, it is possible to see how attractive it is going to be. Restaurants and cafés are opening up, artists are moving in, and soon boutiques will follow, lining the newly pristine waterways. I have high hopes that a cross between Port Grimaud and Venice will emerge! Whatever happens, the area has the inestimable asset of a breathtaking view of the cathedral.

This building alone merits the visit to the city. Trade in cloth, particularly velvets, which are still produced in Amiens, was at its peak in the 13th century and provided the funds to build this testimony of faith and refuge from suffering for an age beset with plague and war. It is incredible that its elegant and infinitely intricate form should have risen in less than fifty years, between 1220 and 1269, resulting in an unparalleled unity of style. The vaulted nave, supported by over a hundred delicate pillars, soars away into neck-cricking distance; take time to boggle at the carving of the 110 choirstalls – you won't find finer craftsmanship anywhere in the world; their 4,000 figures illustrate familiar biblical scenes translated into the life-style of the 16th-century Amienois.

To appreciate such details and to soak up the peace and unsurpassable beauty, arrange at least one visit outside coach hours. One unforgettable evening I had the place almost to myself, with all the saints on the west front golden in the sunset and someone practising on the organ in the shadowy vast interior.

Those who are interested in any depth should buy a more specialised guide than this to do justice to Notre Dame, but to all who visit her, I would say allow more time than you think you might need to absorb her benefices; walk round the whole building to understand the scale and cross the road to sit on the steps opposite for a while to study the west porches, with their army of elongated figures. Look for St. Firmin, the Spanish evangelist who became Amiens' first bishop, on the left porch, and find him again above the stalls in the south aisle pictured against a 15th-century Amiens whose cathedral, belfry and ramparts are all recognisable.

To add authority to what I hope is this brief appetiser, I would quote Ruskin: 'This apse of Amiens is not only the best but the very first thing done perfectly in its manner by northern Christendom.'

To find the old **St. Leu** area from the cathedral, go down the steps to its north, and turn right through a Dickensian alley, where chickens, dogs, cats, rabbits run in and out of hovels and glimpses of interiors from another age can be snatched through open doorways. Then left and across the bridge.

The main shopping area lies in the opposite direction, stretching from the pl. René Goblet, along the r. des Trois Cailloux, through the pl. Gambetta, to the r. Delambre, past the Hôtel de Ville, along the r. Gresset to the pl. Léon Gontier, with its prominent glass Maison de la Culture, where you can pick up brochures and maps. Outside and scattered about the city are dotty 'sculptures' of old bicycles piled apparently at random in a heap and sprayed red, white or blue. Makes a change from statues of generals.

Following this route on a shopping spree: in the pl. René Goblet are **Le Palais des Gourmets**, a *salon de thé*, good for chocolates and pâtisseries. then **Caramelle** for classily-wrapped presents of the local specialities – les macarons d'Amiens and tuiles amienoises. Less classy, less costly are **Le Petit Poulet**, another cuppa stop, and for light lunches, pizzas, and **Miami**, a clean 'n' cheerful bar/restaurant.

The r. des Trois Cailloux seems to specialise in high quality mens' shops – Burtons, Devred, Pastignac – shoe shops from Jourdan to Bata, and even more choc shops. Halfway along, time for a beer stop in the pedestrianised r. Ernest Cauvier, to the left. **Chez Marius** is a 'taverné', with 120 different beers, eight on 'pression'. A sandwich here or at the more refeened **Schaetjens** next door, a *glacier* and *salon de thé*, is most agreeable eaten at a table under the trees outside, a welcome oasis in the city centre.

Department stores **Nouvelles Galeries** and **Monoprix** come next, followed by the enticing smell of hot croissants being sold in great variety from an open stall. Then **Lafarge** for high quality handbags and luggage, and a super choc shop, **Jean Frogneaux**. Turn left in the pl. de l'Hôtel de Ville for supermarket **Codec** and a **Nicolas** wine concessionnaire, but surprisingly nowhere in this sweet-toothed, elegantly-clad, well-shod thoroughfare did I find a good *charcuterie*. To buy everything you need for a picnic you must turn right, and behind the Hôtel de Ville in the pl. Léon de Bouverie is **Fine Digeaux**. The best present shop is also just off the main street – **Actua** in the r. des Sergents – with all manner of ideas for the home and family.

Another good reason for an excursion to the Picard capital is a visit to the *hortillonages* – that unique waterworld as strange as anything dreamt up by Walt Disney. From 15/4~30/9 you can take a boat trip from the Chemin du Halagé (marked off the bvd. de Beauville) – an hour's meander in one of the low, high-prowed punts that give you a duck's eye view of the squares of market gardens crisscrossed with channels, mini-canals – the *rieux* – and larger navigable canals, all irrigated by the rivers Somme and Avre.

'Hortillon' was the name given by Caesar's soldiers to the men who tended these gardens then, and there were vegetable plots here in pre-Roman times. The hortillons get about in distinctive flat-bottomed tarred boats – *bateaux à cornet*. The area latticed with water is considerable and it must be easy for the stranger to get lost in the maze of waterways, lakes and islands.

The black rich soil of the gardens is banked above the waterline. Most of them sport neat rows of bumper caulis, leeks, cabbages – three crops a year they can produce – but there are flowers too and it was the colour that struck me most on a September visit. I had been expecting a wishy-washy watercolour effect of gentle greys and greens – but no, there was a positive riot not only of autumn leaves and scarlet creepers but of gaudy dahlias, mammoth almost-artificial sunflowers, marigolds, asters, golden rod, not to mention purple cabbages, crimson tomatoes and rosy apples on the trees, as shiny and profuse as those in a nurseryman's catalogue. On most plots stands some kind of a shelter – from micro-hut to keep the fishing gear in, to doll's-house bungalows, like 'La Réfuge', all red and white, with attendant gnomes.

I thoroughly recommend an hour's relaxation in this way, preferably on a sunny day, when the water sparkles best as you drift stealthily

Le Prieuré, Amiens

through the water lilies, poplars and willows, disturbing a variety of wildfowl. If you happen to be there on the third Sunday in June, you'll catch the fête des Hortillonages, when the traditional costumes of the area come out.

Even better if you get to Amiens before 30th Sept '87, you can see a *son et lumière* celebration of the 1000th anniversary of the city at the Cathedral (starts 10.15 pm – 35f per person) .

HOTELS AND RESTAURANTS:

➔Le Prieuré

(HR)M *17 r. Porion 22.92.27.67 Rest. closed Fri. p.m.; Sun. p.m.*

There are times – very few and exceedingly far between – when I cannot believe my hotel-questing luck. To find, tucked quietly away in the very shadow of what I think is the most stunning cathedral in France, a little family-run hotel, recently converted from an old priory, with elegant dining room and rooms full of character and comfort, at moderate prices, not yet in other guides, is almost too good to be true. Well, it was and it wasn't.

All these delightful facts do apply to Le Prieuré. The building is quite charming: you enter through a cobbled courtyard, furnished with a sedan chair (telephone) and antique table, into the panelled reception area with bubbling *vivier*; the dining room to the right has elegant high ceilings, corniced with beautiful plasterwork, chandeliers, crisply-laid tables, all very tasteful and reassuring. The rooms vary enormously, as one would expect in a building of such character. All are furnished with antiques. Several look out onto another enclosed courtyard full of greenery, little white tables – very soothing in the heart of a city – and one is in the old chapel, all 380 gothicky with stained glass and steep eves. Four have bathrooms, five have showers (200f), two have neither (170f). Bargains.

So far, so very good indeed. But when I arrived, at the end of a devastating day, to claim my room, booked and confirmed for three nights, there was no-one around. Much ringing of bells and banging of doors eventually produced a flustered M. Boulet, who could not recollect P. Fenn (pretty stupid – I had called in a few weeks earlier to chat to him and he had sent me brochures) and was unfortunately unable to offer me accommodation since a music festival in the city had taken over all his rooms. Fatigue and the thought that all plans and phone calls would now go awry lent desperation and P. Fenn sat on her suitcases and refused to budge until (a) a stiff drink was produced and (b) a room was magicked. The first requirement took half an hour, the second rather longer; when the room was made ready (now 7.30 p.m.) it was in a dark attic, up three flights of stairs and definitely not one of those I had been shown on my first recce.

Further enquiries around the town and from fellow guests confirmed my impressions – the hotel has everything except efficient management. One American said he guessed the dinner was just great when it arrived, but he had got mighty hungry in the meantime. The menus looked most interesting, with lots of regional specialities, and I had intended to eat in on my first night, but discouraged by the reception debacle and empty dining room, I decided otherwise, and discovered next day that local opinion is that I was wise.

So, to sum up this tricky one – I have to award a qualified arrow for Le Prieuré's unique situation and character-full building, modest prices, and I would risk staying there again myself because of these, *but*, second time around, I would get something in writing from M. Boulet about my booking or else take a vacant room on the day, and would not expect the service nor the food to match the potential.

I hope this gives readers a clear picture and I should particularly like their views on this one, especially on the food, to allay my guilt at not having sampled it myself.

➔Hôtel Univers

(H)M-L *2 r. Noyoh 22.91.52.51 DC, EC, V.*

About as different as possible from Le Prieuré, but a very pleasant surprise. Here is a big modern hotel set on a main thoroughfare – all the things I hate most. But the Univers is an example to all other big modern city hotels – its rooms are charmingly and individually furnished with real furniture and cheerful chintzy curtains. The reception and service knocks spots off that of many a family-run hotel, the breakfast is excellent and on time, and if you insist on a side room, whose balconies overlook a green and pleasant park, the traffic noise is minimal. 320-500f is a fair price for an extremely comfortable central hotel. An arrow for pleasant efficiency.

Hôtel Normandie

(H)M *1 bis r. Lamartine 22.91.74.99 CB, MC*

A small family-run hotel set in a side street near the centre. Everyone I asked commented on the friendliness of the owners, M. and Madame Albanese. Rooms are 145-270f.

Le Postillon

(H)M *pl. au Feurre*

A late note from the Somme tourist office in Amiens tells me that this hotel opened at the end of 1986. They say it has a series of rooms with a splendid view of the cathedral. Reports welcome. Rooms 300-500f.

Grand Hotel de L'Univers

➔Aux As du Don

(R)M *1-3 pl.Don. 22 92 41 65 cl. Sat lunch; Sun p,m.; Mon o.o.s; 308-15/9 and one week in Dec.*

A welcome newcomer to the Amiens scene is this cosy bistro in the

St. Leu quartier, decorated with lovely 18th-century wood carvings. The cooking is light, fresh and imaginative, on menus from 110f (mid-week). Here is a recent experience:

Everything was delicious. It was friendly and cosy with very good service. Starters were rillettes anguille fumée, daube de lapin en gelée, fondant d'avocats. Main course noisettes agneau basilic, saumon à l'oseille and magret Xeres. Then came roquefort à l'armagnac, followed by three wonderful desserts, of which the star was cygne glacé, coulis de fruit, so beautiful that I didn't want to spoil the design by eating it – Sue Robinson

Another arrow for Amiens.

Les Marissons

(R)L-M *66 r. des Marissons 22.92.96.66 Closed Sun. p.m.; Mon.; Sat. Lunch. 1/1-10/1, July*

The first of the new restaurants in the soon-to-be-transformed St. Leu area, this 15th-century boat shed has recently been converted into the prettiest imaginable restaurant; it overlooks the canal, with the looming cathedral an unequalled focal point. The owners have chosen the colours of Picardy for interior decoration – yellow walls, blue chairs. Low rafters, fresh flowers, soft lights, classical tapes all make for a soothing and agreeable ambience.

There is a 135f mid-week menu, not bad but with little choice, so I settled for the next one up – four courses for 176f (there is a five-courser for 208f). One should not leave Amiens without trying their much vaunted gastro speciality, pâté de canard, so I fell upon this option as a first course, served en croute, au foie gras, but can't say I was impressed. Perhaps I should have stuck to the fish alternatives, which are house specialities – deux terrines de poissons aux petits légumes, and émincé St. Jacques both sounded good. However, the calves' sweetbreads with pleurottes (wild mushrooms) compensated (could have been filet de boeuf) and cheese and puds were fine, so all in all I think an arrow is just justified for the prettiest restaurant in town, offering good-value high-class cuisine.

1993: Under same management – Côté St. Leu, 4r. des Majots.

Le Mermoz

(R)M *7 r. Jean Mermoz. 22.91.50.63 Closed Sat.; Sun. p.m.; 1 week in Feb.; week at Christmas; 12/7-10/8 AE, DC.*

NO NEWS

Unexpectedly situated in a distinctly seedy area near the station, Le Mermoz was the favourite restaurant of every Amienois I asked. Frankly I found it a bit dull: the dining room is really very boring harsh lights, modern decor, totally nondescript – but the owner Patrick Letellier is certainly as attentive and welcoming a host as one could wish for. When he saw me furtively taking notes from his menu he insisted on giving me one to take home, so I can reliably report that the menus are: 95f – 'Touristique', 110f – 'Poissons', and 190f

'Dégustation'. I was starving on that particular night and was inclined to go mad on the latter but, at the risk of seeming blasé, it did seem to be an uninspired selection of all the old luxury clichés – foie gras, lobster, salmon, magret, sorbet, cheese, dessert. So 'poissons' it had to be.

Not bad – flan de crevettes aux baies roses turned out to be a competent enough seafood mousse, rascasse aux champignons forestiers was as tasty as the ugly Mediterranean fish can ever be, the hot goat's cheese was a commendable variation on the usual cheeseboard, and the dessert was so inoffensive that I can't recall what it was. So I would go if I were you – I'm sure it's all a very safe bet. Just not very exciting.

➔Le Saladin

(RS)S *r. des Chandonniers 22.92.07.15 Closed Sun.*

The idea of sitting down to a salad for lunch is not one to thrill the gastric juices of the French, happily accustomed to the knees-under, napkin-tucked-in-waistcoat daily blow-out. But a few daring foreign ideas are beginning to infiltrate the satisfied chauvinism and the occasional town now risks the sissyness of wine bar and veggie restaurant. To the great credit of the Amienois, they have ventured to give Le Saladin's fare a go, and are now devotees (so that you must go early or book). As so often with late converts, the dedication of this little restaurant, behind the Hôtel de Ville, to the light and the fresh has been totally convinced and convincing. It is so pretty – all pink and white and green, with fretworks of pink flowers around the mirrors, white cane chairs, lettuce-green cloths, beaded pink *fin-de-siècle* lamps and lots of greenery trailing over white lattice. They even have pink hearts on the lav paper!

Obviously the salad rules here, but what salads! Not a limp lettuce or bleeding beetroot to be seen. They cost around 35f for, perhaps, the admirably seasonal salade du marché, with artichoke hearts, ham, cheese, mushrooms, mayonnaise, or there are hot cheese variations like the one I chose – 'Auvergnate' – blue cheese melting on to croutons on a substantial mixed salad, or perhaps 'Savoyarde', with gruyère, or 'Crottin', with goat's cheese.

For cold weather there's 'Assiette Doudou' – piperade and salad – for 40f, or a delicious quiche picarde served with not only salad and mushrooms but very unhealth-conscious chips. Puddings are equally fresh and home-made – alcoholic sorbets like passion fruit with Grand Marnier, apples and calva, or lemon and vodka. For don't-care tea-times the sundaes are good too: 'Forêt Noire' has mint sorbet, choc ice, choc sauce, crème Chantilly; 'Antillaise' has ice creams of coconut, rum, raisins, vanilla, banana and kiwi in a caramel sauce ... I could go on but perhaps I should also tell you about the home-made fruit flans, especially the Tatin brought flaming to the table. Wine costs 8.80f a small pichet, 16.50f a large, and there is a delectable and virulently green house cocktail, whose recipe is an unwheedleable secret.

Now you may say you don't go to France to eat salads and sundaes, but even the most stalwart gourmand liver has to have a rest occasionally and those planning a series of substantial meals will enjoy them all the more if a little abstinence is practised in between the gutsiness. I can't think of a better way to abstain. A valuable discovery and an arrow for originality and high standards.

Le P'tit Chef
(R)S-M *8 r. Jean Catelas 22.92.24.23 Closed Tue. p.m.; Wed. 16/7-14/8.*

Any association with English establishments of the same name is purely coincidental.

Opposite La Maison de la Culture, one of those blank French façades that give nothing away. Inside equally nondescript, but light and cheerful, with fresh flowers and ranks of well polished glasses and copper pans auguring well. Nothing for it but to try it out and I'm glad I did.

The 70f mid-week lunch menu is jolly good value and I recommend it highly to anyone who wants an honest, no choice, no messing meal. Otherwise the somewhat unusual system is that the main course choice determines the price of the meal, entrée and cheese included. My terrine de petits légumes and tournedos au poivre, plus cheese, came to a very reasonable 120f.

The wines are well chosen but more expensive proportionately than the food. Any bottle will cost more than the cheapest menu.

La Corne de Boeuf
(R)M *30 r. de Beauvais 22.91.77.65 Closed Sun.*

A bright and cheerful restaurant specialising in meat of all kinds great hunks of it, and especially beef. You can take it straight, grilled over the charcoal embers, with sauces, or on skewers, but it's all good quality and excellent value at around 30-50f a portion. Nothing-special starters and puds. Recommended locally but needing some confirmation before getting arrowed.

La Soupe à Cailloux
(R)S-M *12 r. des Bondes 22.91.92.70 Closed Mon.*

A pretty little bistro, all scrubbed and spare, in the about-to-be converted region beneath the cathedral. Original and interesting interpretations of traditional recipes on menus that change every day and cost from 60f. Popular with the more restrained young.

Le Pré Porus
(R)M *95 r. Voyelle 22.46.25.03 Closed Mon. p.m. and Tue.*

Diabolical food. But you don't go to Le Pré Porus for a gastronomic treat. Its delights lie rather in its situation.

To the east of Amiens is a complicated network of canals and rivers, always animated with fishermen, rowing boats, the flat-bottomed punts used by the *hortillons*, and even pedalos. On the very banks of the Somme sits this well-known restaurant whose wide terrace overlooks all the cool greenness of willows and water. Nothing could be more agreeable than to sit there on a hot summer's day and allow the slap of the wavelets and the plop of the oars and punt poles to soothe the sticky big-town hassle away.

There was a jovial wedding party taking over one evening when we were last there and that couple's wedding snaps could not have had a more romantic setting, give or take a boozy uncle or two getting in the way.

The hardworking patron is kind and concerned – unusual in a tourist stop like this. Having bagged the best place on the terrace, we found it getting nippy when the sun retreated, but there was no fuss about moving paraphernalia of drinks, place settings and Fenns into an already crowded (the French wouldn't dream of being so silly as to sit outside) dining room. He was so kind that I couldn't bring myself to tell him how awful the first course was (burnt leek flan). When I saw some ghastly floury white-sauced monkfish arrive on the next table I rubbed hands that I had not chosen that, but the shrivelled trout that was my portion was no more palatable and had to be left. Kind patron, upset, made instant amends, and along came as compensation – the monkfish!

Husband sniggered until he saw his order of coq à la bière. Could this mammoth bone really belong? Waiter said, 'It's a big chicken, sir.' Husband tasted and was no wiser; patron took one look and did a Basil Fawlty: 'Actually it's ham, sir, but the flavour is the same.'

No, certainly don't look forward to anything more than the most straightforward of food, that even that paranoid chef they keep in their kitchens can muck up, and don't be fooled by the interesting regional 'Menu Picard' – 95f for regional items like flamiche, mussels cooked in beer, ficelle Picarde, coq à la bière – but take perhaps an omelette, or a drink, or even tea, and sit back and enjoy the scenery.

La Couronne
(R)M 64 r. St. Leu 22.91.88.57 Closed Sat. 14/7-14/8

On the main road heading north, not far from the flamboyant St. Leu church. A pleasant little restaurant, decorated with engravings of old Amiens and a great favourite with businessmen at lunchtime always a good sign.

Generous portions of traditional cooking and local dishes like ficelle picarde and coquelet façon barquaise on a 88f, four-course menu. Desserts are a bit dull, but you probably won't have room for 'em anyway.

Map 10B **ANSERVILLE** 60540 Bornel (Oise) 187 km SE of Boulogne; 21 km S of Beauvais

Turn west off the N1 south of La Mare d'Ovillers. The village is just one street, lined with pollarded limes, and the Coubriche farm is behind a green gate on the right, just round a sharp bend.

➔**Madame Coubriche**
(Chambre d'hôte) 44.22.01.76 Open all year

Nice Madame Coubriche has converted five rooms in an erstwhile stable block of her old farmhouse to extremely comfortable guestrooms. This is the very model of a perfect chambre d'hôte. No family possessions cluttering up the bedrooms, no grubbiness to make you feel guilty about how hard the poor landlady is working, more lights than in many a posh hotel, constant hot water, modern

Mme Coubriche

showers and washbasins, well-chosen wooden (not plastic) furniture, spaciousness and light.

Friend Ann slept here, with private shower and loo, while I had a room in the main house, which was equally comfortable and downright elegant for a farmhouse.

Madame Coubriche has her regulars, her *pensionnaires*, for whom she cooks a substantial evening meal – five courses based on local farm produce for 45f. Early morning squawks alerted me to the sight of the welly-booted patronne conveying two flapping victims to the kitchen, ready for the ultimate sacrifice in that night's coq au vin, and the sight of the generous gratin dauphinois I watched her assembling later in her clinically clean kitchen made me wish I had reserved a place at her dinner table. However, I should caution that a communal meal here might not suit everyone. The other customers on this occasion were all male, smoking heavily, and engrossed in the telly-not my idea of a convivial French mealtime.

But there was no doubt about breakfast, taken at the same table. It was all that I had hoped for – fresh farmhouse butter, homemade jam to go on the hot bread, and as much steaming coffee as even I could drink.

B. and b. is 175f for two, 200f for one, dinner 60f.

Madame Coubriche is a friendly efficient hostess, and the pleasure of country peace combined with a well-run establishment earns a certain arrow.

Map 10D **APREMONT** 60300 (Oise) 220 km from Boulogne; 5 km NW of Senlis

A tiny village near the forests of Halatte and Chantilly.

La Grange aux Loups
(R)M *44.25.33 79 Closed Sun. p.m.; Mon.*

NO NEWS

An attractively rustic inn, warm and cosy atmosphere inside but also attractive for an al fresco meal on the terrace in summer. They specialise in charcoal grills and very good they are too – try the brochette de St. Jacques as a change from the more obvious beef and lamb steaks – but make good use of local game and funghi. The theme may be of country simplicity but the service and settings are sophisticated, which means that three courses à la carte will cost around 200f. Menus at 77.50f and 147f and a good wine list.

Map 4B **ARGOULES** 80120 Rue (Somme) 56 km SE of Boulogne

10 km W of Nampont-St. Martin, on the S. bank of the Authie, on the

D192. One of the most picturesque villages in the valley; the mighty lime tree, from which the Auberge du Gros Tilleul takes its name, still spreads its shade over the village green as it has done for 300 years, and artists find inspiration in the nearby château and Gothic church.

Auberge du Gros Tilleul
(H)S(R)M *All Cards 22.29.91.00*

The Gros Tilleul used to be a legend along the valley and the name of its erstwhile owner, Pierre Bony, is still talked of with the respect due to the best restaurant for miles around. When he died the auberge died with him – first standing desolately empty and then passing through unsuccessful hands. Now fresh hope dawns in the shape of new young owners, M. and Madame Beugé, who say their aim is to restore the restaurant to Bony standards. The menus are ambitious and interesting, at 72-195f and 220f, and I heard more than one local recommendation and approval of what *les jeunes* are doing.

They are also trying gradually to improve the rooms, which are still pretty basic and dark, if picturesquely situated in the raftered eves. They cost from 250f, 295f with bath a double, so a stay here would be not only extremely peaceful but also cheap.

Already reports are coming in of excellent meals taken here, so it looks as though M. Bony's ghost can lie easy at last.

Map 4D **ARRAS** (Pas de Calais) 62000 98 km SE of Boulogne

 *Wed., Sat.*

Arras never fails to amaze and delight me. Why it is so little known and appreciated by English tourists I shall never know. I would rate it No. 1 in the north of France for a winter break, combining as it does so much to admire, with good shops, hotels, restaurants and easy autoroute access.

If you park near the Abbaye St. Vaast, you can walk through three intriguing squares, each one opening out of the last like a layered Russian doll, except that in this case they get larger, culminating in the explosion of the Grand' Place, which must be the largest in Europe and also one of the most striking, surrounded by arcaded Flemish houses, whose ornamented stepped gables, red brick, old stone, create an intensely satisfying total harmony. So perfect is their design, the suspicion that one has stumbled into a stage-setting might well occur, and indeed the apparatus of film crews is often to be seen sprawling across the cobbles.

In fact, an artful but delightful deception has been practised, in that most of these houses are not the 17th- and 18th-century models they would seem, but a reconstruction from the rubble that was left of the great squares after the devastation of the First World War. The extent of the damage of four years' bombardment can be seen in the photographs in the impressive Town Hall, which forms one side of the Place des Héros, and I urge a visit.

Don't miss, on the left as you go in, the figures of the monumental giants, Jacqueline and Colas, that are paraded through the streets on fête days. Like their home town, they have been damaged, restored, and re-built, a commendable statement of municipal confidence in the over-riding and continuous attraction of the best of things past.

The photos, rather badly displayed to the right, show how only a very few of the old Flemish houses still stood, their gables sometimes lurching drunkenly towards the hole left by their neighbours. It would make sad viewing had the renaissance been less thorough and successful.

Then proceed down to the 13th-century vaults to take the lift up to the 250ft belfry, for a not-to-be-missed-on-any-account eagle's eye view of the city. It's a good idea to make this excursion early in your visit to get an idea of the layout and inter-relation of the squares. But I must warn the unsuspecting infirm that at the end of the lift ride there are still 33 steep and winding stairs to climb.

This vantage point is the giveaway for the pseudo antiquity of the houses far below. Their weathered façades might look ancient enough, but the new roofs are definitely 20th century.

The cloisters and refectory of the Abbaye St. Vaast house a museum of Arras; on show are the tapestries which gave the town its name – arras – the weaving of which brought the prosperity that caused houses on the squares to be built for their rich merchant owners. Around the *places* look out for the heraldic signs of the local craft guilds and of the ruling families of the time.

In the 18th-century, porcelain-making became another Arras industry, especially the famous *bleu d'Arras*, displayed in a gallery of the museum.

So vast are Arras' squares that even the extensive markets that take place on Saturday and Wednesday mornings fail to fill them completely. This is one of the best markets in the north of France and a visit contrived on one of these days is well worthwhile. The stallholders, with their bright umbrellas, offer a huge range of goodies, from the heaps of seasonal vegetables at giveaway prices (I paid 3f for a *kilo* of chicory) to the Limoges porcelain. I love its plain white background for serving all manner of dishes and spent a fortune (or saved one, depending on how you look at it) on bargains like fireproof terrines, saladiers, soupiers and an impressive fish platter, which, at 90f, was a third of the price of the one I had bought the previous week in a conventional porcelain shop (I didn't really need two fish dishes but it's female logic to buy a second cheap one to level things out!)

Hôtel de l'Univers
(H)M *Pl. de la Croix Rouge 21.71.34.01 AE, DC, P*

Hotel *Food*

In FE4 I removed the arrow confidently earlier bestowed on the Univers, because readers had not always agreed with my enthusiasm for the place. Indeed sometimes I began to wonder if we had visited the same hotel. Where I had found in this 18th-century ex-monastery elegance, calm, comfort, their unhappy lot was shabbiness, noise and poor service. So this time I challenged the urbane Directeur, M. Gibberon. 'You must have given me the best room,' I said. 'What about the rest?'

'There are the keys,' he said. 'Think of a number.'

So I picked a handful at random, and put on my most critical inspector's hat. And they were all just like mine – tastefully, almost luxuriously furnished, with expensive curtains and bedspreads, new carpets, modern bathrooms, thick towels, warm radiators. I still think No. 11 is one of the nicest, with its steely-blue furnishings, but there are others, with four-posters, and pink themes, and green themes, and floral themes, that are very pretty too.

So why the discontent? Having stayed this year on a Saturday I can vouch that some of it is totally justified. This haven of quiet, set back in a courtyard from the main shopping area, is bedlam when they let out the refectory across the yard for wedding parties. Till 3 a.m. the disco ranted and raved and now I fully sympathise with those readers who viewed the whole set-up with jaundiced eye. Next morning M. Gibberon tactically made himself scarce before I could tackle him, but the receptionist assured me it was not thus every Saturday. But pretty often I suspect. Too bad that a hotel of this standard should allow its clients to be disturbed in this way.

Other complaints centre on the food. The vast dining-room is very impressive, with its tapestries and beams, but the dearth of locals eating there had previously warned me away, and with the alluring prospect of eating at La Faisanderie as an option I had no intention of wasting a good night's eating here. One reader who did writes: *'The potage was like dirty dishwater and the tomatoes stuffed with tuna-flavoured cotton wool. The chicken supreme was barely thawed, covered in luke-warm floury sauce and sticky rice. The navarin of lamb looked like a dog's dinner – all bone and gristle. I can safely say this was the worst meal of six months' eating in France.'* I don't think she liked it much.

Here is another valued view from a reader who visited about the same time as myself: *'For once I part company with your judgment! The hotel was packed with a commercial convention. There was nowhere other than the bar to sit and we found the hotel, and indeed Arras, noisy, and full of unattractive streets. Yes, the two places are worth a detailed look, but we simply could not see the hotel as a 'haven of quiet' and, as I say, it is the one and only time we have been at serious odds with your excellent judgment.'*

Fair enough, Mr. Henderson, but since this is an unashamedly personal and subjective guide, I shall still resolutely back up my own less-than-always-excellent judgment in this case and restore the arrow, with strict limitations: If you do not stay in a courtyard room on a Saturday night, and if you do not eat in the restaurant, you may expect a well-run (excellent breakfast served in room dead on time, immaculate housekeeping) historic and elegant hotel in the heart of a fascinating town, with rooms that are excellent value for this quality, at 290-350f.

Astoria

(HR)M *10-12 Pl. Foch 21.71.08.14 Closed 24/12-8/1; closed 24/12-2/1. Rest. closed Sun. p.m. All Cards*

I have several good reports of this hotel, opposite the station.

'We finally settled on the Astoria on the corner of Rue Gambetta and the Place de la Gare. There is an excellent brasserie, Le Carnot, adjoining, with a wide choice of menu and à la carte. The staff and management are always helpful and friendly and welcome us even after a long absence. Prices are reasonable and the whole place is well kept. The brasserie is well patronised by local people, which is usually a good sign.' – G. W. Berry.

Rooms are 125-300f.

Les Grandes Arcades

(HR)M *8-12 Grand' Place 21.23.30.89 Closed Sun. p.m.*

Hotel *Restaurant*

Reports continue to be favourable for this hard-to-miss hotel. perfectly sited on the Grand' Place. The restaurant too wins accolades:

'The best meal of the trip. Atmosphere, welcome, food, wine all superb. Highly recommended. ' – Richard King.

Rooms from 90-160f, meals from 55f.

Le Régent

(HR)M-L *5 r. A-France, St. Nicolas-les-Arras 21.71.51.09 Closed Sun. p.m.; Mon*

Just outside the town, on a main road, so some of the front rooms could be noisy, but the old building has considerable charm, the furnishings are luxuriously comfortable, and there is a nice garden leading down to the river.

Too far probably to walk into the interesting parts of Arras, and the prices are comparatively high, so I would only choose to stay here if the Univers were full (or I had suffered there like some of my readers). It does have the advantage of an excellent restaurant.

Rooms 290-460f. A la carte only in the restaurant – allow 200f.

Le Chanzy
(HR)M *8 r. Chanzy 21.71.02.02. Open every day.*

Had its ups and many downs, and is not really the kind of restaurant a wise guide writer would even mention, since no two experiences seem to concur. There are so many options, of which dining room, which menu, which speciality to settle for, that one is usually left feeling the wrong choice has been made and if only ... But there is a new chef here and my general feeling is that the Chanzy nadir has been reached and it might be a pity to miss what can only be an upward trend.

What is certain and enduring is that Robert de Troy's cellar is not only *'la plus riche de France'* but is getting richer. He now stores 140,000 bottles and is excavating the chalk caves beneath the restaurant still further to accommodate even more. Ask for a tour, willingly given, and receive a free vinous education.

The cheapest menu is 77f; expect solid traditional cooking – côte à l'os carré d'agneau, andouillette d'Arras.

The rooms vary as wildly as the menus and this time, having received some gruesome accounts, I asked to see them all. The best, at 300f, are not at all bad and the same price buys an apartement in the annexe, but there have been dire reports of temperamental central heating and hot water, so be wary in winter. The cheapest at 150f involve climbing up dreary flights of plastic wall-papered stairs and are frankly not worth the effort.

Hôtel Diamant
(H)M *5 pl. des Héros 21.71.23.23.*

A new little hotel at the foot of the belfry. It's all very pretty, tastefully furnished, with smart new bathrooms, conveniently situated, but the rooms are very small for 220 240f a double.

➔La Faisanderie
(R)M-L *45 Grand' Place 21.48.20. 76 Closed Sun. p.m.; Mon.; 2 weeks Aug.*
★ Michelin

Chef Jean-Pierre Dargent and partner Francis Gauduin say they like it better here than at Pommera. I'm not surprised. They are installed in one of the most attractive buildings – one of the few surviving 17th-century examples in the Grand' Place – in this most attractive town, with a range of local and visiting clientèle who might not have been prepared to drive out to their previous modest little eatery on a main road. I would have driven there because I reckoned the food was the best in the entire area, but am delighted to see La Faisanderie established in a setting befitting its excellence.

It's still agreeably small, with two dining rooms, of which I prefer the vaulted cave, cleverly lit, elegantly furnished, brightened with flowersand lightcolours.

Jean-Pierre has always been a diligent promoter of his region (he worked too at Flavio's at Le Touquet) and the175f menu he calls La *Carte de Notre Région. Pour ne pas oublier du Pays d'Artois et des Flandres.* The other, 'Gourmande' costs 255f; but before embarking on either menu you get complimentary tastes of whatever *amuse-gueule* the chef devises that day. For us it was little money-bags made from a crêpe, tied with a thread of leek, stuffed with baby cockles and tiny chopped root veg, plus mini-tarts stuffed with rillettes of salmon. A promising start.

The home-baked bread at Pommera was always a feature of the house, and the tradition continues here – six different kinds come round in a basket – studded with nuts, encrusted with seeds flavoured with bacon, etc.

Husband and I shared the two menus between us, tasting a hot pâté of wild duck, served with a compôte of wild cherries and onions, and an autumn salad of smoked fish 'de la Mer du Nord'. Had we been feeling more dedicated to experimentation, we might have tried a cassolette of whelks in a garlic cream.

Then a thick slice of local lamb, cut across the bone, served with lingots du Nort – tender white dried beans melting into the garlic and grilled coquilles St. Jacques and langoustines, with home-made pasta. Wonderful.

Two more courses to go, neither of them to be neglected. Husband chose a salad of grilled Maroilles cheese garnished with croutons, followed by pancakes stuffed with local dessert apples, Reine des Reinettes, and a honey ice-cream, while I sniffed my way through an educative regional cheeseboard, by courtesy of the clever Philippe Olivier. The waiter knew all about the cheeses and helped me to whiffers like Le Dauphin, Boule d'Avesnes and Maroilles. With the coffee come irresistible petits fours, for which room should be reserved at all costs.

No doubt that here is one of the best tables in the north and yet another justification for coming to Arras.

La Rapière

(R)M *44 Grand' Place 21.55.09.92 Closed 3/8-31/8; 25/12-1/1; Sun p.m. AE, DC, EC, V*

A pretty little restaurant across the square from the Faisanderie, which readers have liked very much. Probably the best bet in the town for a moderately priced meal, with menus from 69-155f and reasonable wine.

'Starters: pâté and vegetable terrine, both excellent. Main courses: truite au beurre – excellent, well-cooked, plain and simple. Veal served on slice of ham, plus mushrooms. Very good chips. Cheese: small, with choice of three. Sweets: scrummy chocolate mousse. Wine very reasonable at 39f. Alsace pink and tasty, well chilled.' Quentin Gray.

Le Victor Hugo

(R)M *11 pl. Victor Hugo 21.23.34.96 Closed Sun. p.m.; Mon.; Aug. EC, DC.*

Don't miss a walk to the magnificent pl. Victor Hugo, even if you don't intend to eat here.

In one of the 18th-century houses that surrounds the square is this very French, very 'correct' restaurant, specialising in fish. It's for serious eaters, with a preponderance of *hommes d'affaires* at lunchtime.

The food matches the décor – elegant, classic, sober, of high quality.

Prices are puzzling. Menus are 175f at lunchtime, but 95f and 195f, including wine, in the evening. If you think 95f is expensive for a sole, consider that you would pay the same price for an inferior specimen in an inferior restaurant. Here it comes immaculately fresh, steamed, and served on a bed of sorrel. A plump Bresse duck costs 85f and *assiette gourmande* of pâtisserie, which lives up to its name, is 50f.

Les 40 Chevaux

(R)M *13 Cour de Verdun 21.71.02.91 Open every day*

A new venture, which is winning much local approval. Patron Maurice Theret was for 21 years maitre d'h. at Le Chanzy, so he knows a thing or two about restaurants and wine. It looks as though he has transported the best of Le Chanzy's traditions here, and the fact that he is keen enough to open up every day bodes well for an early visit.

The décor's a bit boring, but the food should compensate, if you like reliable, traditional cooking, well-served. Menus from 90f.

I didn't realise there were also 16 rooms here, at 90f apiece, so wastefully missed the chance to investigate. Reports welcome.

L'Ambassadeur
(R)M-L Buffet SNCF *Pl. Foch 21.23.29.80 Closed Sun. p.m. AE, DC.*

I have to include this splendid example of upmarket station buffetry because it is generally approved of, even though I personally haven't returned since I had mould served with my quiche. Michelin did subsequently remove the star and perhaps lessons have been learned, though it still wouldn't be my first choice in Arras.

It's very grand and smooth, with Louis XV-ish décor. A plus point is its promotion of regional dishes, like harengs à la Flamande and that quiche aux poireaux, which I hope is now made freshly each day (have a shifty underneath to be sure). Menus from 125-290f.

Le Win'Stub
(R)S *7 rue des Petits Vieziers 21.51.10.85.*

NO NEWS

A little Alsation bistro, set in an old house in the cobbled pedestrianised street leading to the pl. du Théâtre, good for a modest meal or snack any time.

Inside it's all lace tablecloths, crocheted caps on the fin-de-siècle lamps and café curtains at the stained glass windows, with stylised vines and plastic grapes emphasising the winey theme.

My speciality, 'flamenilkuche', proved to be a kind of light puffy pizza with melting onions and lardons of bacon. At 23f just fine for lunch. Hot tourte alsacienne involved foie gras, for 21f, and tarte à l'oignon was a mere 16f. The choucroute specials were as substantial as even the portly businessmen demolishing them, napkins tucked in necks, could have wished for. Good desserts, like tarte au citron and charlotte au chocolat, and a pichet of wine for 12f make this probably the best bet in town for a cheap meal.

For a beer, coffee or quick snack I can recommend **La Licorne**, a smartish brasserie/café between the Grand'Place and the pl. des Héros. Clean, warm and good loos.

Recommended by locals but uninspected by me are two more suggestions: for fish, considerably cheaper than Victor Hugo, **Le Clam's**, a little bistro with a vivier at 52 Grand' Place 21.07.37.79, closed Wed; and for good fresh salads: **Le Pavillon**, 38 pl. des Héros, 21.71.02.65, closed Mon. lunch.

Map 3B **ATTIN** 62170 (Pas de Calais) 30 km S of Boulogne 3 km N of Montreuil on the N 39

➔**Auberge du Bon Accueil**

(R)S *21.06.04.21. Closed Sun. p.m.; Mon.; Wed. o.o.s.*

Ask anyone in the area where to get a reliable cheap meal and the answer will be the same, 'Try the Bon Accueil.' I nearly gave it an arrow in FE4 and the 100% favourable response it received since then makes one obligatory now.

It's right on the main road, on a bend, and its popularity with French families means there is always a confusion of cars parked with Gallic careless abandon marking the approach. You go upstairs into a large modern dining room, blown-up posters of Alpine scenes on the walls, awful oil paintings, plastic seats, white cloths – nothing exciting décor-wise, but oh so professionally run. The friendly efficient patron, M. Delvoye-Coquet, who speaks excellent English, has eyes in the back of his head. You have only to exhaust wine, bread, finger-wipes, and they are replaced before you realise it. So efficient in fact is the service, with all the waiters running to obey orders, that if you don't deploy delaying tactics you could be in and out in an hour.

The food is and has always been, excellent value, with some interesting ideas, which change daily according to weather, markets and whims. Basically there is a 76f including wine menu from which there is no need to deviate unless you especially wish a supplement like a whole fresh crab for starters or a large steak or lobster on the list of main choices.

A speciality dish included in the basic price when I visited was a croustade of pigs' trotters, served with a sauce tartare – wonderful winter fare. My salad with hot goats' cheese was excellent and the fresh artichokes looked prime specimens (the only time I found these old favourites on a menu during their peak season). Then came a hefty portion of calf's liver with a compote of onions for me; next table were tucking into what was obviously the French favourite home-cooked ham served in a cream sauce with home-made noodles. There is always a good fish dish available, like médaillons of monkfish in a chervil cream sauce. Third course is pudding (my lemon tart was a fluffy and light variation I was delighted to meet) or cheese. The wine list is equally good value.

The whole place is lively, noisy, bustling, always full – an excellent choice for a family meal.

'The patron is a charming man whose restaurant produces unusual but first-class meals. We have visited three times this year and like the atmosphere and friendliness of the place.' – Noel and J. Ashton.

Map 4B **AUBIN-ST-VAAST** 62140 (Pas de Calais) 49 km SE of Boulogne

➔Madame Vézilier
La Gentilhommière 21.86.80.48.

On the N 39, the south bank of the Canche, an undistinguished village.

Hesdin is particularly short of lodging places. Here is the answer for a visit to the area.

M. and Madame Vézilier have only been offering chambre d'hôte accommodation for two years in their spankingly clean, brand-new, manor-style house in a quiet street just off the main road. Just completed are two new bedrooms, making five on offer altogether. They are all smashing. Well furnished, with all mod cons, at 180f a double including breakfast. Being new to the game, the Véziliers are trying hard to please, if that doesn't sound too cynical. Catch them while you can.

An arrow for convenience and a bargain stop.

Mme Vézilier

Map 4C **AUCHY-LES-HESDIN** 62171 (Pas-de-Calais) 61 km SE of Boulogne

5 km NE of Hesdin on the D94. A little town, dominated by the huge grey paper-mills on whose site once stood the monastery where the dead and wounded from Agincourt, only a few kms to the north, were cared for. The name has passed on to:

➔Auberge le Monastère
(RH)M *21.04.83.54. Closed Mon.*

I first met M. Marécaux at a French Workshop in London. He's just the kind of man who would bother to come over to promote his association, Les Trois Vallées. He is enthusiastic about his restaurant too and about his English clients; having worked in England, he has great affection for the country and its people. His recipe is an unusual one. The emblem of the restaurant is a *tonneau* (a large barrel), with a monk drawing off some wine from it and a smaller version of just such a *tonneau* is left on every table for the customers to take as much or as little as they please of the house wine it contains. This is included in the cost of the 100f menu (140f weekends) .

Starters are likely to be the chariot Grandgousier – a vast help yourself hors d'oeuvre buffet, or a dozen Burgundy snails or a terrine de poisson. His main course speciality is pink sea trout braised in champagne; or perhaps pièce de boeuf Henri IV.

M. Marécaux's proudest boast is that he has played with Acker Bilk, so a session at the piano is a very likely outcome to an evening spent in the old beamed room, with open fireplace. If he's not in the playing mood himself he hires an organist at the weekends.

Map 1A **AUDRESSELLES** 62164 Ambleteuse (Pas de Calais) 13 km N of Boulogne

The main coast road, the D 940, swings out to the coast here, via the fishing village of Audresselles. Crabs and mussels are on sale from numerous low Flemish-style fishermen's cottages or from the boats themselves. On a nasty bend by the square is:

Le Champenois
(R)M *21.32.94.68 Closed p.m. o.o.s., Feb.*

M. and Madame Fleury run one of the best fish restaurants in the area. Straightforward dishes of the freshest of the local catch, or specialities like timbale of crab feature on menus at 69 or 149f, but a grilled lobster from their vivier is another most attractive possibility.

Chez Mimi
(R)S-M *21.32.94.00. Open every day, year round.*

NEW OWNERS

I had decided to give Chez Mimi a miss, having been put off by the surly proprietor and a certain seediness, but the locals were outraged: 'You cannot leave out the best seafood restaurant in the area just because of "le corsaire",' they said. Well, they could well be right and I look forward to reports from braver souls than I.

The menu is almost exclusively fish, fresh from the Audresselles boats, with lobsters a speciality. Main courses like sole or turbot around 70f, a plate of moules marinière 20f.

Map 10D **AVILLY-ST-LEONARD** 60300 (Oise) 229 km SE Boulogne; 3 dm S of Senlis

A village just south of Senlis, bordering the forest of Chantilly.

Café de Paris
(HR)S *44 57.22.50*

A misnomer if ever there were one. There are few Parisian touches about this intrinsically simple little auberge on the corner of a quiet village street.

1993: Double rooms 160-200f. Menus from 120f.

Map 4A **LE BAHOT** – see Verton p. 132

Map 10D **BALAGNY** 60760 (Oise) 224 km SE of Boulogne; 4 km E of Senlis

Turn off autoroute at Senlis, exit 8, and follow signs to Crépy-en-Valois. 200 metres after roundabout take first lane to left, marked 'Balagny'.

Madame Hue
(Chambre d'Hôte). Place du Château d'Eau (44)54.41.88. EC

Bump down the lane, under the autoroute and turn left into the village.

Downtown Balagny must be aware of the myriad headlights snaking along so near, must hear the persistent rumble of the autoroute traffic, but chooses to ignore the imposition of such unnatural stress. The triangular village green is rarely disturbed by more than an intinerant mongrel or a diligently pecking chicken. The farmhouses lie firmly enclosed behind their mellow stone walls as they have for hundreds of years and the ambience of the village street owes more to manure and mud than fumes and oil.

A dark green gate faces the traveller, a ring prompts some frenzied barking and there, alert to open up and welcome, are M. and Madame Hue. Their 15th-century stone farmhouse was M. Hue's childhood home and his father's and grandfather's before that, and I doubt if much has changed in that time. The mangers where the beasts used to eat are still there in the kitchen. Madame Hue told me she had never bought a stick of furniture in her life – everything has been passed down through the generations, so that although the general trappings are extremely simple, I slept in her grandfather's splendid Directoire bed, which would no doubt fetch a fortune at auction, and the armoires and carved chests dotted about would make an antique dealer's eyes gleam.

In the living room it's all pretty basic – stone floors, wood ash in hearth (never saw a fire even in November, but the central heating is 20th century) scattered rag rugs. The seating clearly denotes status: Madame Hue gets a bleak wooden bench, her husband an arm chair and the two adored prize-winning dogs, a schnauzer and a French bulldog, a comfortable full-size bed in the warmest corner by the fire.

Guests eat breakfast here at the refectory table. No packaged jam, no plastic butter for Madame Hue. Rather a selection of whatever flavours she happens to have made last. For us it was blackcurrant, apricot, raspberry, and a fluorescent orange confection that had us guessing until she told us it was carrot. The farm butter comes in a slab, the coffee and hot fresh milk in prodigious steaming quantity.

The anglophile Hues are kindness personified; nothing is too much trouble to help their visitors find their way around, advise on restaurants, discuss their plans. Madame Hue will cook an evening meal *sur commande* for those too fatigued from a long journey to venture out again to Senlis. 'Two courses?' I quizzed. '*Mais non – un bon souper,*' was the indignant response. We never sampled the bon souper, but I gather that for 50f you get soup, entrée, meat, veg, cheese, pudding and wine.

So far, so very good, but there are flies in this attractive ointment. This is certainly no place for the infirm or the incontinent. The two adjoining bedrooms in the house are up two flights of steeply winding stairs, with wash basins but no loo or bathroom. M. Hue's evenings were no doubt enlivened by the sight of friend Ann and me skipping skittishly throuqh his living room and kitchen clutching sponge bags and negligées, on our way to the tub, but the arrangement is hardly ideal for the modest, or those who have to rise in the night or have reservations about their bodily functions being general knowledge.

And some might object that the farmhouse is too *familiale*, with evidences of grandchildren's toys and personal belongings in every room. The farmhouse is cosy but I suspect that the lady who wrote to me complaining of dust on top of the wardrobe would have a field day here. And grandpa must have been a shortie – I had to lie diagonally across that bed.

So this must be a very special choice for special people and by no means recommended for all. In favour are most of the things I personally value highly: warmth – of house, water and welcome – perfect situation near autoroute and delightful Senlis yet rurally quiet; excellent value at 120f for one, 160f for two, breakfast inclusive. Against is a certain lack of comfort.

There is also a cottage across the courtyard with two more double rooms and cooking facilities for 600f a week, 92f a night.

Map 6D **BAVELINCOURT** 80260 Villers Bocage (Somme) 113 km from Boulogne; 13 km NE of Amiens

On the D929 then right on to the D115.

M. Noel Valengin
(Chambrer d'Hôte)

NO NEWS

An amazing 1898 manor house in the depths of the countryside, very well preserved inside and out. It has five comfortable double bedrooms for 110-140f, but you must share bathroom and loo. All very peaceful, in pleasantly calm surroundings, wih good reports on both comfort and the agreeability of the owners.

Map 2C **BAYENGHEM-LES-SENINGHEM** 62380 Lumbres (Pas de Calais) 38 km E of Boulogne

Turn right off the D42 just before Lumbres to this peaceful hamlet, tucked into the hillside. Beside the church is:

Hostellerie Le Relais
(HR)S *(21) 39.64.54 Closed Sat.; Sun. p.m., 16/8-3/9 CB AE V*

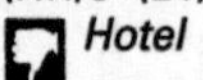
Hotel *Restaurant*

A nice old faded house, white paint peeling a bit perhaps, with four very basic bedrooms for the very basic price of 170-180f. M. Micielski stresses that he runs a restaurant rather than a hotel and is not at all happy if you eat anywhere but here. You would indeed be unwise to do so, since Madame Micielski's cooking is the best value for miles around. Proudly displayed are her diplomas won at Pas-de-Calais *foires gastronomiques.* She cooks whatever is best in the market and in her garden that day, and consequently don't expect her to produce a menu. Her friendly and capable daughter recites the dishes on offer: for 120f fish, meat, cheese and dessert, often featuring home-reared chicken, home-grown veg, with occasional flights of fancy for desserts like cream-filled feuilleté or gâteau glacé. Her home-made jams feature on the breakfast table.

An unusually unspoiled stop in this area and recommended for exceptional honest home cooking.

But don't be as soppy as your author, who ought to know better, who failed to book for a November Sunday lunch, and turned up late, car-fatigued and hungry and had the misery of being turned away from a room bursting with shiny-faced, stomach-patting French families relishing every mouthful of their lunch. Nor, I beg you, follow her unwise footsteps to the next village, where a sign 'Café de la Place' led her to believe that here might be a worthy substitute. She could have got packet soup, overcooked lamb and Instant Whip at home.

Map 4B **BEAURAINVILLE** 62990 (Pas de Calais) 42 km SE of Boulogne

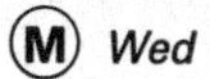

9 km SE of Montreuil on the D 113. See Valley of the Canche.

A sizeable village, with a market in the square on Wednesdays. Alongside is:

Val de Canche

(HR)S *21.90.32.22 Closed Sun. p.m.; Mon.; 15/10-30/10; 24/12-2/1 All Cards*

Very much the centre of activity, with a bar that is rarely empty of local characters.

M. Decobert cooks consistently well. 'Professional' was how a colleague described him, and I would agree. He offers menus at 65, 105 and 140f but has an admirable penchant for *cuisine du terroir* – a terrine of game, local eels – and for these specialities you must look to the carte.

The rooms, at 120-225f, are basic but immaculate; some have their own shower or bath, but it's down the corridor for the loo.

'Visited in November. The rooms, although lacking atmosphere, were nevertheless very clean. We enjoyed an excellent evening meal cooked by the owner.' – Noel and J. Ashton.

'We had a very fine Sunday lunch there, including a delicious smoked trout soufflé, a classic raspberry tart and a memorable pear sorbet with Calvados which practically blew the top of one's head off.' – Jill Thomas.

Map 9B **BEAUVAIS** 60000 (Oise) 168 km from Boulogne.

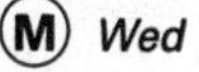

The fact that, having allocated a whole day to 'do' Beauvais, I completed the task in a couple of hours is an indication of its limitations. The 1940 bombardment has left little of interest in this ancient town, standing, as it has done since Roman times, on a strategic north/south route. The obvious exception of course is the tallest cathedral in Christendom, St. Pierre, whose vast bulk dominates not only the town but the whole of the Picardy plain. Unlike Amiens, built with quite unbelievable speed, Beauvais' construction spans many centuries, and indeed it never was finally completed, still lacking a nave and a replacement for the spire which collapsed in 1573.

Its building seemed doomed, a saga of disasters running from the first primitive cathedral built during the Carolingian reign, through collapses, feudal disputes, fires, the Hundred Years War, up to the 16th century when building ceased.

The height of its choir is neck-cricking – 204 ft of it, vertical lines soaring to the extremities of the possibilities of Gothic art. Don't miss the 16th-century rose window in the south transept and the 19th-century astronomic clock, which shows the movement of planets and tides and strikes only the hours between noon and five.

Hôtel du Palais
(H)M-S *9 r. St. Nicolas 44.45.12.58 AE, V*

Not far from the cathedral is this little hotel, built like most of the town in dull modern style, mitigated in this case by the warmth and friendliness of its patronne, Madame Claret.

The rooms, shiningly clean, are comfortably furnished, with cheerful flowered wallpapers, and the plumbing works. If you have to stay in this rather dull area, you would be made most welcome at Le Palais. Rooms are 105-250f with bath.

Marignan
(R)M (R)S *1 r. de Malherbe 44.48.15.15 Closed Sun. p.m.; Mon.; 1/2-21/2. All Cards*

In the main shopping street, with two options – a smartish restaurant upstairs, with menus from 98f and a bar/brasserie downstairs, which I, in common with an encouraging number of local office workers, found ideal for an inexpensive lunch – cheerful, bustling atmosphere, good well-cooked food.

Map 9B **BEAUVAIS-WARLUIS** 60122 (Oise) 170 km SE of Boulogne

4 km S of Beauvais on the N 1.

Le Petit Provençal
(R)M *44.02.30.20 Closed Sun.; 14/7-15/8; 20/12-31/12*

NO NEWS

A useful main road stop. A small and pretty provençal-style restaurant, with a cellar bar where you can taste and take away wine from a vast and discriminating selection.

No menu, but portions are generous, so two courses should be ample. Carte dishes are based on traditional cooking, with little signs of Provençal influence apart from pigs' trotters à la Marseillaise (96f for two people). Otherwise, a wild mushroom salad costs 32f, a plump Bresse chicken served with leeks 62f, and pears cooked in Bordeaux 20f.

Map 4A **BERCK-PLAGE** 62600 (Pas de Calais) 42 km S of Boulogne

A vast sprawling agglomeration whose approach roads seem to go on for ever before they end on the busy seafront. Here those unfortunates who suffer from diseases of the bone are pushed out to catch the sea air on strange mobile beds. Not a Fenn favourite, I have to admit. Personally I find the combination of their obvious misfortune with the brashness of the 'amusements' and scruffy bars a depressing one, but the beach, 12 km long, extending to the mouth of the Canche, is magnificent and the number of year-round residents and visitors ensure some good restaurants, much favoured by locals for Sunday lunch outings. The **Agora**, for the more energetic, is a modern indoor sports complex right on the seafront.

Le Homard Bleu
(HR)M *48 pl Entonnoir 21.09.04.65 Open all year All Cards*

An agreeable refuge from the nearby prom; a comfortable restaurant serving mostly fish dishes including an excellent soupe de poisson and some regional specialities like caudière berckoise. Menus from 65f. Rooms, which could be noisy, are of very assorted standards 195-230f.

L'Entonnoir
(H)S *Sun. p.m.; Wed. o.o.s. 21.09.12.13 Closed 15/12-15/1 AE, V, EC*

Almost opposite, another restaurant with a feeling of solidly reliable bourgeois good value. Rooms 185-230f. Menus from 58f.

Restaurant Edward
(R)M *bvd. de Paris 21.09.07.98 Closed Sun. p.m.; Mon. o.o..s.*

NO NEWS

For those in transit not wishing to get embroiled with the main drag, Edward's on the outskirts is a good bet. Ignore the unpromisingly dull façade to take advantage of imaginative cooking at moderate prices. Edward is an Englishman illustrating to the French that it is possible to serve, for 115f, fresh salmon marinaded in lime, then a fillet of beef with wild mushrooms, Philippe Olivier cheeses and charlotte russe with strawberry sauce. Well worth the money, but he does have other commendable menus at 48.50f and 69.50f. Under the same management at the same address is the **Hôtel la Molière** with rooms from 50-104f, open year round.

Map 3B **BEUSSENT/ENGOUDSENT** 62212 (Pas de Calais) 32 km SE of Boulogne; 10 km No of Montreuil

Take the D127 to Beussent and cross over the river. Then turn immediately left, following the Course* for 1 km.

Au Bon Accueil
(R)S *Restaurant Debove. Hammeau d'Engoudsent 21.90.70.63. Lunch only; closed Tues.*

This one deserves a book all to itself. It happily refutes the cynics' put-down – that no small restaurant can survive being highly praised in an English guide without letting standards drop or character change. Readers have flocked to the little café/restaurant to sample Madame Debove's hospitality and been unanimous in their praise. Obviously there's something about the place that encourages the putting of pen to paper because no other establishment has such a bulging file. And yet nothing has changed since I first wrote about it six years ago (except the prices, which have doubled but are still excellent value). You still get four or five courses, according to the mood of the house, the weather, the market, and how many other clients are waiting. You have no choice, but are invariably happy to leave it all in Madame's capable hands, confident that, whatever arrives on your plate (which might well be altogether different from your neighbour's), it will be copious and good.

Trout from the Course figures regularly, pheasant in season, gigots of lamb, roast beef, duck, with some variation of hors d'oeuvre and a pudding that could be a hot apple tart or maybe a rum baba oozing with booze, or sometimes just prime fruit. There will always be a host of locals tucking in and on Sundays you would be very foolish not to book.

Little Madame Debove pops in and out, greeting arrivals, miraculously getting food to tables in the right order (not that it matters much – it's often all on the same plate), assisted nowadays by her son, who does much of the cooking. The only obvious 'improvement' is a smart new sign on the road, indicating that Restaurant Debove is now firmly on the map. So long as it continues like this, it will certianly remain on mine.

Here is what Professor Glyn and Ruth Daniel, local residents, have to say:

'Glad to be introduced to this. Got on very well with Madame, who seemed very perky. The food was delicious. We had hors d'oeuvres,

trout, roast chicken and pork with prunes (all on the same dish), salad and a delicious covered apple tart.'

From Derek Sheffield: 'This establishment just about sums up for me what France is all about. A fantastic hors d'oeuvre, seven appetisers on one dish, trout with new potatoes, mange-tout and a delicious sauce, a cream tart with puff pastry and raisins, ten perfect cheeses and two French beers, all for 72f.'

The price now is 70f for lunch, with good and reasonable wine. Thank you Madame Debove for backing me up so handsomely.

1993: Now run by daughter.

* See 'Valley of the Course', p. 86.

Map 3B **BEUSSENT/ZERABLES** 62212 (Pas de Calais) 29 km S of Boulogne; 12 km N of Montreuil

Just a signpost on the D127, following the valley of the Course*.

Café Restaurant Cocatrix-Grémont

(R)S *Hameau de Zérables 21.90.73.39 Always open*

The 'always open' says it all. Readers have been delighted with the atmosphere of this modest little restaurant, where the family Grémont-Delame have been known to open up to frantic knocking on a dark and dirty night and to cook the refugees, sole customers, a made-to-measure meal. With smiles. Not that the surprisingly large dining room is often empty. On Sunday it fills up with locals who are well aware of the value on offer.

Even with a new coat of whitewash, this is no beauty – an incongruously modern building down a track which leads to the romantically named Lacs d'Amour. But the consensus has overwhelmingly been in favour of ignoring the plastique and concentrating on the grub.

The cheapest menu is now 55f for three courses. which usually includes local trout, but if an omelette and frîtes is what you fancy, don't hesitate to ask.

Map 4C **BLANGY-SUR-TERNOISE** 62770 Le Parcq (Pas de Calais) 77 km SE of Boulogne

11 km NE of Hesdin on the D94.

An unattractive stretch of country, but for those who prefer to use the yellow Michelin roads, Blangy might well prove a useful stop. Right on the road is:

Relais du Ternois
21.41.85.60 *Closed Mon.*

NEW MANAGEMENT

Some of the most interesting food around, cooked by the young Pascal Henneguelle. No carte, but on menus at 45f, 65f, 85f and 130f you can sample: mushrooms stuffed with a gratin of spinach, a ragout of snails with morilles, magret of duck with pears, escalope of veal with a shrimp sauce, a plum tart for dessert.

All very good news. The bad is that the service is slow and disinterested and the ambience is not warm. Locals shake their heads and say apologetically, 'les jeunes!'. News of any experiences here particularly welcome, because, with the right attitude and some more experience, it could be a winner. Menus 60-130f.

Map 2B **BONNINGUES-LES-ARDRES** 62890 Tournehem sur la Hem (Pas de Calais) 28 km E of Boulogne; 10 km S of Ardres

Turn off the N4215 km W of Boulogne at Nabrighen on to the D 224, then turn right on to the D 21.

Le Manoir
(Chambre d'Hôte) 21Route de Licques. 21.82.69.05., 21.82.56.21. EC

A nice old shuttered manor house in the village centre, set back from the road in its garden. It was Madame Christiane Dupont's family home and now she has furnished six spacious and comfortable rooms for guests. The bathrooms are modern, the furnishings tasteful, and I think Le Manoir could be a godsend for those wanting a peaceful stay in the country, only a few miles from the ports. 120f for one person, 200f including breakfast.

An arrow, I suspect, as soon as I have managed to stay there myself, which I promise will not be long.

Map 4C **BOUBERS-SUR-CANCHE** 62270 Frévent (Pas de Calais) 76 km SE of Boulogne

Boubers regularly wins the Lauréat International for the best *village fleuri*, and certainly flowers do tumble out of window boxes and flowerbeds in every garden in the village street. It is dominated by the gates of its château, next to the church with its espaliered trees. The bench opposite is a good place to stop for a picnic, or there's:

La Crémaillère
(R)S *pl. de L'Eglise 21.03.60.03*

You can sit outside this little café in the square and watch nothing very much happen. Good for an omelette and chips, or just a beer. Menus at 90 and 110f.

L'Ile Flottante
(R)M-S *r. Principale 21.03.62.37 Closed Weds*

NO NEWS

Named, I suspect, not after the meringuey sweet, but because the Canche rushes round a little island just here, by this pretty little restaurant. It is most agreeable to sit in its colourful garden in the summer or in the cosy dining room, hung about with copper pans, in colder weather. Menus from 70f.

Map 2A **BOULOGNE-SUR-MER** 62200 (Pas de Calais)

 *Wed., Sat.*

The Hôtel d'Angleterre I cannot recommend. This is the name given by the French to the old debtors' prison in the Haute Ville, filled in the 18th century with refugees from the English law, who had fallen into debt again here across the Channel.

Boulogne has always had an attraction for the English. It used to be an elegant resort, much favoured by the Edwardians, who built second homes overlooking the sea and the river. They felt at home here in the British colony across the water, enjoying the fine stretches of sand, the chic parades along the prom, the first thermal baths in Europe, the Parisian shops, the superb restaurants. They brought their families for long summer months to benefit from the briny air of the outlying villages of Wimereux and le Portel. Boudin loved to paint the scene.

It takes some imagination now to picture how it must have been. The waterfront still bustles but not with Edwardian ladies and their entourages; nowadays it's ferry boats, cargo-ships and fishing boats. Boulogne is France's first *port de pêche.*

Most of the catch gets canned or frozen or driven, at the high speed the French admirably apply to transporting perishables, to Rungis, but stalls along the front usually have some mussels or something flappingly fresh to sell to the housewives or day trippers.

Industrialisation has swallowed the banks of the river Liane, where factories and building yards and garages mushroom. (I've never seen so many garages.) The lavish Edwardian villas and hotels perished in the last war. Their 20th-century reincarnation in the *basse ville* is indiscriminately concrete.

The Boulonnais have Napoleon to thank for the town's prosperity. He cast his acquisitive imperial eye across the narrow strait of water that separated him from another potential outpost under his command and set logical plans afoot to conquer the 'damp soil' of

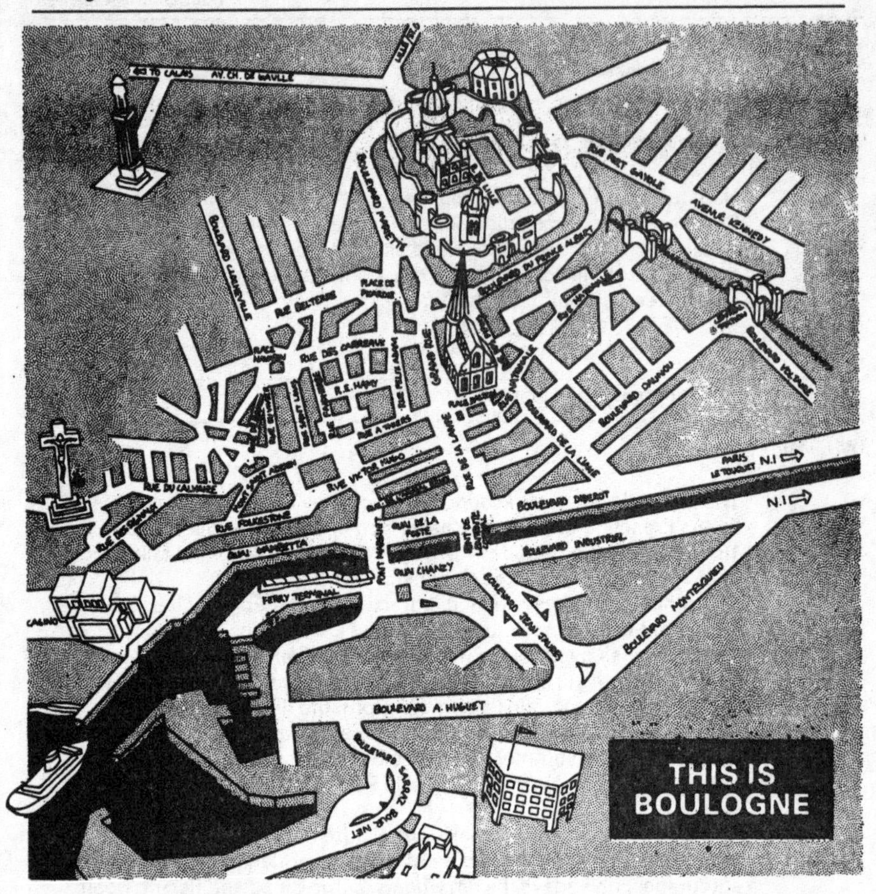

England. In 1805 the bay of Boulogne along the coast to Ambleteuse was filled with a huge invasion fleet, awaiting his command to sail north. On a commanding plateau behind the town the supporting troops encamped. How menacing it must have been to have looked seaward from Folkestone and seen there the tall column he set up in honour of his Grande Armée.

By one of those fascinating twists in timing, at the critical moment he was diverted from the action that would certainly have changed the course of history by the Austerlitz campaign and Nelson's victory over his fleet at Trafalgar, but in the meantime he had enlarged the port to harbour 2000 ships and Boulogne has never looked back.

In fact Napoleon wasn't the first general to use Boulogne as a stepping-off base for the submission of the British. Julius Caesar had set off trom here in 53 BC with the same idea. Henry VIII redressed the balance somewhat when he did the reverse crossing in 1544 and annexed Boulogne for six years.

The British may not rule nor live here any more, but they still come to do their shopping in the lower town. If they care at all to picture how the old Boulogne must have been, they must climb up the Grande Rue to the old town, the 'Haute Ville', where the ghosts still linger.

Once inside the encircling 13th-century ramparts, the frenetic 20th century down below is forgotten. I like it best in winter, when the mist swirls, the cobbled streets are empty, footsteps echo and the square built in honour of the crusader Godefroy-de-Bouillon has no anachronistic cars confusing the prospect. There are fine and historical buildings here – the 18th-century Hôtel de Ville, the Hôtel Desandrouins, also known as the Imperial Palace – Napoleon's invasion HQ – the library built on the site of an ancient convent, and the 13th-century Gothic belfry (climb up for a stunning view on a clear day).

You can – and should – walk all round the ramparts, punctuated by the four massive gates, on the gravel path laid between the rosebeds, with a fascinating lay-out of the city and seascape far below. If you're planning a picnic, you can buy the ingredients in the *haute ville* and eat it here, or on a bench in the well-groomed lawns and gardens just outside the walls, facing crescents of old and dignified grey houses.

But the focal point of the *haute ville*, of the whole town, and indeed of the whole area, since you can see it for miles around, is the imposingly-domed cathedral of Notre Dame, named after an apparition of the Virgin, in the 7th century. A procession in mediaeval costumes, perpetuating the centuries-old prilgrimage in her honour, still takes place on the last Sunday in August. On other days her wooden statue, crowned with gems, stands in the central chapel of the vast 19th-century basilica.

Underneath is a labyrinth of subterranean passages and rooms, with vestiges of a 3rd-century Roman temple. Only a hundred or so years ago, a remarkable 11th-century crypt, with painted pillars, was discovered here by the builders of the existing cathedral. Edward 11 of England married Isabelle of France there.

Cobbles can be hard on the feet and if all this stopping and staring makes you long for a cuppa, you could do no better than make for the *salon de thé* and *chocolatier* run by two charming ladies, **Béthouart** at 46 r. de Lille.

On the way down the hill again, stop off at the museum (closed Tue) and look at the paintings of some of the artists who loved the old Boulogne – Corot, Boudin, Fantin Latour.

Then on to the cobbled pl. St. Nicolas, bounded by brasseries and bars, well patronised by thirsty Brits. They might like to know that outside the church of St. Nicolas is a public WC with an appealing notice: 'chalet de refuge'.

On Wednesday and Saturday mornings the square and its adjacent streets is the site of the biggest market in the region. Farmers and

Boulogne

their wives cage their two rabbits, four hens, one duck, tie up bunches of herbs, assemble their goats' cheeses, cut their lettuces, make up posies, pick wild mushrooms and set up their wares alongside the itinerant market-men with motorised bases from which to sell charcuterie or dairy produce, and the technicolour vegetable stalls, overflowing with whatever fruit and veg are in season. This is the best French shopping experience of all.

A more modern approach is via the hypermarket – the mighty **Auchan**, 8 km outside the town off the N 42 St. Omer road. Open 9 a.m. until 10 p.m. Monday to Saturday, always packed with compats loading up with cheap beer and skittles. For those who want to make a day of it under the one roof – and thousands do – the Flunch cafeteria is not at all bad for good-value refreshment. Efforts are currently under way to upmarket the produce on offer here and the cheese and charcuterie stands are particularly admirable.

Food shopping in Boulogne is a pleasure easily realised because most of the more interesting shops are grouped together in the central grid of streets, within a short hump from the port. The most famous gourmet stop is of course **Phillippe Olivier** in the r. Thiers, whence cometh the cheese course for many a prestigious English restaurant. A visit here is an education, especially if you can buttonhole M. Olivier and get him to show you round the caves where 200-odd varieties are cosseted. Ask advice as to best seasonal choice and buy farm butter and crème fraîche while you're about it.

Even more unusual for English visitors though is **Idriss.** 24 Grande Rue, an Aladdin's cave of a shop, glowing with all manner of preserved exotic fruits, stacks of glacéed baby cumquats, kiwi fruit, mangos, greengages, quarterings of lemon and orange peel – twice the colour, twice the flavour of the chopped-up, tubbed kind back home. Pears and apricots and peaches look dried not shrivelled, nuts tumble from sacks. spices are ranked in glass apothecary jars.

A welcome new delicatessen has opened up at 35 Grande Rue – **La Comtesse du Barry**. Upmarket preserves from all over France, some prepared by top chefs, make good presents. Tins of crème tartinière aux deux saumons et à la vodka, followed by cuisse de canard aux ris de veau aux oignons fondants, and a petit soufflé à la poire could make up a whole cheating meal.

Down the same road nearer the pl. Dalton choose picnic desirables from **Derrien**, the best charcutier in town, usefully open on Sun. a.m. and proceed to **Lugand** for pâtisserie and coffee, picking up some chocolates there or across the road at **Léonidas.** (On the other hand the locals prefer to make for the bvd. Daunou near the railway station to buy their cakes and chocs at **Géneau**, n. 38.) **Le Cornet d'Amour** in the r. Thiers (with another in r. de la Lampe) is another pastry/tea shop favoured more by Boulonnais than by Brits.

Dotted about the town are high quality boutiques for clothes and shoes; Les **Nouvelles Galeries** in the r. Victor Hugo is the more upmarket of the two chain stores (**Prisunic** the other).

For wine-buying there are several options, apart from the hypermarket. My first choice would always be **Le Chais,** where you can park easily and load up the car. To find it, drive up the bvd. Daunou, turn sharp left after the railway bridge into the rue des Deux Ponts. The owner is unfailingly informative and helpful, whether its 'vrac' or plonk you're buying or a major investment of some of the quality wine he stocks in his mammoth warehouse, all at very competitive prices. You can wander around, learn a lot, and have free tastings (closed Sun., Mon. and two hours for lunch). However, if time does not allow this additional excursion, there are three branches of **Les Vins de France,** with the one in the r. Nationale the most helpful, all usefully open on Sunday mornings. Or you can resort to the supermarkets, like the **P.G Supermarket** (open 9-8, Mon-Sat.) which has roof parking, just behind the Hotel Ibis.

Don't overlook the r. Nationale for clothes shopping; here are **Anastasia, Cloé, Reflets de Paris, Bergamote** – all classy dressers and **Prestige** for men. **La Maison du Rideau** in the same street has good wallpaper and fabric ideas, a little different from the home range. On the corner of r. Faidherbe and the r. Victor Hugo is an excellent bookshop, **Duminy,** to buy local maps and guides; **Kiabi** a huge clothes shop in r. Victor Hugo at most reasonable prices for all ages; **Lacroix** unisex clothes; see if French trousers are really a better fit; **Caprice Cadeaux** at 24 r. Nationale, for fine china and presents. The manager Jacques Bellanger is also the President of the **Boulogne Shoppers Club,** which gathers 50 shopkeepers in Boulogne giving British customers special discounts and other facilities. A special card is sent on receipt of an English (18p) stamped addressed envelope. **Parfumerie Gilliocq** at 6 Grande Rue, take back one of the 100 different perfumes, or other beauty products – all beautifully wrapped.

If you need a chemist or doctor out of opening hours, you must ring the police, who will direct to you the one on duty; for emergency petrol supplies there is a Total garage on the industrial estate on the N 1 towards Paris, open from 6 a.m. to midnight. soon it will be programmed to take credit and purchases all night. Or the Mobil on the St. Omer/Calais road is open all day and every night except Tue/Wed. The banks are open Mon-Fri, 8.30-12 and 1.30-5., but if you do get caught out penniless, **Scalbert Dupont** at the ferry terminal and at the hoverport stay open every day from 10-1.30 and 3-7 p.m.

For extra-early breakfasts, the **Bar Hamiot** on the front is an experience; it opens, as it has done for many years, at 5 a.m. to feed the fishermen, straight from unloading their boats. Their favourite warming tipple is a café bistouille – strong black coffee laced with cognac.

The Tourist Information Centre, where they speak English and will arrange hotel bookings, is on the other side of the river from the town, Pont Marguet. (21)31.68.38. Open every day July and August 10 a.m. till 7 a.m. Rest of the year except Sun. and Mon. 9 a.m. to 12 p.m. and 1.30 p.m. to 6 p.m.

Nausicaa

Centre National de la Mer, Boulevard Sainte-Beuve 62200, Boulogne-sur-Mer. 21.30.99.99. Open April to September from 10 am to 8pm, October to March from 10am to 6pm.

Any extended visit to Boulogne would be incomplete without a trip to Nausicaa, France's marvellous national sea-world. A hi-tech reconstruction of life beneath the waves using smells, sounds, atmospheric music, changes in temperature and light, which transports you into an underwater world to interact with the fish as you pass in semi-darkness past aquariums boasting sea-life from plankton to sharks. There are touch tanks where children can tickle the tummies of friendly skate and visual effects give eyeball to eyeball contact with lobsters and crabs; humans are given the impression of being caught with a shoal of tuna in a net and eerie ocean depths are explored as if from a submarine.

All explanatory signs are in English and French. This is an ideal day out for both adults and kids. Adults 45f and under 12s 30f; there is also a bar/restaurant, library and cinema running a continuous projection of films about the sea and its environment.

Restaurant du Nausicaa
(R/B)M *21.33.24.24.*

Both bar and restaurant are open until 11 pm each evening, 7 days a week – although the exhibition closes at 6 pm (8 pm March–October).

The bar only serves snacks, sandwiches, pain au chocolat, hot dogs etc. with a special deal for 25f which gets you 3 oysters and a glass of wine. The restaurant serves a lot of sea-food dishes, as you'd expect, with whole sections on the menu devoted to delicious oysters, fruits de mer, shell-fish and fish. It is about £10 for a main course à la carte or you can try the good value menus at 145f or 210f. There is a children's menu too at 40f for 3 courses. I highly recommend the whole complex as an edifying family excursion.

The Morin Country Slow Train
12 rue du Cloître 62200 Boulogne-sur-Mer 21.80.83.92.

This old train, built in 1951, was recently rescued by a group of enthusiasts who, against all odds, lacking the support of politicians and other adminstrative bodies, have spent *all* their spare time raising money to get her back on the rails and running the weekly sortie to Desvres, a gentle pottery town some 18 miles out of Boulogne. Meandering through the countryside at a sedate 10 mph, the train leaves behind the industrial estates and docksides of Boulogne and enters a sort of rural bliss of cows, hens, little gardens and tiny stations. Brightly painted in blue and yellow the little locomotive is a real winner with kids and a great source of relaxation for the older generation.

HOTELS

The hotel situation in Boulogne is not good. Those who are seeking a pampered weekend must look further afield. I can only suggest a few tried and tested old British favourites:

Le Métropole
(H)M *51 r. Thiers 21.31.54.30 Closed 21/12-5/1 All Cards*

The Métropole has many loyal devotees, who are faithful to the very friendly management. They particularly like the attractive little rear dining room, where breakfast is taken. Rooms from 310-390f.

Le Faidherbe
(H)M *12 r. Faidherbe. 21.31.60.93*

Don't be put off by the grim exterior – it's all very much nicer with a log fire and a cheeky parrot to greet you. The modern bedrooms are very pleasant and well equipped, at 190-300f. But there have been booking problems, so take extra care.

La Plage
(H)M-S *124 bvd. Ste. Beuve 21.31.45.36 Closed Mon; 20/12-28/1; Rest. closed Sun. p.m. o.o.s.*

CHANGE OF MANAGEMENT

A deservedly popular, very French little hotel on the front, with two look-alike sisters in charge. It's bright, clean, inexpensive and the food is so good that even in winter the dining room is full at weekends. Substantial menus start at 62f.

The rooms are pleasantly furnished. A double with bath costs 125f; cheaper versions start at 85f. It is always tempting to take one with a balcony overlooking the sea, but even in winter the traffic noise is considerable and I think that light sleepers would be wiser to opt for a room at the rear, especially at busy times.

An arrow for good value, good food, pleasant atmosphere.

Le Castel
(HR)S *51 r. Nationale 21.31.52.88 No News*

NO NEWS

Here is a reader's alternative suggestion, just round the corner from the pl. Dalton – although a M. Evrard has just taken over ownership.

'Room 85f for two – clean and well decorated. Very friendly people and excellent cooking. Set meal 47f – the best meal of the holiday: home-made soup and plenty of fresh herbs or prawn cocktail with large prawns, followed by cod in lemon sauce or succulent pork, then good chocolate mousse.' – Rosemary and Claire Hancock.

Hôtel de Londres
(H)M *Place de France 21.31.35.63.*

Similar in standard to the Faidherbe, the Hôtel de Londres is to be found next to the bus depot in Place de France. Thankfully there are no night buses (hours 8am to 6.30pm) and so your night's sleep will not be disturbed every 5 minutes. The staff here are very friendly and there is a wide range of clean, good value rooms. Doubles with shared bathroom from 110f, with bathroom and TV from 150f and a room for 3 about 280f.

RESTAURANTS

Here is a different story – one eats better than one sleeps in Boulogne, with a choice of two Michelin stars in the vicinity. (See Pont de Briques p. 130.)

La Matelote
(R)L *80 bvd. Ste. Beuve 21.30.17.97 Closed 15/6-30/6; 23/12-18/1; Sun. p.m. EC, V.*

Tony Lestienne earned his rosette by combining the best of both *nouvelle* and *ancienne* disciplines. His currently pink (I liked the yellow better) restaurant is a fair step along the front, opposite the Casino, but even mid-week o.o.s. it is always full (so do book). He is not afraid to offer up traditional dishes like a *daube* of beef, which goes down a treat on a winter's night, and his fish is always excellent – simply cooked but served with the kind of sauce, like a fluffy sabayon flecked with herbs, that earned him that star.

His pâtisserie is always outstanding so go for any feuilletés on the menu – it was an outstanding asparagus version when I was last there, but the crab is recommended too – and leave room for the desserts. Tempting nibbles and/or Philippe Olivier cheeses at either end. Wines will push up the bill considerably. Allow 250f if you eat à la carte, or 160f if the menu of the day suits.

La Liègeoise
(R)M-L *10 r. Av. Monsigny 21.31.61.15 Closed Sun. p.m.; Wed. AE, DC, EC, V*

Alain Delpierre continues to draw the businessmen for weekday lunch, and the families for Sundays, to his black-and-yellow decorated restaurant, opposite the theatre, bedecked with an over-abundance of plastic foliage. His daily menus at 95f (not weekends) are excellent value, not to be missed by those who wish to sample French cooking by an up-and-coming young chef of considerable talent, but for a focal point to a Boulogne jaunt I would go for the 155f

'Promenade gourmande', where small portions of five dishes, interrupted by a sorbet, rounded off by the ubiquitous Philippe Olivier's best, give an even better idea of his range, and less ground for the complaint that 'that nouvelle muck doesn't fill you up'.

The wine list is extensive, well chosen and not expensive.

L'Huitrière

(R)M *11 pl. de Lorraine 21.31.35.27 Closed Sun. p.m.; Mon. All Cards*

Nothing wrong with the freshness of the fish at **Hamiots**, if you don't mind the hassle of a smoky brasserie, but nowadays there is another fishy option in Boulogne. Philippe Cardon's little restaurant, tucked away in a corner of the r. Faidherbe away from the less discriminating day trippers' eyes, is a welcome newcomer.

You have to go through the shop which sells smoked fish, oysters and fresh prawns to take away, and then squeeze through the sliding door into a pint-sized dining room, full of businessmen at lunch time (so book). It's all blue and white and fresh and functional and for serious eaters, especially if you order the plâteau de fruits de mer, served on seaweed on a hollowed cork bark – an excellent deal for 115f, but requiring time and industry.

I recommend the 120f menu, with two fish dishes and the house version of apple tart, more Yorkshire pudding than pastry. Otherwise a single fish dish from the best of the morning's catch, like sole or halibut, will cost around 95f, as will the Flemish dish *waterzoi* – an assembly of assorted poached fish. Muscadet sur Lie 70f.

➔Le Ste. Beuve

(R)S *16 r. de Pot d'Etain 21.31.32.33.*

Turn left off the r. de la Lampe to find in a side street this nice old stone house where Boulogne's most famous son, the philosopher and writer Ste. Beuve, was born. This has now been transformed into the kind of restaurant that is all things to all men. If you want chips with your boeuf bourguignon that's O.K. with the accommodating owners, but there is more, much more. Somewhere a chef with imagination is lurking, or how else would my skate arrive with segments of pink grapefruit nicely cutting the batter in which it was cooked? Let us hope that he doesn't just give in. (Every time I go the ratio of Brits to French is higher.)

The menu value is the best in town. For 75f, including ¼ bottle of wine or beer, you get three courses of the ilk of crab and whelk salad with a 'whisky' sauce, or hot sausage on potato salad, followed by a brochette of fish with shrimp sauce or an escalope of veal with port wine sauce, then a respectable cheeseboard or dessert. I tried the tarte maison, which varies according to the season, but was in my case 'aux poires' with the pears professionally fanned out on the bed of crème pâtisserie and glazed with apricot.

Don't go for a gourmet experience; rather for excellent value, well-cooked food in comfortable surroundings, with the management still new enough to be trying hard. An arrow before it gets too popular.

➔Le Fats Domino
(R)M-S *80 r. Victor Hugo 21.30.94.60.*

At the extreme end of the r. Victor Hugo, also visible from the seafront. Currently the favourite of every local I asked value-for-money-wise. In the evenings you get even more value because of the jazz sessions in the stone cellars. The food is not only cheap, it's interesting. There is a useful "Express du Midi" lunchtime formula – 2 courses like magret de canard and a plateful of different sorbets and appropriate coulis for 60f. An arrow for good value, good food.

➔Chez Jules
(R)M-S *Pl. Dalton 21.31.54.12.*

Welcome renaissance of an old favourite; excellent fish, from a bowl of moules to a seafood brochette suspended on a kind of gallows. Rillettes on 90f menu left for help-yourselfers. Cheerful bustling noisy atmosphere. An arrow.

➔Bar Hamiot
(R)S *1 r. Faidherbe 21.31.44.20*

Hamiot's commanding position, on the sea front on the corner of the main r. Faidherbe, might well cause the British traveller in search of a real French meal to pass on by, suspecting it to be full of compats. He would be wrong to do so, for trippery though the outside may appear, crowded, noisy, smoky though the interior, Hamiot's is more than a tourist trap. It goes on doing what it has always done since the well-known local family Hamiot first opened up this fishermen's favourite – dishing up no-frills honest nosh at honest prices. It's a popular with the Boulonnais as with the British, and you should be firmly bottoms-down by 12.30 if you want a lunch table. The excellent menu, fishy-orientated, costs 55f always including the fish of the day, fish soup and mussels, with nothing-special cheese and pud. Arrowed as an honourable Boulogne institution.

An-Bascaille-Là
(R)M-S *16 pl. Godefroy de Bouillon 21.80.57.30.*

Almost impossible to eat well in the *haute ville,* alas, for which I suppose we must blame the sightseers and tourists who allow the restaurateurs to cash in on them. At least An-Bascaille-Là is sometimes good (when the patronne is there). Their 65f menu is certainly better than average, and their West Indian dishes have some character, i.e. avocat farci à l'antillaise, salade de la jamaïque and veau à la caraïbe. Wines pretty dismal, but you can always drink punch.

'Very crowded cheerful atmosphere. We had 48f menu, all plumping for enormous plate of moules marinières. The men had a vast chunk of pork, the women chicken, followed by three cheeses in perfect condition. House wine 25f. We think excellent value for money.' – Moira Fletcher.

Le Petit Caporal
(R)S *60 r. Nationale 21.91.11.40 Closed Sun. p.m., Mon., Wed. p.m.*

St. Léonard is sufficiently far from the centre of Boulogne (4 km on the N1) to miss the tourists. Le Petit Caporal is the only restaurant I know that caters primarily for the Boulonnais, and all the better for that. It's small, cosy, friendly, with a set menu much approved of by the local businessmen at lunchtime (so go early). For 70f you get three courses, like moules à l'oseille, terrine de poisson, sauce cressonnette, or mousse d'oie au cognac, followed by osso bucco, poulet basquais, rognons au porto, plus cheese or pud.

La Houblonnière
(R)S *8 r. Monsigny 21.30.55.30 Closed Sun.*

If you're only here for the beer, there are 100 different varieties to get through at la Houblonnière, from Yorkshire Ruddles to Japanese Sapporo. A dish of the day makes admirable blotting paper.

La Providence
(R)M-S *8 r. du Bras d'Or. 21.31.58.22 Closed Tues.*

The owner of La Crêperie, r. de la Lampe, and the mâitre d'hôtel of La Matelote have joined up to open this new restaurant and are offering all types of dishes from delicious stuffed pancakes to delicately cooked fish or meat for a wide range of prices from 50f to 120f. Messrs Cazier and Painset both speak English.

Map 2B **BOURNONVILLE** 62240 (Pas de Calais) 19 km E of Boulogne; 6 km N of Desvres

Some of the prettiest countryside in the North is to be found due east of Boulogne, in the forests of Boulogne and Desvres, along the tracks of the river Liane, up hills, down dales, past sleepy undiscovered villages. Easy and very pleasant to get lost in the maze of one-track lanes either side of the D 127 and I often find myself in Bournonville, hub of five mini-roads, by mistake. So I park the car, cross over to look at the stream, and count the French cars and sometimes even coaches that have somehow found their way to:

Auberge du Moulin
(R)S *21.33.31.87*

Without the indication of these usually reliable straws in the wind it would be a temptation to pass this one by. Ramshackle is a useful word, well-applied here, though we now have a door firmly fixed to the outside loo.

In FE4 I issued a challenge:

'For any reader who can eat every mouthful on the cheapest menu and I mean all the vegs, a modicum of bread and the cheese course, I will pay for the next meal he eats there. With admiration. Valid for the whole of 1985.

Here's what to expect:

Course 1 Smoked salmon cut like a steak, or rather two steaks.
2. Tongue – two more steaks, with copious carrots and lots of gravy.
3. Gigot of lamb. Three steaks this time, with enough mashed potato and haricots to feed a family.
4. Salad.
5. Cheese. And I shall expect any contestant to try every variety.
6. Tarte aux pommes. And every crumb. With cream.'

The year wore on and regretful letters arrived: 'We almost made it! Five courses, yes. Six courses – impossible.' I thought I had got away with it. Then came the following from the Park Cellar Wine Society of Sittingbourne.

'You will be pleased and a little surprised that a representative group of the above Society embarked on the above challenge on 8th November 1985. Five members took and with great gusto consumed the meal plus a soup to start (before the salmon!!) and two members had two different sweets!!

We have to declare the challenge well and truly won. Now for the prize?

We enjoy your books enormously and follow your recommendations. A letter from you acknowledging a successful challenge that can be displayed in the Society's tasting room and a copy of your next book will be ample reward.'

They let me off lightly.

The menu, content unchanged, is now 85f, but just as good value, as numerous happy guzzlers have testified.

The Valley of the Canche

The river flows out into the sea at Etaples.

Follow the north bank from Montreuil on the tiny D113 for a pleasantly peaceful traffic-free rural ride. You can zig-zag across at will over any of the several bridges to visit Brimeux, Beaurainville (p. 57),

Aubin St-Vaast (p. 52) down to Hesdin (p. 100).I wouldn't recommend the obvious extension of the drive to Frévent, a dull, unfriendly little town, with a disappointing hotel, and the Logis at Monchel I thought incongruously over-sized and over-priced for its rural standing; a more rewarding halt is at Fillièvres (see p. 97) or there's Boubers, the prettiest of all the 'villages fleuris' along the river (p. 62).

Map 2A **LA CAPELLE-LES-BOULOGNE** 62200 (Pas de Calais) 5 km E of Boulogne

On the N 42.

Auberge de la Station
(R)M *139 rte National 21.83.32.54 Closed Mon.; Sun. p.m.*

A useful stop, bang on the main road, and a member of the Auberges du Boulonnais Association, which means consistently high standards – or else.

'Excellent value and although portions are not overlarge, they are all beautifully cooked.' – Terry Barnett.

There is a bar, a very pretty, rustique dining room and, in the summer, service at the tables in the rear garden. Food aims at 'style campagnard', with menus starting at 70f.

The four rooms were being renovated when I was there, but I fear that however nice they are, they will be noisy – all slap on the lorry route. They will cost around 150f.

1993: Now by-passed by lorry route.

Cap Gris Nez (17 km N of Boulogne)

Map IA. Turn off the D940 on to the D 191.

We all know that the swimmers make for Cap Gris Nez, but how few of us bother to do the same. We should. Just 4 km off the main coast road, lies this impressive headland, the coast of Albion clearly visible on most days of the year, an attractive little beach nestling in the bay, with sand for digging and rocks for clambering over. No shortage of refreshment:

La Sirène
(R)M *21.32.95.97 Closed 10/12-24/12; Sun. p.m.; Mon. o.o.s.; Lunch only from Sept. to May, except Sat. CB, V, MC*

Another good example of how the French do not see a well-known beauty spot as a licence to cash in on rotten catering. The Sirène would be a good restaurant wherever it were placed; situated as it is, with big glass windows making the best of that view, it is highly to be commended for continuing to serve what many locals consider the best fish in the district.

'Still the favourite place for a lobster treat,' writes Dr. Glyn Daniels.

On Sunday lunchtime it is full of local families enjoying their weekly blow-out. The windows (even on a beautiful sunny day) firmly closed and steamed up, so that nothing shall distract them.

There is a menu at 90f, most expensive fish dishes like sole or turbot will come to the same. There is a bar, too, if a drink is all you need, and even in winter there is usually some company there.

Les Mauves

(HR)M *21.32.96.06 Closed 15/11-1/4 All Cards*

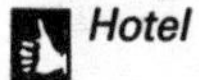 *Hotel* 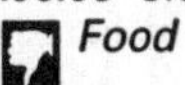 *Food*

Vastly improved since my last visit, and now a really comfortable little hotel – low, stone-built, white paint, nice garden, on the approach road to the Cap. The bedrooms are modern and functional. The dining room is attractively rustic, with blue plates on the dresser, carved chairs, polished floor, and there is a little bar in which the guests can mingle.

Rooms cost 230-390f. Menus from 98f.

Hôtel du Gris Nez.

(HR)S *21.32.96.37 Closed Tues.*

I am ashamed to have ignored the Hôtel du Gris Nez for so long. I ought to know by now that a bar full of regulars is a good sign and not mind pushing my way through them to ask to see the rooms.

When I did so eventually, Madame Peiriaux took me in hand and showed me every one of her spotlessly clean bedrooms, bargains at 110-150f a double.

Lots of fish on the menus, served in a spacious rear dining room with bay windows overlooking the valley. But the biggest clue to the kind of treatment guests here are likely to receive was Madame P's information, 'We're meant to be closed on Tuesday, but of course if I have guests who want to stay, I always let them.'

'Very friendly service. It was full of French at 5.30 but when we ate at eightish we were the only ones. Menu at 65f – shrimp cocktail, fish soup, fruits de mer, then steak, chicken, cod, skate or langoustines. The ladies shared an enormous platter of fruits de mer at 120f. Would highly recommend.' – Moira Fletcher.

Pavillon Bel Air

(Chambre d'hôte) 21.87.30.15

Hard to miss, on the corner opposite the Hôtel du Gris Nez; bright cheerful pine-panelled rooms at 131f and 163f a double, exclusive of an unusual range of breakfasts. You can have simple at 18f, through eggs and bacon at 20f, up to 25f for petit déjeuner maison – the works.

The young owners, Georges Bally and Josette Vassuer, are friendly and anxious to make their guests' stay a rewarding one. They show them films of the attractions on offer in the area, including the fossils on which they are experts. and are always ready with maps and advice.

Map 7B **CAULIÈRES** 80590 (Somme) 130 km S of Boulogne; 7 km W of Poix-de-Picardie by the N 29; 28 km SW of Amiens

Not a very interesting stretch of country, but a useful stop on the main road is:

Auberge de la Forge
(R)M *22.40.00.91 Closed Tues. p.m.; Wed.; 3/2-18/2; 10/8-17/8 CB, AE.*

Determinedly rustique with beams, open fire, and horsey accessories on the walls, but chic with it. Alain Mauconduit tries to please all worlds with his cooking, sometimes traditional, sometimes modern, sometimes Picard, sometimes Perigourdine (he used to work there), sometimes Norman from across the nearby border.

He uses a lot of fish in modern dishes, like a ragout of brill served with prawns, but piles on the calories with a superb hot apple tart. There is an 85f menu but I would recommend the next one up, at 110f, as being especially good value, or the 130f, even better.

Map 10C **CHANTILLY** 60500 (Oise) 223 km SE of Boulogne; 93 km S of Amiens; 49 km N of Paris

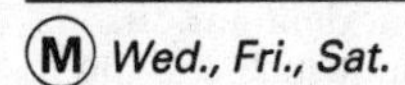

Wed., Fri., Sat.

However high the expectations for the château of Chantilly, however well-briefed, it must be a blasé traveller indeed who is not bowled over at the first sighting of this stunning arrangement of turrets and gables, swimming above the blue-and-green geometry of lakes and lawns. The scale is vast, the site inspired, the interest limitless. Take a full day, I urge you, to appreciate it all.

For us, very sadly, it was a day of such driving rain and bitter wind that even I could not face the tour of the gardens, the clever formal lakes, the walks through the forests, the photographing that I had been so greatly looking forward to. So I have an excellent reason for returning.

Once in the proximity of Chantilly, the château creeps up on you when you least expect it – many different aspects appear suddenly through the woods, from the surrounding lanes, the town. From

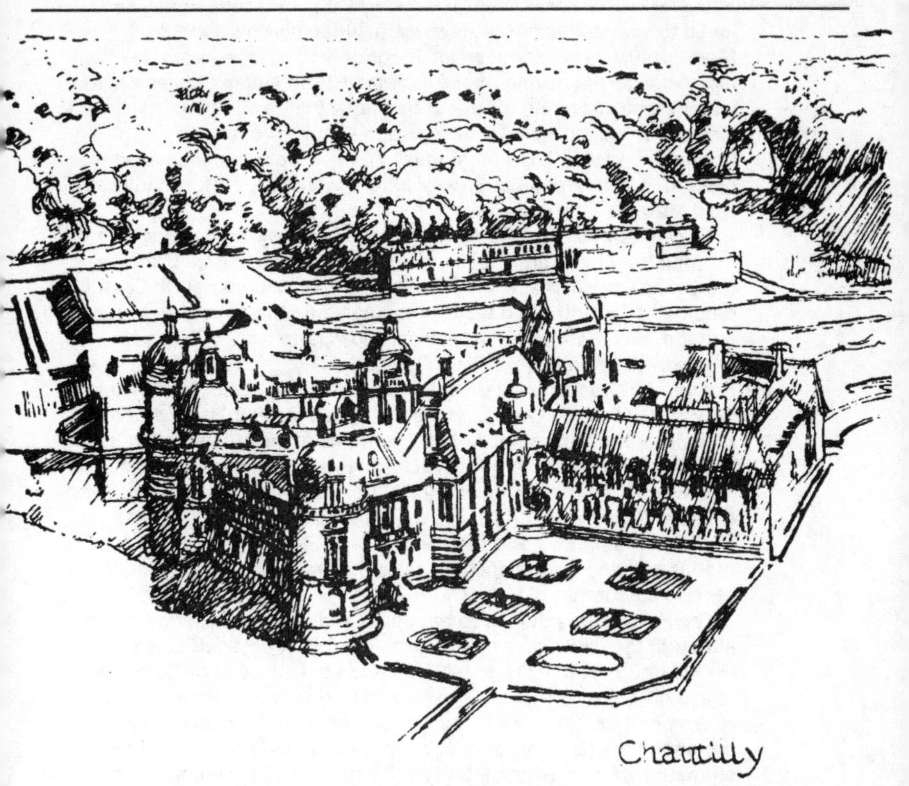

whatever angle, set off by its great park, the lure is compulsive.

You will need a far better-informed and comprehensive guidebook than this one to learn more than a smattering about the château's history, lay-out, treasures, but just to whet the appetite.

The statue on the terrace outside the Grand Château is of Anne (masculine) de Montmorency, Grand Constable of France, who served six kings, from Louis XII to Charles IX, as diplomat, soldier, art collector, friend and companion. His wealth and influence is inconceivable in modern terms. From being a childhood friend and brother-in-arms to Francois I, the trusted adviser to Henri II, he was sufficiently close to Catherine de Medici to suggest to her the latest cures for sterility. By the marriages of his twelve children he was connected to many branches of the royal family. When in 1528 his family seat at Chantilly was demolished, he set out to build a replacement that would make even royalty envious.

The Renaissance-style château that was the result of enlisting the finest artists, craftsmen, designers and gardeners of the time, did just that. Charles V visited and was charmed, Henri IV, 'Le Vert Galant', loved to stay there after Anne's death, when his son Henri de Monmorey was host, and coveted not only the gorgeous château but his host's gorgeous daughter Charlotte. His little plan to have his way with her, by arranging for her to be married to the timid and, with any luck, complaisant Henri Ist de Bourbon-Condé, rebounded when Charlotte and Henri had other ideas and fled from the fate worse than death to a honeymoon in Brussels, from which they refused to return until after the King's death.

They inherited Chantilly in 1643 and the château was handed down through their heirs until 1830; their son, the duc d'Enghien, known as the Grand Condé, made it his life's work to further embellish Chantilly, employing Le Nôtre to transform the park and the forest, the fountains and the lake, to the wonder they are today, and were to Louis XIV, who copied them at Versailles.

It was Le Grand Condé's great-grandson, 'M. Le Duc', Louis-Henri de Bourbon, Prince de Condé, who constructed the stables, one of the most important architectural achievements of the 18th century. It was closed during my November visit, until Easter, but I am sure that a tour would be of enormous interest, and not only to the horsey. They call it 'a Musée Vivant' because the visitor can not only look at sculptures, paintings and models of horses, but see many different breeds of living horses and witness equestrian displays in 18th-century costume.

The Revolution put paid to the upper storeys of the Grand Château, although the Petit Château alongside somehow escaped destruction. On his return from exile, the 78-year-old Louis-Joseph de Condé wept to see his beloved château and park in ruins. He and his son decided to restore it exactly to its former glory, rebuilding the château and replanting the gardens, and for a while Chantilly rediscovered the animation of its pre-Revolution peak – the glittering setting for balls, receptions and hunting parties – but after the revolution of 1830, when his cousin Louis-Philippe came to the throne, the incumbent Duc de Bourbon (last of the Condés), fearing that another exile could not be far away, hanged himself, thereby closing for ever the Condés' association with Chantilly.

He left Chantilly to his great-nephew, the Duc d'Aumale, fifth son of Louis-Philippe, who after a period of exile after the 1848 revolution, caused the fifth Grand Château, the one that exists today, to be built, in the Renaissance style. It is him we have to thank for the fascinating and varied collection of pictures and *objets d'art* in the museum today.

I was delighted and surprised at the range and quality of the paintings and greatly intrigued by their juxtaposition. At the time when the Duc d'Aumale was amassing his collection, all manner of treasures from all over the world could be brought at bargain prices and his keen eye roved over and settled upon Italian primitives, contemporary l9th-century paintings, Flemish masterpieces, Gobelin tapestries, mediaeval manuscripts. As he acquired new possessions, he grouped them, not as a museum-keeper would have done by period or by artist, but, like any more humble collector, according to his preferences. This has the effect of keeping you on your toes – no skipping an unpromising room, lest you miss a peak, like Raphael's *Three Graces*, or an Ingres, a Filippino Lippi, a Memling or a Van Dyck.

In the same room as the Raphaels are forty exquisite miniatures from a 15th-century *Book of Hours*; the miniscule and revealing portraits on enamel in the Cabinet des Gemmes I found equally rewarding. Don't miss Queen Victoria.

The Château and park are open form 1/3-14/11 every day, except Tuesdays, from 10.30-4.30, and from 15/11-1/3 at weekends, from 10.30-4.20. (tel: 44.57.03.62.).

Trust the French to capitalise on a natural asset. A day spent in Chantilly is guaranteed to work up a thirst and appetite. Not for them the plastic caff, but the maximum exploitation of an existing bonus the old kitchens. These have been transformed into:

La Capitainerie
(R)M *44.57.15.89 Closed Mon.; Tue. Lunch only*

NO NEWS

The mediaeval foundations have been excavated to reveal light creamy stone pillars supporting vaults and arches. With bright pink cloths and white iron tables, it's now a delightful place for rest and restoratives. I can't claim it's a gastro-excitement but everything is fresh and well-cooked and the service is as elegant as the setting.

The set menu is 90f; friend Ann and I, trying to avoid the *crises de foie* that would surely follow two large meals a day, asked if we might share a menu, and indeed one between two proved more than enough, since course one was a choice of hors d'oeuvres from a central table, enabling two plates to be filled with crudités, pâté, prawns et al. Then came a trout in crisp batter which we split down the middle, and another help-yourself range of seven or eight puds; three did us nicely!

Back in the town, there are plenty of good restaurants to cater for the Parisian day-trippers and the racegoers, but a strange dearth of hotels. I didn't find one I could recommend. They say it's too near Paris, but I would have thought rooms could have been easily filled with tourists who wanted to stay outside in the greenness. Look at Gouvieux p. 98.

➤Tipperary
(R)M *6 ave. du Ml. Joffre 44.57.00.48 Open every day AE,DC*

First at the post, with my money firmly on the nose. Tipperary used to be a famous restaurant, went into a decline, and now is straining to be up front again, with the handicap of (ill-informed) poor form.

Its décor is a delightful evocation of its 19th-century prime, with hilarious cartoons by local artist Bizetsky (musician, erudite wit, sculptor, part-time station master too) who, during the Second Empire, drew local personalities, like racehorse owner le Duc de Hamilton, portrayed lumpishly on an elephant because his weight precluded him from riding 'comme gentleman-rider', or le Comte de Lagrange, first French owner of a Derby winner, Gladiateur, portrayed as a satyr, equine hindquarters as aristocratic as top-hatted, cigar-smoking head and torso.

Newish owners, M. and Madame Greffe, speak fluent English and are friendly and welcoming hosts. With their encouragement, young chef Brice Auriault produces inspired food. The 85f menu certainly cheered us up one wet and dismal day when no-one else in the town wanted to give us a late lunch.

We were off with a salad, generous with the kind of prawns that were alive that morning, strips of smoked eel, salmon, herring and avocado. Then into the straight with a leg of duck stuffed with wild mushrooms, accompanied by rarely perfect veg. But, best of all, at the winning post was the superb dessert, which alone would have won an arrow from me – a terrine striped with chocolates – dark milk and white – richness cleverly combined with bitter pink grapefruit.

Even at this modest level, with an order for a mere half bottle of wine, complimentary pâté and nibbles are offered.

Every day there are 'suggestions' which can be incorporated into the menu, like a salad of chicken's livers, quenelles de brochet with a saffron sauce, or pancakes stuffed with pears and orange jelly.

Don't go in a hurry though – the service is more a jog than a canter. Apart from that, I can't fault the place, especially as M. Greffe's smile never wavered when we asked to share a menu !

Le Relais Condé

(R)M *42 ave. du Maréchal Joffre 44.57.05.75 Closed Mon.; Jan.; Aug. AE, DC*

A charming little restaurant conjured up from an old chapel, popular with those involved in the nearby racecourse.

Best stick to the 95f menu, which often includes regional dishes, served in the *nouvelle* style. Interesting new possibilities like cabbage stuffed with langoustines alternate with old favourites like goujonnettes of prime sole. Be prepared for a 250f-ish bill à la carte. Pricey wine list too.

Relais du Coq Chantant

(R)M *21 rte. de Creil 44.57.01.28 Open every day AE, DC, EC*

The first name on everyone's list if you ask a Chantillais where to eat; its attraction is not immediately obvious – a boring modern building on the main RN 16 approach road. Inside is totally predictable plush,

Le Tipperary

tapestried, reverent, elegant, gleaming, smooth, efficient. Triple glazing baffles the traffic noise and you could be in any good French restaurant in any French town.

It's the food that's exceptional. Alain Deboves was voted best cook in the l'Oise in 1980 and he hasn't slipped since. His cooking is varied and interesting and you can always rely on the 150f menu (280f on Sunday) to offer something different, like a terrine of rascasse wrapped in leeks, tarragon-herbed raviolis stuffed with lobster, but trad dishes like fillet of beef in a Saumur Champigny sauce are equally praiseworthy. Outstanding desserts bow to the seasons.

Stray from the menus and it could cost upwards of 250f. Splendid wines, which can also be bought at very fair prices to take away.

Les 4 Saisons

(R)M *9 ave. Leclerc 44.57.04.65 Closed Mon.; 3/2-25/2 AE, DC, EC*

NO NEWS

A curiosity in France to find a Scandinavian restaurant. This one is an offshoot of a well-established Paris restaurant, Flora Danica. To Denmark must go the credit for the light and airy 'garden style' restaurant, the flowery terrace, the smiling service, and dishes like blinis with smoked salmon, wonderful Scandinavian pickled herrings and the perfect freshness of the fish, but the French cannot help imposing their own image on anything to do with food, and the game dishes that were being served in November were as traditionally gallic as any.

The name of the restaurant is gallantly supported – emphasis is placed on using seasonal ingredients – in autumn, a bavarois of sweet peppers spinkled with walnuts. The desserts are good, too, with the exploitation, rare in France, of rhubarb, in a delicious compôte de rhubarbe, crème vanille, light years away from the stewed grey shred and lumpy custard of school dinners.

Crêperie la Cour Pavée

(R)S *136 r. du Connetable 44.57.23.41*

A good choice for a light lunch of crêpes, galettes, ices, or for coffee and teatime, with an unsuspected light courtyard, glassed-in at the rear.

Map 8A **LA CHAPELLE-AUX-POTS** (Oise) 163 km S of Boulogne; 15 km W of Beauvais

Turn north off the N31 on to the D22 for 1 km to this tiny village, whose name indicates its main occupation – pottery.

Hôtel de la Gare
(HR)S *44.80.50.27 Always open*

Hotels de la Gare are invariably good news; I could not pass by this prim, little, quintessentially French specimen without investigating, and came across what I think will be a treasure – and the cheapest bed in the book.

A spotless, perfectly acceptable double room here costs 96f. And the menu will set you back another 52f!

The owners are friendly and welcoming, the situation in peaceful countryside just off a main road is strategic, and I look forward to more reports.

Map 6A **CHÉPY** 80210 Feuquieres en Vimeu (Somme) 100 km S of Boulogne; 20 km SW of Abbeville

For the map-proficient the most attractive way to approach Chépy from Abbeville is to turn off the D925 south at Mionnay on to the pretty D86, taking a right turn towards Chépy, as time and inclination suggest. Otherwise its the D925 towards Eu, and the D65 left. It's the usual story – get off the main roads and a maze of Michelin white lanes reveal totally unspoilt rurality. Chépy boasts a station, and again as usual in France, you have only to find the station to find a good restaurant too:

➔**Auberge Picarde**
(H)R-S *pl. de la Gare 22.26.20.78 Closed Sun.; last fortnight in August CB*

Thirty years ago the Henocque parents opened their restaurant opposite the station and it has been a local rendezvous ever since. Now they have semi-retired to run the **Auberge Picarde Hotel** (H)S *pl. de l'Eglise, Chépy. (22.26.22.29.)* with eight very simple bedrooms, clean and wholesome and cheap, leaving their son and daughter-in-law to carry on the family tradition in the restaurant.

Having graduated from the hotel school in Amiens, Alain is well qualified to do this and added his own touches, like home-made bread, and free appetisers and petits fours. He uses nothing from the deep freeze, makes his own pastries and sorbets and is altogether very good news indeed in this wilderness.

He offers a mid-week 80f menu and a daily speciality at 35f, which I can heartily recommend. The 95f menu is a bargain worth travelling some distance for, with specialities like paupiettes of salmon with chives, magret of duck with figs and a wonderful pear mille feuille coated with caramel.

Arrowed for unusual quality and value, in a new venture.

Now with 25 rooms at 220-350f.

La Côte d'Opale

From the mouth of the Somme to the Belgian border the coast has been labelled 'Opale', because of the milky waves that batter its chalky cliffs, and the flecks of colour reflected from fleeting northern sunshine. The most spectacular stretch is between Boulogne and Calais, where the coast road climbs and dips between rolling farmland, with little to interrupt the seaward view.

A series of fine beaches extend north to Cap Gris Nez. **Wimereux** is the best-known, biggest, busiest, with a choice of hotels, shops and restaurants (see p. 154). West-facing **Ambleteuse** is often neglected by English visitors because it involves turning off the main road and has few commercial attractions, but here, protected by the 17th-century Fort Mahon, is a range of rocks, sandy beaches, dunes, and the estuary of the little Slack offering interesting paddling. Once a naval station, it was used by Napoleon to base his flotilla for the projected English attack.

Audresselles has a lot of character, with its low, typically northern cottages, fishing boats known locally as 'flobards' pulled up by trolley and stranded like whales in the main street. Added attractions are the good beach and le Champenois (see p. 53).

But my favourite is **Cap Gris Nez** itself. Turn left off the D940 and take the D191 to find the delightful sheltered cove already described on p. 76.

The Valley of the Course

Probably the biggest success of the early *FE*s. Numerous readers who had known the area well but always belted down the main roads, never dreaming that an infinitely preferable route south lay just a few kms away, discovered the delights of the valley of the Course. They willingly followed instructions to divert to the little D127 from Desvres to Montreuil and follow the valley of the rushing sparkling little river via flowery unspoilt villages like **Courset, Parenty, Recques, Beussent,** to eat at ridiculously cheap rustic restaurants like **Madame Cocatrix** at **Zérables,** the **Auberge d'Inxent** and above all the indefatigable **Madame Debove** at **Engoudsent.**

Each year I feared from the very number of enthusiastic letters that the valley would lose its intrinsic charm to a stream of GBs; but on each subsequent visit I failed to meet more than one or two on any day's perambulations. And perambulation is the right pace at which to explore the valley. Use it as an attractive quiet route from A to B if you must but, far far better, leave time to divert left and right, picnic along the river and discover a stretch of countryside that would be unremarkable perhaps further into France but is fast disappearing from the North.

The café/restaurants continue to please and although their prices have gone up, their value for money has not changed. They are listed alphabetically, along with one or two new discoveries of similar simple excellence in the villages a few kms away from the river.

How long the rare unsophistication will endure I dare not think. My heart sinks at every new board up advertising building plots for sale, at every raw bungalow that jars one back into the 20th century. Most of these are second homes and the alliance between their owners and the old residents is thin. It's as though two separate existences run parallel but never converge – the one lived out in mod-conned weekends, the other in intense year-round rusticity lived in picturesque crumbling barns and farmyards and the fields behind them, leisure hours spent no further away than in the cosy dark and smoky bars to be found in every village.

Admittedly the population of the Course is not easy to know. Here is a description of their habits and tastes of 150 years ago. Their ancestors live on:

> 'The population is exclusively agricultural. The men are generally strong, well-built, of medium height. They tend to make too frequent use of the bars and spirituous liquor, which makes them irritable, noisy and even quarrelsome. They have no particular amusement except skittles and cards and nowadays prefer the latter diversion. They never go to dances except those held in their own villages on fête days.'

For this book I have been able to extend exploration to the lanes and valleys on either side of the river and was enchanted to find that, if anything, the charm increases (as the bungalows thin). The valley is a deep one and its steeply-wooded slopes are more extensive and attractive than I had imagined. As for the villages, it seems one could go on for ever discovering a succession of time-warped sleepy crossroads, flowery cottages, churches, ponds, bars, fruity-smelling farms and the streams that run into the Course, each with a name too grand for a trickle – the Baillonne, the Bezinghem, the Brimoise. By the side of the latter, at pretty **Montcavrel**, I picknicked and zizzed for an hour or more one sultry August day, exhausted by the coastal hassle just a few kms away. and only a boy on a bicycle, fishing rod on shoulder, discovered my childish penchant for paddling.

Accommodation though found I none. Only the **Relais Equestre** at Inxent can I still wholeheartedly recommend. But for a hearty lunch, a drink, drive, walk, cycle, al fresco meal, the Course still takes a lot of beating .

Map 10D **COYE-LA-FÔRET** 60500 (Oise) 232 km SE of Boulogne; 5 km S of Chantilly

 *Sat.* Turn east off the N16 on to the D118.

Auberge des Etangs
(R)M *1 rue des Clos des Vignes 44.58.60.15 Closed Mon. p.m.; Tue.; Feb DC*

The persistent rain and darkness of a November tour precluded a much-looked-forward-to visit to the lakes, les Etangs des Commelles, in the forest nearby; the ideal combination would have been an autumn walk through the beech trees followed by lunch at the Auberge des Etangs.

Its outward appearance is a let-down. I had envisaged views over the water; this is on the corner of two busy roads. However, the food compensates for much.

Take the 140f menu – beignets de cervelle, sauce tartare, homemade duck confit, cheese platter, soufflé au Grand Marnier. All the ingredients are Rungis-fresh, and the service from François Cologiacome is friendly and efficient.

Hôtel de la Poste
(HR)S *Grande Rue 44.58.64.18*

Uninspected but included on the strength of local advice and the scarcity of alternative modest accommodation in the area. Reports please.

Map 5B **CRÉCY-EN-PONTHIEU** 80150 (Somme) 65 km S of Boulogne, 19 km N of Abbeville

Like many another mourning Picard town, there is a war memorial in the main street of Crécy; what is unique about this one is the date on the inscription, which reads, 'To the memory of the Frenchmen who died defending their Fatherland, the 26th August, 1346.'

The other side of the cross commemorates the bravery of Jean of Luxembourg, the blind King of Bohemia, brother of King Philippe, who opposed Edward III. Determined to 'strike a blow for France', he ordered himself to be tied to his horse during the battle, where he was slain along with 1300 French knights, the cream of the French nobility, and 30,000 men-at-arms.

To this day, in recognition of his gallantry, the Prince of Wales wears his badge of black shield and plumes.

There is not much else to mark the site of the battle, whose name if not details every schoolchild knows. The windmill on the edge of the battlefield, where Edward III received news of the progress of the conflict and ordered that his sixteen-year-old son should win his spurs unassisted, is no more. On the lonely hilltop site above the plains of wheat fly the tattered flags of Bohemia, Luxembourg, France – and the Union Jack.

Quite obviously Crécy has great potential as a tourist centre; apart from its great historic interest, it lies strategically on the route south, with only the lovely forest of Crécy between it and Abbeville, where accommodation is limited. Four years ago, researching for *FE2*, I described the **Canon d'Or** in the main street – a perfect little country inn, old, beamed, dark, polished, with gingham curtains. The only snag then was the formidable owner, with the equally formidable name, Madame Vigeant-Grand'-Eury, who knew she could fill up her hotel without bothering to be polite to her customers. So the news that her children had succeeded her boded well and I booked and confirmed a double room with bath, looking forward to the good news without the bad.

I relate the outcome for several reasons: (1) because it makes me feel better; (2) because it illustrates how badly money can be spent in France without the aid of a good guide!; (3) it provides an answer to those letters that start off 'what a lovely job you have' and, most importantly; (4) to guide readers away from similar mistakes.

Not only no bath materialised, but no cupboard, no towel, no bedside lamp. When I asked where I could hang my week-long crumpled clothes in my dwarf-sized room, the answer was over the chair. The bathroom, shared by the whole hotel, was along an unlit, paper-peeling corridor.

Dinner was at 7.30 – or else. Only one other table taken, by Germans. I feared the worst – and boy was I right! For 85f (the price I would have paid to eat well in Abbeville) I was served crudités soaked in vinegar, terrine de saumon (look how good it all looks on the menu!) like violently pink fish paste ,and entrecôte bordelaise, stringy and grey. Tinned vegetables are inexcusable at any time of the year; in July they were an outrage. Commercial ice cream for pudding, and we were still only on 8 o'clock. By now the chef was settled in front of the telly (I don't blame him – he clearly had nothing to do in the kitchen except open packets and tins), the Germans had gone to bed, it was raining outside, and the nearest bar was 19 km away, so I watched an American sub-titled film with the chef.

'Would I like breakfast?' 'Yes, please, in my room.' (Couldn't face that gloomy dining room again.) 'Sorry.'

All totally unnecessary. I longed to say, 'Let me into your kitchen, let me boil one of the beautifully fresh artichokes I bought from the shop opposite, let me cook an omelette with fresh herbs, let me slice a fresh peach into some wine – it would take me all of ten minutes and cost half of your pretentious rubbish. Let me put flowers in the bedrooms and carry a tray upstairs if that's what the customer wants. It would cost me nothing and I bet my hotel would be full, not about to shut down as yours inevitably will be. Tourist-traps like the Canon d'Or don't deserve mugs like me, who meekly ate up my disgusting plastic breakfast, and paid my outrageous bill of 320f.

I should have listened to my readers and gone to:

La Maye
(HR)S *13 r. St. Riquier 22.23.54.35 Closed Sun. P.m.; Mon. o.o.s.; Feb. EC, V, P*

Such an undistinguished outward appearance and a seemingly boring menu deflected me. But readers and locals alike agree that though both the rooms and food are simple, they are both good value (and infinitely preferable to the alternative!) Rooms 250-310f, menus from 70f.

Map 5A **LE CROTOY** (Somme) 68 km S of Boulogne

Fri.

On the north bank of the Somme estuary, but claiming to have the only south-facing bank in the North of France. This may well be, but what with the decidedly bracing air that always seems to be whipping up the waves here, one thinks more of Skegness than St. Tropez. It's a lively little town, faded with the saltiness, a favourite excursion for a walk along the promenade, to watch the fishing boats unload their catch, or to dig sand castles. Another famous attraction is:

La Baie
(H)S (R)M *Quai Léonard 22.27.81.22 Open every day*

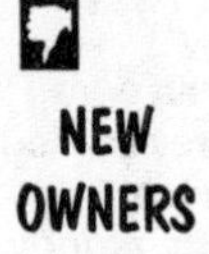

Or rather it is Mado, the seemingly eternal patronne, who is the principal attraction. The dishes, moules Mado, sole Mado, turbot Mado, indicate how powerful is her personality. Her advanced years have no influence on her style, and the beads and bracelets still jangle a warning of her approach from table to table, giving the wrong bill, arguing with the customers. The chihuahua doesn't feature in her bosom any more but the white parrot still welcomes the customers; perhaps he too is getting old – he was having trouble with the first line of the Marseillaise.

Depending on the season and mood, there are two distinctly different ambiences to choose from. The inner sanctuary is a warm Victorian clutter, full of the French, who don't allow sea-views to distract them from their food; the terrace gets the tourists, who like to see what is going on outside too. Both rooms are usually full soon after midday, year round, so booking is strongly advised. Decidedly fishy menus from 90f.

The rooms have always been occupied when I have wanted to look, which I thought boded well, but readers tell me that they are extremely basic. At 96-142f they probably are.

'It still needs a good cleaning and painting, but at £10 a night for the best view and the food, how can you complain! Between the two of us we consumed over two nights: oysters – excellent (but the bread was stale), crab, snails, turbot, sole – superb, steak – tough, apple and apricot tarts – good, and charlotte chocolate – excellent.' – Moral appears to be to stick to sea food.'

Map 3A **CUCQ** 62780 (Pas de Calais) 35 km S of Boulogne

Ⓜ *Wed., Sun. 1/6-30/9*

A pleasant well-groomed residential outpost of Le Touquet, just 3 km north. Look out for a sharp bend in the D940 Berck road and to the right is:

➛**Chez Claudine**
(R)M *21.94.65.11 Closed Wed*

Well worth the drive for the best bargain in the Touquet area. Run by three young men, who offer two formulas: in the brasserie you pay 75f for as much as you can eat from the *table suédoise*, with forty hors d'oeuvres to chose from, then a plat du jour, which offers two fish and two meat dishes daily, then pâtisserie. With wine and service included, this is a winner, especially for a family meal where you can fill the kids up for the day.

More elegant, more calm, overlooking a pleasant rear garden, is the alternative restaurant, with a 125f menu, including lots of seafood.

Both popular year-round and often frenetic in summer, so definitely book.

Auberge de la Renaissance
(HR)S *20 pl. Verte 21.94.75.54 No News*

NO NEWS

It's a hard act to follow Claudine, just across the road, but here is a totally different experience. A nice old house, very French, less smart inside than out, with a 65f menu of four courses. Simple, honest food – Bayonne ham, haddock, lamb chops and fruit. Summer outside tables.

The rooms across the yard are very basic indeed, but if you have only 80f to spare (or 110f with shower) this could be the answer.

Map 2B **DESVRES** 62240 (Pas de Calais) 19 km SE of Boulogne

Ⓜ *Fri.*

On the D341. A little industrial town, best-known for its pottery copies, for the most part, of traditional designs from other European potteries. Its vast market square slopes dramatically down the valley and I can never find my way out, since the road signs all seem to be pointing backwards, and there are eight choices of exit. If you are clever and hit the D127 you are at the starting point for a very pleasant drive down the valley of the Course. The D253 will lead you through the Forest of Desvres to Bournonville (see p. 74), whence you can make a little tour of the wooded, hilly region, with vistas down to the Liane north of Desvres, by turning left on to the D254 to the pretty village of Cremarest and down by D238 to regain the red D341 back to where you started from, with a view to refreshment at:

→**Café Jules**
(R)S *11 pl. Léon Blum 21.91.69.72 Lunch only V, AE*

A typically French café on the market square, but very much more attractive within than one would expect. Often undiscovered by tourists but well-known to the locals as the best value around. 85f buys a splendid mid-week three-course meal, with a daily-changing menu. The Sunday price is 138f.

Café de l'Agriculture
(R)S *pl. Léon Blum 21.83.07.72*

'The restaurant is nothing special but clean and tidy with (my wife's comments) beautiful white net curtains! the meal we found exceptional – terrine, juicy fat steaks cooked the way we asked, good frîtes, Camembert and a quarter of a tarte aux pommes each. All this for 45f including service, will make us call again next year.' – Michael Weeks.

Plat du Jour 36f.

Map 5C **DOULLENS** 80600 (Somme) 93 km SE of Boulogne; 28 km S of St. Pol

An agreeable old town on the river Authie, with some gabled houses retaining their picard character.

Hôtel Aux Bons Enfants
(HR)S *23 r. d'Arras 22.77.06.58 Closed Sat. All Cards*

The friendly M. Louette makes no pretensions about his hotel. 'Familial,' he says firmly. And none the worse for that. His rooms are simple but perfectly adequate for an overnight stop, at 100-170f, with a good dinner for 70-150f.

One big advantage is that there is a spacious car park at the rear of the hotel, firmly locked up at night. A possible disadvantage is that the front rooms could be noisy, so ask for one *au calme*.

Le Sully
(HR)S *45 r. d'Arras 22.77.10.87 Closed Mon.; 17/6-1/7*

Several readers have recommended this friendly, small (only eight rooms) hotel. If you can master its opening times, it's a very good bet. Rooms are a very reasonable 175-250f and menus start at 59f, with cheap house wine.

Map 4B **DOURIEZ** 62870 Compagne les Hesdin (Pas de Calais) 51 km SE of Boulogne

On the D119, the north bank of the Authie.

Douriez is quite a sizeable village, with a wide market square, in one corner of which an archway leads to:

M. et Mme Robert Graux
(Chambre d'Hôte) 21.86.33.95

A find, particularly in this area of limited accommodation. Here are four very upmarket b and bs in a newly converted 19th-century manor house. The rooms are extremely comfortable, bright and light, with all mod cons, and cost 180f including breakfast for a double. M. and Madame Graux are friendly and helpful, and can recommend excursions and restaurants nearby. Saulchoy and the Val d'Authie restaurant are five minutes down the road for those who don't like to travel far between bed and board.

Map 7C **DURY-LES-AMIENS** 62156 Vis en Artois (Somme) 106 km SE of Boulogne

6 km S of Amiens on the N1.

La Bonne Auberge
(R)M *22.95.03 33 Closed Sun p.m.; Mon. o.o.s. AE, EC, V, P*

A more than useful stop on the Nationale, avoiding central Amiens' traffic hassle. In fact even those safely installed within the city should consider driving the 6 km out of town to eat at the consistently reliable, un-chi-chi food prepared by Raoul Beaussire.

The auberge has tables and umbrellas and flowery window-boxes outside, but is nothing special at all within. The large mock-rustic dining room just gets on with the serious business in hand, with little attempt to match the appeal of the food.

There is an excellent value 88f menu. After that it gets a bit complicated. There is a 150f fish menu, which includes half a Breton lobster, a 169f version that includes wine, and an elaborate 280f blow-out, which includes neither. The desserts are the least good items on the menu; save the space for the excellent cheeseboard.

This is the place to sample Amiens' celebrated pâté de canard en croûte. It appears on the more expensive menus or à la carte for 60f.

Map 3B **ENGOUDSENT** See Beussent p. 60

Map 6B **EPAGNETTE** 80580 Pont Remy (Somme) 82 km S of Boulogne

2 km SE of Abbeville on the D901.
A useful stop on the Beauvais road:

La Picardière
(R)M *22.24.15.28 Closed Tue. p.m.; Wed. AE, DC, EC, V, P*

NO NEWS

Too good to use just for an emergency stop. Regional cooking from several areas by Michel Savreux-Dreuillet. From Picardy he takes recipes for layered pancakes (ficelles), trout and terrines, from nearby Normandy, recipes from the Vallée d'Auge, like a hot sausage cooked in a brioche, and from the south-west confit of goose and magret of duck. Choose one of his speciality charlottes 'au fruit' or 'pralinée' or crêpes for dessert, and take time to choose wisely from a prestigious wine list.

Menus are said to include 'boisson' but I failed to check what this involved. They start at the odd price of 48.57f but the one that earns the red R in Michelin is the 134f which, if it really does include wine, must be a snip. Good parking, a flowery terrace to escape to for a drink and an elegant '*cadre rustique*' make this a highly recommended suggestion, lacking only a few confirmations to make it an arrow.

Map 6B **ERONDELLE** 80580 Pont Rémy (Somme) 93 km S of Boulogne; 12 km SE of Abbeville

A devil to find. The village of Erondelle lies between the D3 from Abbeville and the Somme; from here take the D12 towards Huppy.

La Renardière
(Chambre d'Hôte) 22.27.13.00

Reassured by the signposts to La Renardière, follow the road that winds unexpectedly spectacularly higher and higher through the woods until at last it bumps down a long drive to arrive at an eccentric, mock-Gothic large house in a pheasant-breedery.

It's all just like home, with family clutter in the hall, but very well maintained and immaculately clean. This is classified as a luxury chambre d'hôte, and the three bedrooms are spacious and comfortable, at 450f for 2 people including breakfast, which strikes me as rather expensive, except that Madame's Thaon's welcome is warmer by far than that of most hotel receptionists, and the site and peace are both gratifying. All reports favourable.

Map 3B **ESTREE** 62170 Montreuil (Pas de Calais) 37 km S of Boulogne

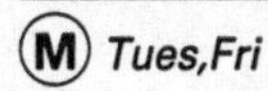
Tues,Fri

4 km N of Montreuil. Take the St. Omer road and turn left on to the D150.

The last of the picturesque little villages that line the Course, which runs wide and deep here, separating Estrée from its twin hamlet, Estréelles. There is still no love lost between them, ever since their ancestors fought on opposite sides of the Wars of the Roses, Estrée being Catholic and Estréelles Protestant. Side by side, they maintain separate churches, separate mayors and separate schools. The only hotel along the river is:

Le Relais de la Course
(HR)S *21.06.18.04*

NEW OWNERS

This used to be my regular stopping place in the Course valley and one of the most successful arrows in FE1 and 2. Then, with the kind patron's sudden death and new ownership, the dissatisfied letters started arriving, with complaints about service and food. Nowadays it's a Perhaps. I met some perfectly happy clients, who liked the food and thought the 55f menu good value (the 60f and 70f versions looked promising too), but locals don't go there and hoteliers tell me that guests who eat out at the Relais only do so once.

However, its situation is both strategic for Montreuil and the coast and extremely pretty, with river running by, and the simple rooms (one with bath) are not expensive at 140f a double – so considerable pros must be weighted against the cons:

'Wonderful. All of us agreed it was the best meal for all our holiday.'

or

'Surly patron, broken bedside lamp, no loo paper, tough ham (other choice on menu not available, although there were only two other people at dinner that evening), requests to drink up so that bar could be closed at 9.30.' – Hm.

Map 3A **ETAPLES** 62630 (Pas de Calais) 27 km S of Boulogne

Just across the river Canche from Le Touquet's razzamatazz is a real French fishing town which gets on with its marine business year round, tourists or no tourists. No prizes for guessing what eating here will be like – simpler, cheaper, fishier.

Lion d'Argent
(HR)S *21.94.60.99 Closed Tue.*

CHANGE OF OWNER

Take a ramble round the market on a Tuesday or Friday, then drop in to the pub on the square for an honest no-nonsense 58f worth, as many of the local shoppers and stall-holders will be doing. Take, say, a bowl brimming over with mussels, a fillet of haddock on a bed of spinach, an unorthodox but good tarte aux pommes (like an English custard tart topped with caramelised apple slices and doused with more than a sprinkling of calva), all dished up with a smile by the charming young Madame Pierreuse, and you'll have had more than your money's worth. For single dishes from the carte, crêpes étaploises, stuffed with seafood, or turbot poached and served with cream and apples, Vallée d'Auge style, are good choices, and palatable house wine from Herault costs only 29f.

The décor is a bit bizarre, from a casual trombone to the pipi boy with discreet flower, but the liveliness and good humour of the place makes even the plastic flowers acceptable. Only the dread pop musak might spoil it for some, myself included. Rooms 180f, menus from 55f.

Les Pêcheurs d'Etaples
(R)M *quai de la Canche 21.94.06.90 Open every day year round*

A guarantee of the freshness of the fish in this dominating modern building, right on the quayside, is that it is run by the marine co-operative of the local fishermen – so whatever lands on your plate was probably swimming that day. The view from the picture windows overlooking the river and all the activity of the fishing boats pulled up alongside makes it a good idea to book a window table or get there early.

For those English starved of fresh fish back home, this would be a very satisfactory destination for a getaway meal, winter or summer, and take-home souvenirs could be whatever the boats have landed that morning, sold in the fish shop below the restaurant or from stalls on the quayside.

Readers have agreed that the menus at 90f and 120f have been good value, but more ambitious dishes are also on offer on the carte, like suprême de barbue soufflé au Noilly, or coquille de daurade gratinée à la fleur de thym, and the étaploise version of a bouillabaisse should make good recounting back home.

Au Marin Joyeux
(R)S *78 rue de Rosamel 21.94.64.79 Closed Wed.*

The local taxi-driver and his family run this little bistro one street back from the main coast road. Predictably fishy menus at 85f.

Map 5A **FAVIÈRES** 80120 Rue (Somme) 61 km S of Boulogne; 5 km NE of Le Crotoy

Turn right off the D940 on to the little D140, into the flat marshy countryside, with villages that no-one ever bothers to explore, to find in the centre of the hamlet:

La Clé des Champs
(R)M *Route de Rue 22.27.88.00 Closed Sun. p.m.; Mon; 4/1-13/2; 31/8-11/9 DC, CB*

A spruce little restaurant, newly acquired and smartened up by Jean Flasque, son of the previous owner. He used to teach at the hotel school in Amiens and now has the opportunity to practise what he preached. Inside all is flowery and bright and the rural theme makes a pleasant change from the coastal ambience. Menus start at 73f (108, 128, 155f), with fish from Le Crotoy featuring strongly – brill cooked with mustard – but more meat in evidence than in most other local restaurants – veal chops with a julienne of lettuce, calves' sweetbreads in Burgundy with two kinds of mushrooms. In August the puddings were encouragingly seasonal – charlotte of strawberries and a bavarois of peaches. Definitely worth watching.

Map 4C **FILLIÈVRES** 62770 Le Parcq (Pas de Calais) 72 km SE of Boulogne; 10 km SW of Hesdin

On the D340. Just a hamlet, with a strangely-domed church, standing above the millpond on the Canche.

Vieux Moulin
(HR)S *21.47.93.42 Open all year EC*

A modern little hotel by the side of the water, looking less romantic than its originator, the old mill, but coming up trumps with good value menus and clean, if modest, accommodation.

'Our comfortable room overlooked the rushing millpond just across the road. Here you help yourself from a large dish of home-made pâté at dinner, and to dishes of butter and home-made jam at breakfast. "Have you eaten sufficiently?" and "Would you like some more coffee?" typify Madame's friendly attention at this small in-the-country inn. Deserves better write-up from you in next FE please.' – R. B. Harrison.

I rush to make amends. Rooms are 180f and menus start at 75f.

Map 10D **FLEURINES** 60700 Pont Ste Maxence (Oise) 223 km from Boulogne

7 km N of Senlis , on the N17.

Auberge de la Biche au Bois
(R)S *27 rue de Paris 44.54.10.04 Closed Wed*

NO NEWS

Expense accounts will no doubt make for the well-known Vieux Logis at Fleurines but local information is unanimous that this is a better bet. As the name suggests, game is the speciality but the chef is also proud of his regional dishes.

Unfortunately I hit a Wednesday to visit, so can't report further, except to say that the menus start at 55f.

Map 10C **GOUVIEUX** 60270 (Oise) 224 km SE of Boulogne; 3 km W of Chantilly

Between the D924 and the N16 in surprisingly rural and attractive countryside.

Château de la Tour
(HR)M *44.57.07.39 44.58.19.37 Closed 28/7-12/8, Rest 15/7-12/8 AE, V, P*

A château built at the turn of the century in rolling parkland, with spacious green views down the valley from its flagged terrace.

Its patronne, nice Madame Roland Jadas, has decorated all the 15 rooms *à l'ancienne*, ie. with real furniture, chandeliers, swagged curtains, but the bathrooms attached to every one are not *ancienne* at all. They function as efficiently as the rest of the hotel.

There is a pleasant salon and dining-room, light and airy by virtue of tall windows and high ceilings. All very good news anywhere, but particularly in this area of great interest and scant accommodation. The bad news of course is that it is difficult to get in. Rooms from 265-390f.

La Renardière
(R)M *Hameau de la Chaussée 44.57.08.23 Closed Tue. p.m.; Wed. 15/8 -30/8; 6/1-25/1 No News*

NO NEWS

A really pretty little restaurant set peacefully in a hollow just off the D924 on a lane that soon crosses the river and offers attractive walking.

It's all predictably rustic chic, with beams and flowers and smiles too, and the food is very good. Take the 87f menu for, say, a terrine of rabbit, farm chicken, or veal liver with cassis, cheese, and bavarois of seasonal fruit, or stick to one course on the charcoal grill.

Map 6B **HANGEST-SUR-SOMME** 80310 Picquigny (Somme) 23 km S of Abbeville

On the D3, this little town is famous for its watercress, grown down by the bridge across the river.

Restaurant du Canard
(R)S-M *22.41.70.90 Closed Wed.; Sun. p.m.; Feb. No News*

NO NEWS

If you imagined that a restaurant named after a duck, in a town *sur-Somme* would be something rustic on the banks of a river, you'd be wrong. This one is a bulbous modern building opposite the station! That disappointment aside, the rest of the news is good. Denis Poidevin is a very good cook and his wife Francette a very good hostess. Between them they please the population not only of Hangest but of many of the neighbouring villages with straightforward cooking of regional dishes, like ficelles picardes and of course many variations of their namesake, the duck. On Sundays you should certainly book. Everything is fresh and here is one simple restaurant where you can rely on the sauces being properly prepared and presented. Menus at 43.25f, 61.80f, 78.30f and 101f.

Map 2A **HARDELOT**, near **NEUFCHATEL** 62152 (Pas de Calais) 20 km S of Boulogne

A strange hybrid of a place, quite unlike anything I can compare it with in England. Here is a half-developed resort, trying hard to mirror Le Touquet's glossiness but only half-succeeding, by reason of its rawness and lack of character. Amenities there are a-plenty – natural ones like pines and dunes, and contrived – wide avenues, expensive villas, flowers, and a sprinkling of smart boutiques, but there is no heart and out of season it's a shut-up desert. However, there is no disputing the excellence of the beach, with miles and miles of fine sands. The swim-insistent might have to walk a fair step to catch that far-receding tide. Not so crowded on hot days as Le Touquet and well worth a beach visit, with plenty of snack possibilities; try **La Bonne Franquette** for a light lunch or, better still, buy a picnic and eat it in the shade of the pine trees.

The little **Pré Catalan**, hidden in the woods, used to be a favourite, but now after a devastating spell as a children's home, it's been taken over by an English company and is, to say the least, shabby and un-vacuumed. So how pleased I was to find a promising new alternative:

Villa Souleïa
Chambre d'hôte 90 Ave. François 1er 21.83.73.95.

Far nicer than to stay in a plastic hotel is to be a guest in the home of

M. et Madame Cecot. You can't miss it, at the roundabout approaching the town, a substantial villa set back deep in the pine trees. There's a nice garden and terrace for sunshine and an extensive lounge for bad weather. The well-furnished, cheerful bedrooms are 220f a double, including English breakfasts. Christa Cecot will cook an evening meal *sur commande* for 100f, including wine. Both she and her school Director husband speak English.

Hôtel Regina
(HR)M *av. François 1er 21.83.81.88 Closed 1/12-1/2. Rest Closed Sun p.m.; Mon. o.o.s.*

A modern hotel, set back from the approach road to the town, with double rooms from 299f.

'We found a very nice hotel, the Regina, very warm, clean and quiet and pleasant. A double room with bath bidet and w.c. cost 180f, and an excellent restaurant with a good menu at 60f.' – Peter Charles.

Le Restaurant du Golf
3 av. du Golf 21.83.71.04

Most agreeable to sit here by the picture windows, to contemplate the encompassing greenness and to listen to no more raucous sound than some hearty chirrupping and the occasional click of connecting club and ball. Far too good for the golfers to keep to themselves is the **Jardin des Saisons**, with menus at surprisingly modest prices, considering the classiness of it all. 95f is the cheapest.

Note: Between the village and nearby **Condette** is the castle where Charles Dickens stayed with his friend Ellen Ternan and wrote *Hard Times* and *Bleak House*.

Map 8B **HAUTE ÉPINE** 60690 (Oise) 149 km S of Boulogne; 25 km S of Poix; 5 km W of Marseille-en-Beauvaisis

Au Bon Coin
(R)S *44.46.23.62 Closed Tues. p.m.; Wed. No News*

NO NEWS

A useful stop, on the D930, and open on Sun/Mon. Patron J. P. Mille won first prize in the Nice hotel school and his cooking is way above average in this area. 44f buys four courses. Reports please.

Map 4B **HESDIN** 62140 (Pas de Calais) 61 km SE of Boulogne

(M) *Thurs*

Those who watched the Maigret t.v. series may have a sense of *déjà vu* in Hesdin. Its cobbled streets, vast market square, nice old houses, encircling boulevards, hump-backed bridges were all pressed into service to lend attractive background for the shooting.

The town lies at the confluence of the rivers Canche and Ternoise, and is crisscrossed with rivulets. All very soothing and quite different from anything else in the region.

Its history is much more turbulent. Once the frontier of the old Hapsburg Empire, it was founded and fortified by Charles V of Austria in 1554, but fell to the Spanish, until 1639, when Louis XIII regained it for the French; this mixed pedigree has resulted in a delightful assortment of architecture. The imposing Hôtel de Ville was originally the home of Charles's sister, Mary of Hungary, then converted into a town hall a century later, with the addition of a sumptuous loggia. The 16th-century Notre Dame church survived the town's vicissitudes, along with a few contemporary houses, and Renaissance buildings line some of the streams in picturesque juxtaposition with more recent grey stone houses. There are even some mediaeval remains, including a castle, out at Vieil Hesdin.

The market square is still the centre of the town and on Thursday mornings the farmers from the surrounding villages set up their stalls to form one of the best markets in northern France. Wander round, feast the eye and nose, then take a seat outside one of the square's several bars to make the most of the colourful scene.

The little town makes a charming centre to the little-appreciated area all round it. The most attractive approach is to take the D 108 from the north, through the delightful villages of **Embry** , with stream flowing by and white folly church on hill, and **Lebiez**, on the Créquoise. **Wamin**, centred round its château, is another pleasing hamlet if you're in the detouring mood. This will lead through the Forest of Hesdin, amongst whose oak and beech wild boar are still hunted. Picnic tables in the glades are one answer to a lack of alternative eating suggestions in the town itself.

And of course there's always **Agincourt**, or Azincourt as the maps have it, to visit. The field where one misty October morning in 1415 Henry V covered himself in glory, capturing or killing 10,000 of the French nobility, is now a flat expanse of open ploughed land, wood-bordered, with no more excitement than a rough granite memorial monolith on the field where the English camped, near the D 104 from Blangy. A good deal of imagination has to be used to picture the scene, as it must have been; I find the blankness rather eerie, perhaps because I know that 6000 French soldiers are buried here in a grave-pit, beneath the roadside calvary.

Hôtel Trois Fontaines

(HR)M *16 rte Abbeville-Marconne 21.86.81.65 Rest Closed Sun p.m. P, AE, V*

I include this one merely because accommodation in the town is so scarce and because, lying on the outskirts of the town, it does have the merits of being peaceful.

The ten bedrooms are in the annexe, motel-style, their French windows looking on to a well-tended garden. They are all exactly alike, simple, clean, with good bathrooms. 300f.

I would have thought it was all unexceptional, if dull, but reports have been very mixed about both food and hotel. One reader took his wife there for her birthday and scored top marks for doing so; another, quite rightly seething after a no-hot-water, rotten meal experience wrote, 'I consider you do a disservice to include this establishment in your book.' Well, disservice or not, in it goes again, with the same warnings that readers must make up their own minds if it would suit them. It certainly doesn't suit me – when I tried to book, in order to make up my own mind again, the offer of a room was smartly withdrawn unless I agreed to eat in. I've done that once and don't propose to repeat the experience.

The **Hôtel des Flandres** gets an even worse press, so I can suggest nothing in the town itself except perhaps **La Chope** (HR)S (48 r. d'Arras 21.86.82.73. closed Fri. 15/09-15/06) which has a very basic 7 rooms at 108f for two and a simple menu at 53.20f. But do look at Aubin St. Vaast, p. 52.

L'Ecurie
(R)M *21.86.86.86*

Just off the main square, through a gateway, into a courtyard, and on to a large room contrived out of the old stables, with assorted horsey impedimenta hanging on all available surfaces. Madame greets, smiles, is friendly and efficient, the lunch-time scene is encouragingly busy with local businessmen. Three quite interesting menus, at 65,80 and 110f.

Restaurant Leroy
(R)M *19 r. du Général de Gaulle 21.86.80.87*

This too was recommended by a Frenchman who knows what he's talking about gastronomically, but my personal feeling about it is that its heyday is over and that the management don't care that much. It's a sober, solid kind of typically middle-class French restaurant, with reliable and substantial if a trifle dull food on menus from 80f. You won't go far wrong but you won't feel like writing to me describing the high spot of the holiday.

Oh dear. And that's just about Hesdin, which is a great pity, since the little town could be such a useful stop. You could always try **La Belle Epoque** in the rue Arras for a light lunch, crêpes, pizzas and tea, but otherwise I should make for nearby Huby-St. Leu, p. 104.

Map 2A **HESDIN-L'ABBÉ** 62360 Pont de Briquec Ste Etienne (Pas de Calais) 7 km SE of Boulogne

Le Manoir
(R)M *Route Nationale 1 21.33.57.74*

NEW MANAGEMENT

'A modern building in traditional style. Quite elegant with lots of fresh flowers and real plants in copper pots. The tourist menu at 60f was very good value, being tasty, a little different, well cooked and nicely presented. A very convenient stop for lunch for travellers from the 9.30 boat from Dover.' – D. J. Jolliffe.

I feel Mr. Jolliffe has done all my work for me. Le Manoir is indeed a welcome addition to the N 1.

Hôtel Cléry
Probably (H)M *21.83.19.83 In the village centre.*

When I went in search of the Hôtel Cléry in November 1986 I found a scene of complete chaos. Floorboards were up, an army of workmen surged about, lighting was by dangling bulb. But there was already no doubt in my mind that, given only a few prerequisites, here will be a winner.

There was no disguising the stunning façade of the 18th-century manor, elegantly white and grey, approached by a fine avenue of trees. Napoleon is said to have stayed here and I don't blame him.

Inside the house, the plasterers were restoring ceilings whose delicacy and finesse were already obvious; the staircase was indubitably fine, and the bedrooms, whose scale I could appreciate if little else, were flooded with light from elegant long windows.

More I cannot tell you at the time of going to press, except that the owners, M. and Madame Osseland, are confident that the hotel will be ready to welcome their first customers in spring 1987. The only possible reasons that this could not be a success are that the welcome should fail, that the prices should be too high, or that – and heaven forbid – the whole house were furnished in orange vinyl. We shall see.

1993: Rooms 300-540f. Breakfast 50f.

Map 9C **HONDAINVILLE** 60250 Mony (Oise) 188 km SE of Boulogne; 22 km SE of Beauvais

Le Vert Pommier
(R)M *44.56.53.60 Closed Sun. p.m.; Mon., Aug.*

'Château, owned by Air France, dominates the village, which is well-kept and centres round the church. Round the corner from the green is Le Vert Pommier, run for the last eight years by M. Gilant, a very keen

tennis player, who allows his guests to work off their lunch on his smart court. A very classy looking place, with white damask tablecloths and napkins and real flowers. It's an old converted French house with beams and attractive entrance with blue-and-grey tiles on the floor.

The speciality is fish. The 79f menu offers terrine de lapin, lapéreau à la moutarde. The carte is expensive, with main dishes costing 78-90f. Pretty garden. It is a restaurant I would go several extra miles to visit.' – Annabel Greenwood.

1993: Allow 200f.

Map 5A **LE HOURDEL** (Somme) 108 km S of Boulogne; 11 km NW of St. Valéry sur Somme

I cannot say I find the Hourdel promontory attractive. Sometimes marshy, sometimes duney, always dotted with caravans, the coast road (la route Blanche), optimistically coloured green by Michelin, may be unusual, with the mountainous dunes flicking their sand in drifts along the way and the waves pounding the stony beaches, but linger-worthy? No. Cayeux is a horror of dingy caravans, unkempt holiday bungalows, glaring neon and blaring 'amusements'. But the little port of Le Hourdel, right on the point, does have a fishing fleet which brings in its catch to:

Le Parc aux Huitres
(HR)S *22.26.61.20 Closed Tue.; Wed. o.o.s.*

A Logis de France, but lacking the *accueil* that that organisation generally deems important. The rooms are not bad, at 120f, with shower, but personally the vibes weren't right. A fishy meal here though might be a good idea, with a 70f menu offering lots of choice straight from the boats. Book on Sunday.

1993: No longer a Logis.

Map 4B **HUBY-ST.-LEU** 62140 Hesdin (Pas de Calais) 61 km SE of Boulogne

1 km NE of Hesdin on the St. Omer road. An unremarkable hamlet, with a steep hill climbing out, on which to find:

La Garenne
(R)M *Anciene route de St. Omer 21.86.95.09. or 81.65.97. Closed Tue.; Wed. lunch; one week in Feb.*

A wildly romantic spot, as rustic as its name (a *garenne* is a rabbit burrow), with overgrown garden and terrace and two ancient rooms to choose from, one all beamed and log-fired, and the other in the 16th-century cellar. Run by two men, Bernard and Didier, it has enormous character and ambiance, and an evening enjoying them both would be well spent. Stick to the cheapest menu at 125f – St. Jacques gratinées, duck breast with green peppercorns, cheese and dessert – or expect a monumental bill via the carte or heftier menus.

'Our find of the trip. A traditional building both inside and out, with a dining room furnished in heavy French style with magnificent raised open fire at one end and candle-lit tables and heavy drapes. The service was excellent and the Saturday evening clientele were all local parties. We had the 87.50f menu, the next one up being the gastronomique at 188f! We paid 15f extra for really good langoustine thermidor, then my wife had brochette of lamb cooked at the open fire and I had escalopes in roquefort sauce. The pudding was the best dessert we have ever had, a concoction of cream, sponge, blackcurrants and cassis. We had a very good Muscadet sur Lie at about 80f. This would be a thoroughly recommended place and we shall detour to go there again as often as we can.' – Dr. H. W. D. Hughes.

Map 3B **INXENT** 62170 Montreuil (Pas de Calais) 32 km S of Boulogne

One of the prettiest villages along the course of the Course. Follow the path beside the church to arrive at a stretch of the river to walk beside without a road intervening. It flows fast and wide here and if you hang over one of the bridges long enough you may see one of the cunning trout that is liable to arrive on the plates of:

Auberge d'Inxent
(HR)M *21.90.71.19. Closed 15/19-15/10; Mon. p.m.; Tues. All Cards*

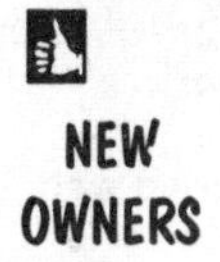

Parking opposite (take care on bend). The best-known and undoubtedly the most picturesque of the Course's restaurants, old and beamy and all hung about with wistaria. The menus don't change over the years, because the Auberge's customers come here specially to eat the trout and chicken variations it does best. It is most agreeable to sit outside on the terrace or by the winter log fire and eat simple food served stylishly. On sunny weekends the influx is considerable and service can be under stress, so don't go in a hurry.

The Auberge is an institution. Elizabeth David wrote about it in 1960 in her definitive *French Provincial Cooking*: 'In a certain country inn in the village of Inxent, in northern France, although the house, the dining room and the service are very modest, the cooking is famous both because of the excellence of the materials employed and the skill and simplicity with which the dishes are chosen and presented. There is very little choice. You will probably start with a trout, killed on the spot and cooked au bleu, served with melted butter so white and creamy that it practically is cream. Almost certainly the next course will be a chicken – plump, tender, roasted a delicate gold in butter, so full of flavour, the cooking so perfectly timed that you begin to wonder if you have ever really eaten a roast chicken before.'

1993: Rooms 350-450f. Similar menus from 85-190f.

➔Le Relais Equestre

(H)S *21.90.73.70.; 21.90.70.34.*

There have certainly been changes here. The Bourdons have divorced and Madame has left the establishment to her husband's care. But those, like me, who feared that another favourite was about to bite the dust, need hesitate no longer. If anything, the changes have been for the better and where I came to mourn, I left rejoicing. Hence the arrow.

The idea of an establishment caring for horses and humans is a doubtful one – the horses usually come off best – but here the non-equestrians should have few complaints about their stabling and oats. There are now seven bedrooms in this old farmhouse, in M. Bourdon's family for generations, and I found them the very model of what simple country bedrooms should be. Their rough-cast walls are whitewashed, the beds are brass or oak, with crocheted coverlets, the floors are scrubbed, rug-scattered, the flowers in jugs everywhere are wild or rambling Dorothy Perkins roses. In the modern bathroom (note singular) the water runs hot, constant, free.

Once the divorce settlement is sorted out, M. Bourdon plans a programme of improvements, which should answer one reader's dissatisfaction:

'We found the Relais charming and very quaint and were pleasantly received by M. Bourdon and had a choice of five rooms. We decided on the two upstairs ones, being intercommunicating and the more picturesque. The rooms were adequate but only just (no tooth glasses, nowhere to hang clothes, no curtains). I had a feeling a woman's touch was missing.'

It was indeed, but now the curtains and fittings that departed with the lady of the house are being replaced and the woman's touch is supplied by M. Bourdon's sister. I found the combination of the charming hardworking host and his daily helps worked well and when the gardens get their share of attention, and more bathrooms are installed, a stay here will be even more desirable.

As it is, the peace and beauty of the place, the good breakfast served on the oak tables in the old kitchen, M. Bourdon's welcome and concern, the ideal situation for beach and Montreuil, make it a wlnner.

There are all kinds of horsey deals, for children and grown-ups, beginners and experts, with full pension thrown in with the use of the

Le Relais Equestre

animals, and I should think the prospect of galloping along the sands and rambling through the quiet surrounding lanes would be most appealing for family holidays. Full details from M. Bourdon.

Double room costs 180f.

Map 4B **LABROYE** 62140 (Pas de Calais) 56 k m SE of Boulogne; 10 k m S W of Hesdin

The big D928 crosses the river here, bringing its share of heavy traffic through the little town, popular with fishermen. For the lorry-drivers, but far too good to keep to themselves, is a Relais Routiers:

Chez Georgette
(R)S *21.86.83.10 Closed Sept.*

I consider this one a promising find. I came across it at lunchtime, when, alas, I had no appetite for more than a sandwich by the river, but the sight of the cheerful little dining room, full of French guzzlers demolishing steaming platterfuls of chicken and fresh veg nearly made me change my mind. Only the thought of a dutiful dinner already booked stopped me testing what I suspect might be a future arrow. Reports particularly welcome therefore.

The friendly patronne likes the English (but I saw not a whisper of a

G.B.) and obviously aims to please. Her three-course menus are 65f with charcoal grills and cous-cous said to be specialities.

Map 4B **LA LOGE** 62140 Hesdin (Pas de Calais) 61 km SE of Boulogne

5 km NW of Hesdin, by the N928 and D108, or through the forest tracks.

The forest of Hesdin is a winner. The lanes cut through it, dip into valleys, and rise between the deep shade of the beeches. Picnic tables are dotted about but even in high summer there was only a scattering of other cars to dispel the illusion that here was a secret retreat. To the north of the forest, on a crossroads is:

L'Auberge de la Forêt
(R)S *21.86.86.52.*

NO NEWS

Alas, the 'camping' behind the Auberge swells every year and I don't blame those who pass by the uninteresting-seeming café with the brashness of the camp right behind it. But do not dismiss too lightly the idea of stopping. For those who are prepared to penetrate the front bar, venture through the kitchen where, of a Sunday lunchtime, a welter of large perspiring ladies are heaving heavy casseroles out of ovens, and arrive at the rear dining room, always full of French families tucking into the enormous meals that M. Godet, son-in-law of the previous owner, dishes up. Menus at 55f offer plenty of variety of no-frills, good value nosh, with ne'er a fellow countryman to be seen or heard.

Map 2C **LUMBRES** 62380 (Pas de Calais) 42 km E of Boulogne

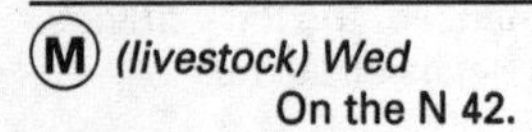

(M) *(livestock) Wed*

On the N 42.

➔**Moulin de Mombreux**
(H)M (R)L *21.39.62.44 Closed Sun. p.m.; Mon. 20/12-1/2. AE, DC, EC, V, P*

The awfulness of the surroundings – the juggernauted Nationale, the dusty paper mills, the mean little town of Lumbres – all accentuate the unexpected charm of this old water mill on the little river Blequin. The rusticity is calculated however – once inside the converted millhouse all is chic and sophisticated, from the downstairs bar, up the corkscrew stairs, to the food served by Jean-Marc Gaudry.

His culinary skills are supported by years of cooking at some of the best restaurants in France, and his Michelin rosette is a well-established one. Le Moulin is one of the most expensive restaurants in the area, but accept the fact that a treat is worth paying for and you will get good value for money.

You may well be lucky with the three-course daily menu at 220f and then you will get a bargain, but sometimes, although of uncompromisingly high quality, it may seem a little dull, and then I counsel the 'dégustation' at 385f. For me it was restrained portions of hot ducks' liver pâté served on a bed of interesting salad, a chunk of freshly poached lobster flecked with herbs and fillet of lamb served in a superb sauce flavoured with truffles. The cheeses are P. Olivier of course and the dessert a refreshing gratin of oranges.

There are always some interesting dishes on the carte, like some imaginative ravioli stuffed with a baby langoustine and served on a bed of chopped cabbage in a light cream sauce, but then you must expect a bill of around 300f, if you choose the least expensive wine. Compare this with the equivalent in England.

Just a word of criticism – what a pity that the dread pop music should penetrate so incongruously here, and do the waiters have to

Moulin de Mombreux

stand so superciliously waiting for the lift to hoist up the orders? Otherwise an arrow for excellent food in charming surroundings. The accommodation does not match up to the luxury of the restaurant – the rooms are tiny and thin-walled, but attractive enough and not expensive at 140f a double. Stop press: Building has commenced on a new wing, with three-star bedrooms, ready autumn 1987.

1993: Now with 14 rooms (L) from 480-650f.

Map 10B **LA MARE D'OVILLERS** (Oise) 180 km SE of Boulogne, 9 km E of Hesdin

---

19 km S of Beauvais on the N1.

Le Bec Au Vent
(R)S *N1 44.08.67.10 Closed Mon. p.m.; Tues.*

NO NEWS

Madame Coubriche (see Anserville p. 41) recommended this one in preference to the better-known Auberge almost next door. And how right she was. I much preferred its atmosphere (rustique, cheerful), food (generous and honest) and prices (menus from 55f) to those of the opposition.

Map 4B **MARESQUEL** 61286 (Pas de Calais) 48 km SE of Boulogne, 9 km E of Hesdin

---

10 km SE of Montreuil turn right off the N39 on the D130 for signposts to:

Château de Ricquebourg
(Chambre d'hôte) 21.90.30.96

'Château' in French can mean anything from Versailles to a dilapidated country house. Think in terms of the latter here. High on a hill overlooking the verdant valley of the Canche is an old manor house, potentially beautiful, given a good deal more time and money than its owner, Madame Pruvost, has been able to apply. As she said when she saw me, unaccompanied, 'We are a household of women here.' She and her two attractive daughters run the place, and the *élévage* of pigs and chickens that supply raw material for the Château's table.

Since she has been doing b and b she has been able to make improvements to the old house and the extensive damp patches on the staircase were being dealt with when I last visited. The bedrooms remain mercifully un-smartened – three vast doubles, with stunning views over valley or orchard, furnished with valuable old oak furniture, heavily carved. You share a bathroom and pay 190f for two, including breakfast, eaten in the gorgeous farmhouse kitchen. Evening meals, by request, at 90f for three simple courses of mostly farm produce.

Don't, I beg you, think of staying here if you like to play safe in a hygienic plastic cube, but if a warm welcome, country peace and the simple life appeal, this could be for you.

Map 4A **MARQUENTERRE** (Somme) 60 km 5 of Boulogne

At the ancient town of Rue (where cosmetic rouge originated) take the D 4 westwards to the well-marked **Parc Ornithologique** (22.25.03.06.). The area is well-named – Marquenterre, the sea that enters the land; here there are sand dunes and mud flats and the kind of opalescent light that gave the coast its name, so that water and land and sky merge. It's all a very worthwhile excursion for the non-expert as well as the bird-fancier, with hides dotted about from which to observe the 300 different species of birds that are known to visit this 500-acre reserve. Binoculars are provided and the whole enterprise is admirably well organised. There are restaurants from 60f to 200f.

Map 1A **MARQUISE** 62250 (Pas de Calais) 13 km NE of Boulogne

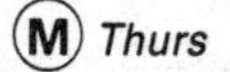

Most travellers know the main road through Marquise, but few realise that behind it there is a little town, with market in the square.

Le Grand Cerf
(R)M-L *ave. Ferber 21.92.84.53 Closed Sun. p.m.; Mon.; Feb. CB, DC, EC*

A well-known staging post to generations of Englishmen toiling down the N 1. Le Grand Cerf is an old coaching inn, far smarter inside than anyone would guess from its dusty exterior. The main dining room, in fact, is a bit too impressive, intended for serious eaters and *groupes*. Make for one of the smaller rooms if possible – far prettier and less pretentious.

The youthful chef, Jean-François Lemercier, has impeccable credentials. He trained at the great Le Flambard in Lille, and was twice a finalist in the contest for Meilleur Ouvrier de France. Perhaps he lacks the panache of Christian Germain at Montreuil, or perhaps he is discouraged by a British clientèle – for the most part looking for an *en route*, good value, set meal rather than leisurely gastronomic excitement – but he does not seem to have reached his full potential yet.

I have not been thrilled with the cheapest menu (at 135f) but I suspect that, in order to do justice, one should go on to the next one up at 175f, and sample some of his fish dishes like oyster soups, ragout of seafood, sole cooked 'en papillote', or some of the game specialities appropriate to a restaurant so-named, such as hare cooked in Sauvignon or a casserole of pigeon and wild boar.

1993: New chef. Menus from 120f.

Map 3A **MERLIMONT** 62155 (Pas de Calais) 38 km S of Boulogne

Between Le Touquet and Berck Plage, well marked on the D940.

BAGATELLE
If you want to abandon your progeny for a day and not have 'em mind a bit, Bagatelle, the biggest 'pleasure park' in Northern France, is the place.

You fork out £3.30 per child and leave them to decide which of the thirty odd attractions best deserves their attention. They can try all of them if they wish. As often as they wish. If you feel you should be roughly in attendance, it'll cost another £4.20 per adult, but 60 acres should be enough to lose them while you suss out the Big Wheel on their behalf, or take mother-in-law out on the pedalo.

A few especially attractive items are not included in the entrance fee. If you fancy being terrified in the ghost train or deafened in the shooting gallery, take extra francs.

Open late March to early October 10 a.m. to 7.30 p.m. 21.94.60.33. – and there are restaurants and free picnic areas.

Map 8B **MONCEAUX** 60940 Cinqueux (Oise) 154 km SE of Boulogne; 12 km NW of Beauvais

On the D 901 .

Auberge de Monceaux
(R)M *1r. de Gen. Leclerk 44.84.50.32 Closed Wed. p.m.; Thur.; Jan.*

NO NEWS

Nothing exceptional, but a useful stop on the main road, with a guaranteed welcome, comfort, and well-cooked food. Fillet of turbot with langoustines, sweetbreads normande (with cream and Calvados) are the kind of substantial traditional dish to expect on the carte. No menu. Allow 160-200f for three courses.

Map 3B **MONTCAVREL** 62170 Montreuil (Pas de Calais) 30 km SE of Boulogne

6 km NE of Montreuil by D 150.

One of the prettiest villages in the Course area, on the edge of a plateau dominating the valley of the little Brimoise. It boasts a château dating from the 12th century, with moat and *donjon*, but gets overlooked by the motorists who follow the valley of the Course northwards on the fast and attractive D 126.

Map 3B **MONTREUIL-SUR-MER** 62170 (Pas de Calais) 38 km S of Boulogne

Sat

Montreuil retains the 'sur-mer' suffix as a reminder that it was once, at a time when the French kings controlled very few provinces, France's only royal port. Nowadays the river Canche has silted up, so that the estuary is some ten miles away. You can still get a glimpse of the sea though from the ramparts surrounding this most fascinating and unique town – certainly my favourite in all the Pas-de-Calais.

The rampart walk is a must. I timed myself all round – 40 minutes but at any stage it is possible to take a path back to the nice old houses and cobbled streets that make up the town centre – so even if the trip is a brief one, do make the effort to walk at least a part of the way above the rolling farmlands, the valley of the river, the lighthouse that marks the estuary, Le Touquet, the old monastery of Notre Dame des Prés, and the variegated roofs of the town.

A deviation here from the N 1, which passes swiftly below the abrupt north cliff on which the town is built, will bring swift rewards. Cross over the river, wind up the steep hill, already conscious that something special is waiting at the top, under the bridge, and approach the town via its oldest quarters. The Cavée St. Firmin, picturesquely cobbled, with 17th-century cottages clinging precariously to its slopes, will be familiar from many a postcard.

The pl. Darnétal – tree-lined, fountain playing – is a good first stop. Park here, visit the Information Bureau in the corner, take a drink or meal at **Le Darnétal** and walk behind it to visit the former monastery church of **St. Saulve**, part 12th century, with a magnificent flamboyant Gothic nave. Montreuil takes its name from the original monastery (monasteriolum) founded there in the 7th century by St. Saulve, bishop of Amiens.

Follow the Grand Rue (or better still cut through the quiet back streets) to the Grande Place, particularly lively with its market on Saturday mornings, but always a good beer stop, with several bars to choose from. Douglas Haig, who had his headquarters here in the first world war, is commemorated by a statue.

Behind the Château de Montreuil is a lovely peaceful green patch,

Montreuil.

ideal for picnics, leading to the **Citadelle**. Open from Wed.-Mon., it was built in the 16th century and subsequently modified by Vauban. Commentaries in all manner of tongues can be arranged by paying a suitable fee and pushing the appropriate button.

It is fitting that such a special town should have its special hotel, and I have no doubt that if money were absolutely no object I would look no further than:

Le Château de Montreuil

(HR)L *Chaussée Capucins 21.39.62.44 Closed 15/12-26/12; 2/1-15/2; Rest. closed Tues. lunch except July and Aug AE, DC, EC, V. P Completely refurbished*

There is always a danger of underestimating any hotel as well-known as the Château. Perhaps I was hesitant to heap praises in previous editions because I could hardly believe that anyone did not know already about this, the only luxury Relais et Châteaux hôtel in the Pas de Calais, and also because I realised that its prices were beyond the means of many of my readers. English visitors have been faithful to this most English of French hotels for generations, even during a bad patch, when I felt distinctly disloyal for raising a lone voice of criticism. Since Christian Germain took over, however, he who criticised would be very hard indeed to please. And I found that the letters about the Château, far from carping at the prices, repeat time and time 'the high spot of our holiday', 'a perfect meal in perfect surroundings', 'worth every penny'.

It is this latter aspect that I am most concerned with because FE above all is interested in value for money, and after each visit I come away more than ever convinced that in its class the Château is unbeatable.

Take into account that here, in a favourite old town, strategically placed for port and seaside, in an elegant house ('château' is misleading – think rather in terms of a large English country house) peacefully set in a well-tended colourful garden, with swimming pool and terraces, luxurious bedrooms (some magnificently eccentric, some more modest, all different, so check when booking), efficiently organised

Then think of the food (even if a stay is out of the question – the hotel is often full); a meal here should be contrived if at all feasible. Christian Germain trained with the Roux Brothers, and it would indeed be interesting to compare prices and quality of what he offers with those of Le Gavroche or the Waterside (any rich reader who eats regularly at both, please contact). For those counting pennies and calories, the 220f no-choice four-course lunch menu is a snip which I am perfectly sure the English comparison couldn't even consider. Here are two sample menus for April, and note how simple they appear to be, making full use of whatever is best in the season's markets:

Fresh asparagus ('aux pointes violettes') with mousseline sauce
Escalopes of salmon with ginger
Veal chop with shallots
Tarte Tatin
and
Marinaded salmon 'en Gravad lax'
Red carp, cooked in Rhône wine
Breast of Licques chicken, with tarragon
Champagne sorbet

COMPLETELY REFURBISHED

The simplicity is admirable but perhaps misleading. The complementary sauces are from no amateur's whisk. Their stock bases are the real thing, lovingly reduced, thickened, stirred and tasted. But the principle of serving nothing but the freshest ingredients, which have travelled the shortest distance to the table (in the case of the herbs, from the Château's garden), is the important factor which causes the oohs and aahs from freezer-numbed palates.

However, in order to see what Christian can really do (and for a taste of the cuisine which will eventually earn him a second Michelin star, I bet) go mad and order the 'Menu Surprise'. At 280f it still fares well with English comparisons.

The 'surprise' is that Christian does the choosing for you and there's no guarantee what you will get. You are asked if you suffer from any allergies or strong dislikes and then get what he feels like cooking, based on whatever looked best in the market that day. There may only be enough for one or two portions – no matter, some lucky diner will benefit from these, others will take something else that Christian thinks might please them. I was 'surprised' to see not the sorbet that arrived on my neighbours' plates but a sauté of girolles turn up on mine. 'I remembered that you left your sorbet last time,' is the kind

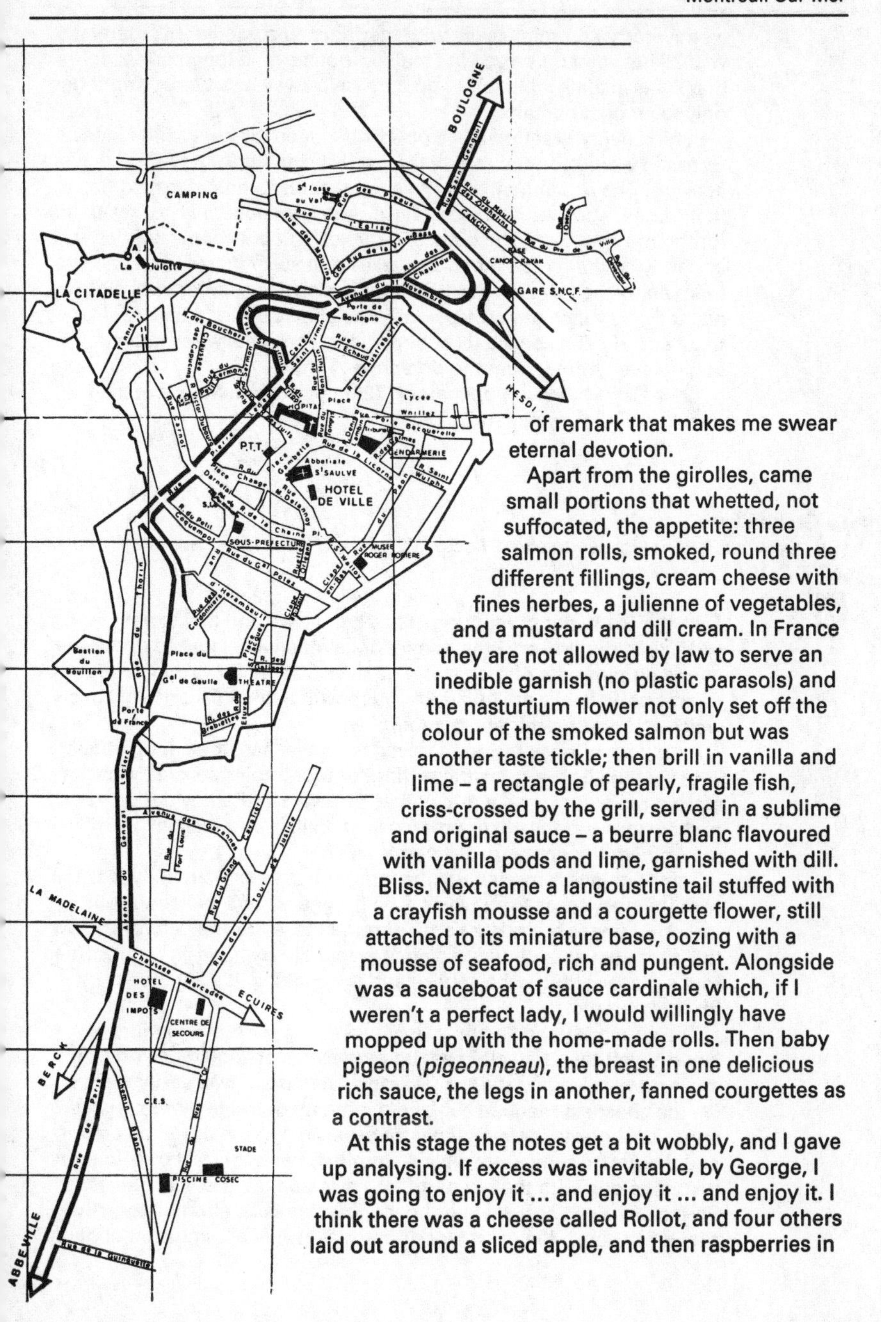

of remark that makes me swear eternal devotion.

Apart from the girolles, came small portions that whetted, not suffocated, the appetite: three salmon rolls, smoked, round three different fillings, cream cheese with fines herbes, a julienne of vegetables, and a mustard and dill cream. In France they are not allowed by law to serve an inedible garnish (no plastic parasols) and the nasturtium flower not only set off the colour of the smoked salmon but was another taste tickle; then brill in vanilla and lime – a rectangle of pearly, fragile fish, criss-crossed by the grill, served in a sublime and original sauce – a beurre blanc flavoured with vanilla pods and lime, garnished with dill. Bliss. Next came a langoustine tail stuffed with a crayfish mousse and a courgette flower, still attached to its miniature base, oozing with a mousse of seafood, rich and pungent. Alongside was a sauceboat of sauce cardinale which, if I weren't a perfect lady, I would willingly have mopped up with the home-made rolls. Then baby pigeon (*pigeonneau*), the breast in one delicious rich sauce, the legs in another, fanned courgettes as a contrast.

At this stage the notes get a bit wobbly, and I gave up analysing. If excess was inevitable, by George, I was going to enjoy it ... and enjoy it ... and enjoy it. I think there was a cheese called Rollot, and four others laid out around a sliced apple, and then raspberries in a strawberry and mint sauce with meringue and vanilla ice cream. It was all heaven and served in small portions over a long period, so that I was actually able to get up and drive away afterwards (far better only to stagger upstairs).

Behind every great man is a good wife, or so they say, and Lindsay Germain would certainly seem the perfect counterpoint to Christian's cooking. She is bilingual and takes great pains to help guests make their dinner choices. Take her advice. And her concern is not reserved for the big spenders. The baby of a (typical) hippie couple niggles and is clearly spoiling their meal. She takes him away in her arms and lets them enjoy their dinner. A smart couple arrive for dinner and, giggling but still every inch the professional, she shows them to their table, baby and all. The service throughout is impeccable, with Lindsay behind every move from the *personnel.*

1993: Demi-precision obligatory. 725f per person. Menus at 270f (lunch including wine) and 380f.

➔La Grenouillère

(R)L *La Madelaine-sous-Montreuil 21.06.07.22 Closed Tues. p.m. and Wed. o.o.s. AE, DC, V*

Take the D 139 out of Montreuil for a km or two and hit instant rusticity in the flowery little hamlet of La Madelaine, tucked under the imposing ramparts of the town. The river Canche flows wide and deep here and the banks are invariably lined with patient fishermen. Lovely walks and good picnic spots abound.

An old farmhouse facing the river, whitewashed, low, hung about with wisteria, is the romantic setting for Montreuil's second Michelin-starred restaurant, and a drink on its terrace, soothed by the proximity of the water and the sheer prettiness of it all, is an excellent preliminary to another gastronomic treat.

Temptation to 'smarten up' the interior has been mercifully resisted, with the tipsy frogs from which 'The Froggery' gets its name, still frolicking under their dark varnish round the walls, the beams are low, the floor uneven and the ambiance resolutely *rustique*. When it comes to the place settings, the service and the cooking, it's another story – far from simple.

The young Roland Gauthier, increasingly growing in confidence since he left the Château to set up here five years ago, goes on from strength to strength, and the last meal I had there was easily the best. On the cheapest menu at 190f, I ate three memorable dishes: quails eggs, just cooked, sitting on pastry bases in a sauce based on cream and the *jus* from mussels which, chopped, gave contrast of colour and texture, along with the red of tomato dice and the green of chives. Perfection. Then cubes of plump langoustine tails, alternating with monk fish cooked in meat stock (how clever!), in an emulsion of garlic cloves boiled till their harshness became sweet. Spinach noodles, home-made like everything else here, centred the dish.

These were exceptionally fine dishes, but Roland excels in that often-neglected course – the dessert. Here he uses imagination and flair to conjure up the irresistible lime mousse, fragile, airy, set in fragrant jasmine tea cream, or two chocolates – dark and white-swirled together in an almond-infused sauce.

Excellent value, but be warned, the wine list can push up the bill alarmingly. The cheapest bottle, a Pouilly Fumé, cost 110f.

1993: 4 newly decorated rooms cost 300, 400 and 500f.

Le Darnétal

(R)M *pl. Darnétal 21.06.04.87. Closed Mon p.m.; Tues. All Cards*

No lack of *accueil* in this little inn on the corner of the square, all freshly painted in brown and white, with geraniums spilling out of window-boxes and white tables on the pavement. Genial patron, Robert Bureau, likes nothing better than greeting old friends and making new ones, and at the slightest excuse out comes the champagne and the complimentary coupe. Mock-regretfully, he claims it's the only drink he's allowed nowadays.

However engaged with friends at the bar though, his eyes are everywhere to ensure that other clients are welcomed, led to their tables in the delightfully cluttered room, with its warm friendly atmosphere generated by lots of flowers, lots of bustle and bright red tablecloths.

I love it, especially in contrast to the more serious and international style of the Château and La Grenouillère, but the food is not just second best. I met a local lady here (it's hard not to meet someone) who said she never ate anywhere else 'the best value for miles around'. Nothing *raffiné* about the cooking – it's hefty portions of the like of boeuf bourgignon or coq au vin, with interesting items like a gâteau of celery with two sauces – a substantial chunk of terrine, crunchy with celery plonked between a shellfish and butter sauce, dished up with more enthusiasm than finesse. All this for 58f, washed down with a demi-litre of Côtes du Rhône for 30f, is what eating in France is all about.

The more ambitious menu at 89f includes hot oysters, a mousse of pike with crayfish sauce and a unique soufflé of skate. Cheeses are good, desserts less so, and the wine list is an interesting one, assembled from M. Bureau's happy exploration of the different wine-growing areas.

There are five rooms available, at 120f a double, which I suspect are like their patron, stronger on atmosphere than rectitude. One reader warned against, but I look forward to trying them myself and reporting what I'm sure will be an interesting experience.

1993: Excellent chef. Menus now from 90f. Rooms 230-260f.

Hotel Central 'Chez Edouard'
(HR)S

All that a little French hotel should be. Pleasantly old-fashioned, run by two young sisters. The snag is the choice you have to make between being disturbed by the traffic in the main hotel (but it's not a main road and quietens down completely at night), and the church clock which strikes in your ear if you stay in the annexe alongside. The rooms are 280f, menus from 68f and not easy to book as this is a very popular little hotel.

The food in the restaurant, Chez Edouard, is worth making a special visit for, bedding or not. Either the 59f or the 88f version is good value, incorporating dishes like a salad of smoked ham, red mullet poached in vermouth, roast goats' cheese, Philippe Olivier platter, charlotte of apples. Nice atmosphere, good for families.

'A first-rate choice – clean, good beds, excellent bathroom and the best breakfast of our tour' – Emlyn Lloyd.

1993: Now called **Le Shakespeare** (HR)S. Rooms now 280f, menus from 68f.

Brasserie de la Place
(R)S-M *pl. du Général de Gaulle 21.06 08 65.*

A new bar/restaurant/salon de thé, which calls itself a *grande brasserie française*, in the market square. It's bright, clean, and wholesome, with an obliging patron, and has three menus, from 67f; a good place to take the family perhaps, since it also does a *menu enfant*, and is open for an early supper. Its speciality is omelettes so it could be useful too for a light lunch.

Hôtel de France
2 r. Coquempot 21.06.09.36. Closed Wed., Thurs. o.o.s. All Cards

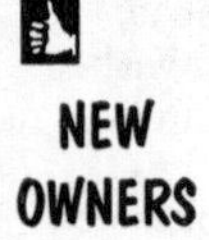

I know there are some good rooms in this historic old inn, where Laurence Sterne once stayed, because one day I had a sneaky look at them. I'd pulled the old bell chain across the courtyard, where it optimistically says 'Reception', and hammered on the door, and coughed and hallooed and, when absolutely nothing happened, I decided in desperation to explore further unescorted. I came across a couple of delightful, spacious rooms, well-furnished à l'ancienne, heard that the food in the adjoining restaurant was excellent, and looked forward to returning another day.

When that day came, it was altogether another story. Our room was plain miserable and so was the welcome. Was I sure I had booked? No, we could not have a bath. No, we could not have a shower. No, we could not have another bedside light. No, the restaurant was not open. What time did we want breakfast? Slammed door.

Now I know I am always reminding querulous readers not to expect the Ritz for 90f, and maybe at this price we could have forgiven the peeling paint, the cheap stained carpet, the long walk to the loo, the mean light switches that make you run to catch the next one, and the thinness of the walls, all on the grounds of economy, but a welcome to tired travellers on a dark and dirty night costs nothing, and its absence is unforgiveable. We spent the night clinging to our respective sides of the V-shaped mattress, listening to the thuds, bumps and curses coming from our worse-for-wear neighbours, until the traffic roar started up again outside (bang on a nasty main road bend), when we thankfully departed. So, the message is: do consider the France if you can get one of the best rooms, for 200f, and do try the **Restaurant du Roy**, on which all reports are highly enthusiastic, but forget the idea of a cheap night's sleep.

1993: Rooms now 180-380f

Le Relais du Roy

(R)M *58 r. Pierre Ledent 21.81.54.44. Closed 14/11-1/3*

NO NEWS

Here is a report from someone luckier than I in finding this attractive little restaurant open:

'Beside Hôtel de France, but not under same management. Ate two excellent meals during three-day stay, but on both occasions the restaurant was very quiet, with only a handful of people. Starters: mushroom roulade and an assiette of meats. Main: lemon sole with lots of tarragon and veal brochette, very peppery, with rice. Cheese: different from usual offerings; Sweets: good chocolate mousse. Very cheap wines – 44-50f. Menus 75f.' – Quentin Gray.

Hôtel Bellevue

(HR)M *21.06.04.19 Private garage All Cards*

Here's better news. There are new young owners here, the first hotel to catch the eye on arrival in Montreuil, clinging to the steep approach hill. M. and Madame Heno are making great improvements, smartening the place up, and here are patrons who know all about welcome. Their plans for the future include the building of a side terrace to catch the evening sun; already the bedrooms are refurbished (200-270f) and the food (80-130f) is served in a cheerful dining room, warmed by a big log fire. Unfortunately all the rooms face on to the road, but M. Heno swears that the traffic stops at night and plans for double-glazing are in mind.

A nice friendly atmosphere, with locals using the bar, and a welcome addition to the (difficult) hotel situation in this popular town.

Map 3A **LE MOULINEL** – see ST. JOSSE p. 135

Map 4B **NAMPONT-ST-MARTIN** 80120 Rue (Somme) 51 km S of Boulogne

Very confusing to have a Nempont and Nampont so near together. This one is a stone's throw further along the N 1.

Les Contrebandiers
(R)M *22.29.90.43. Closed Tues. p.m.; Wed. o.o.s.; Oct. CB*

NO NEWS

Inside is a delightful surprise – ancient beams, flagged floors, huge chimney-piece – all very rustique indeed and a pleasant contrast to the 20th-century hustle outside. M. Garnier, the new patron, has ambitious-sounding menus from 72-170f but I think this is not the place to push the boat out. Rather enjoy the surroundings and eat simply and as cheaply as possible. Well recommended locally but our test meal was a let-down.

Map 7C **NAMPTY** 80160 Conty (Somme) 116 km SE of Boulogne; 16 km SW of Amiens

For those approaching Amiens from the south, the best tip I can pass on is to do so by the yellow D210, or the white D8, both of which are a much more agreeable way of getting into the city than the parallel N 1. The little D8 follows the valley of the river Selle, on the banks of which stands an erstwhile paper-mill:

Le Moulin de Rigauville
(R)M *22.42.12.36. Closed Sun. p.m.; Mon.; Tues. p.m.; 28/7-28/8*

Not as romantic as one might imagine from the c.v. The mill is not very old and not very beautiful, and the large dining room lacks charm, but its site is enticing enough, especially in the summer, when meals can be eaten outside on the terrace by the little river; it is certainly a very popular spot with the Amienois.

Commendably the owners have not cashed in on the lure of the position by the water; the food is well cooked, from prime ingredients, particularly the fish, which features in the 150f *menu poisson*. The five-course 200f menu would make a splendid celebration but the cheapest 110f version is equally commendable and good value.

In the next hamlet, *Neuville-les-Loeuilly*, is another possibility:

La Petite Auberge
22.42.70.76. Closed Tues.; Wed.; 10 days in Feb.

Superb fish again in this narrow little restaurant on the hill in the village centre. All very pretty, warm and welcoming inside, thanks to the friendly owners, Daniel and Cécile Saguirez. Frustrating for those, like me, fish-starved in the country back home, to find such perfectly fresh specimens delivered to this deeply rural situation, some distance from either the sea or the Paris markets. But take advantage of the perfect plateaux de fruits de mer here, 150f for one person, 250f for two, with stylish presentation. Menus at 95f and 120f.

Map 6C **NAOURS** 80114 (Somme) 102 km SE of Boulogne

20 km NW of Amiens by the N25 and D60. Hard to believe that there were days in the summer of '86 that were unbearably hot, but in August there was one such, when the car became intolerable and the town streets sizzled. It was a Sunday and as most of Amiens had shut up anyway, it seemed to make sense to get out into the country, and even more sense to go down a cave!

Those at Naours, a village in peaceful but unremarkable countryside, are no ordinary caves, being carved out of the chalky soil around 300 AD and only re-discovered in the last century. 3000 metres long, with 26 galleries from which lead off rooms for 300 families. Much imagination is needed to visualise how these families, with their animals, lived down here, in a mini-town complete with market squares, crossroads, stables, wells and chapel. Since the time they were scratched out they have been used for refuge from all kinds of wars and pestilences.

An hourly tour walks you round, behind a candle-bearing (French-speaking) guide (wear sensible shoes and take a cardi – it really is cold down there). As a finale there is a museum of the arts and crafts of Picardy, with appropriate voices booming out from the model craftsmen and women.

A useful excursion for a hot day – or a wet one.

Map 4B **NEMPONT-ST. FIRMIN** 62600 Berck Plage (Pas de Calais) 51 km S of Boulogne

A useful staging-point bang on the N1, where the departments of the Pas-de-Calais and Somme join.

La Peupleraie
(H)M *22.29.98.11.*

I list this brand new hotel purely for its functional value – no detour necessary from the N 1 but set back in the trees far enough to escape the worst of the traffic fret. Forty rooms all have bathrooms, at 230f. They were so new when I inspected that the carpets were still being laid, but the furniture and furnishings looked adequate enough. Across the road, in a different *département*, is:

Chez Alysse
(R)S *21.81.20.42.*

A better-than-average main-road stop, with log fire in cold weather to cheer the traveller. Menus, with good fish dishes, from 75f.

Map 10C **NEUILLY-EN-THELLE** (Oise) 199 km SE of Boulogne; 30 km SE of Beauvais

(M) *Fri* Turn off the N 1 east on to the D609, after La Mare d'Ovillers. The little market town of Neuilly is 4 km on.

L'Auberge du Centre
(HR)S *44.26.70.01. Closed Mon.*

It was thanks to the darkness and dirtiness of the November night that friend Ann and I decided we could not face driving any further on towards the fleshpots of Chantilly and would take pot luck in Neuilly. Well, not absolute pot luck, since I had done some homework a day or so earlier, met the friendly patron, Daniel Tessier, approved of the spotless little rooms upstairs (78f or 89f with a bathroom) and noted that the restaurant was bright and cheerful – just what was needed to revive two car-lagged ladies.

My hunch proved right. We ate for 57f as well as we might have done for treble that amount in a smarter location. Ann's three-course menu included grilled sardines, boeuf bourguignon, and a good cheeseboard (90f buys a fish course as well), while I tried some of the house specialities to see what the young chef was made of, and was well pleased with my feuilleté of leeks and wild mushrooms (28f) and an original and highly successful gratin of crab and avocados for 43f. 75cl of house wine at 12f was the cheapest I found anywhere in the region.

Arrowed for unsophisticated charm, good food, excellent value.

Map 9B **NOAILLES** (Oise) 172 km SE of Boulogne; 12 km SE of Beauvais

 *Thurs* Turn west off the N 1 near the Hôtel de Ville.

La Table d'Hote
(R)M *44.03.35.35 29 r. Annoepel Closed Sun.; Mon.; evenings except Fri., Sat.; Aug.*

Within the severe restrictions of the opening hours and the limitations of size (only 30 covers), here is an attractive little restaurant with other considerable advantages. It has great personality and is family-run, Gisèle Parent making the most of seasonal products with daily changing menus, her son in charge of the wines, and daughter generally helping out. No set menu, but dishes like foie gras with grapes for 58f, salmon with sorrel for 68f, confit of duck with a mousseline of turnips 64f and an excellent cheeseboard for 24f.

Not in other guides yet but very popular locally, so booking advisable.

Le Manoir de Framicourt
(R)M *44.03.30.16. Closed Wed., 20/12-2/1. AE, DC, EC*

NO NEWS

Turn left at Blainville, 2 km north of Noailles, on to the VO road, with the Manoir clearly indicated.

A stunningly beautiful 18th-century manor-house, quintessentially French with its white shutters and grey solemnity, all shadowed by a venerable cedar. It's set deep in the countryside, with no traffic to disturb a *déjeuner* if not *sur l'herbe, sur la terrasse.*

And the food lives up to the setting. Stick to the 103f, wine inclusive, menu (the carte is ridiculously expensive and no more interesting) for a feuilleté stuffed with mussels, a duck à l'orange, good cheeses and a pavé de Beaufort.

Le Moulin de Blainville
(R)M *44.03.31.00 R closed for dinner o.o.s.*

2 km north of Noailles on the N 1. A picturesque old watermill set on a main road usually spells disappointment. The temptation to cash in on setting and site is usually too much for the patrons to resist, and food and customers don't matter too much as long as the coffers fill up easily. Le Moulin de Blainville is an honorable exception.

Step down into a charming, beamed, stone-walled room, lined with tapestries, lots of flowers, big log fires, part of the 17th-century mill, or eat on the terrace in summer sun, soothed by millstream streaming. The food is interesting and well cooked, but à la carte only. Say 150-200f.

Map 1A **ONGLEVERT** (Pas de Calais) 14 km N of Boulogne

Turn right off the D940 on to the D191, opposite the turning to Cap Gris Nez. La Maison de la Houve is down a well marked track on your left.

→**Maison de la Houve**
(Chambre d'hôte) 21.83.29.95.

If proof were needed of my dedication to *French Entrée*, the revelation of La Houve must be it. How now will I be able to rely on a night's cossetting, without queuing up to get it?

This a chambre d'hôte *extraordinaire*, and Madame Danel is an extraordinary lady. I cannot see her sliding down the slippery path to complacency as some less strong-minded patronnes have been tempted to do. Her personal standards are far too high – higher I would say than in most luxury hotels.

It has taken her two years to convert her old stone farmhouse to receive guests, and she says she has only just begun. To my mind it is

already as near perfection as makes no difference. The character has been retained – flagged floors, stone walls, huge log-burning hearths, tiled stoves, the old pump, shuttered windows looking out on to a courtyard. but Madame Danel has not been tempted to sit back and capitalise on the undoubted natural advantages of site and character. Interior walls have been knocked down to make two vast reception rooms. The rear walls have given way to stretches of plate glass, to take full advantage of a stunning view. I bet that few people would guess that this was the allegedly dull Pas-de-Calais. The rolling hills and valleys, with never a house in sight, stretching as far as Cap Blanc Nez, with the sea sparkling away and the boats bobbing across the span, is more like Devon than Devon.

Inside, the rooms are dignified and spacious. Guests can sit in the galleried drawing-room, before a log fire in winter, more comfortable than in many a grand hotel.

Madame Danel's motif is a rose; it crops up on her cards, notepaper, road sign, and the six rooms are named after roses: 'Distinction', 'Super Star', etc., with the colour pink recurring. Ours was 'Grand Siècle' with giant pink roses rampant over the green trellis on the toile that covered the walls. The coverlet was crocheted, numerous lamps worked, the flowers were fresh, the carpets deep, the bed huge and sinfully soft. Between us and the room next door came a bathroom, equipped with expensive modern shower (bathroom down the corridor) and luxuriously deep towels and bathrobes.

Along the corridor led off other rooms, all quite different but all stamped with a distinctive style; Madame Danel is a magpie and her *petites collections* of decanter stoppers, dried flowers, straw hats are all put into service to make the visitor feel a guest in a home and not in an institution.

And what a spoiled guest! Never before in all France have I found a thermos of early morning tea outside my door, on a silver tray, with delicate china and a rose in a vase. (Even the thermos was pink and white) Never before have I been offered a hottie in the bed (quite unnecessarily – the house is wonderfully warm), nor come down to a breakfast table laid with a precious antique lace cloth, pristinely starched.

By now expectations for breakfast were high and we were not disappointed. Not only standard hot croissants were on offer but gourmet versions, stuffed with frangipane, sprinkled with toasted almonds. Five different pots of jam, all home-made, butter in a silver dish, unlimited coffee in a pewter jug. The orange juice was freshly squeezed of course.

Madame Danel is as elegant as her house, but the reverse of intimidating. She loves to show off the treasures of her home and have them appreciated. She has lots of plans to go on improving La Houve and I suspect such is her enjoyment in the project that they will never be finished. Perhaps next year the garden she has visualised, full of roses naturally, will materialise.

She gave us warm hugs on departure and we swore we would go back soon. If we can get in.

1993: From 140-215f for two people, including breakfast.

PITTEFAUX 8 kms E of Wimereux on the D233

Anyone doubting that perfect unspoiled countryside can be found within ten minutes of the port should be dragged to Pittefaux and made to recant. In one of the few houses set around a château in deepest farming country lives the kind Englishman, David Sweetman, who first alerted me to his 'local'. This is unselfishness indeed one might think but the fact is that without year-round support from more than just a few local gourmets, some of these utterly charming and worthy establishments will have a hard time to survive. Conscience cleared on that point I can heartily recommend a visit to:

→Auberge Le Souverain Moulin
(R)M-S *21.83.33.35. Closed Sun. Mon;and Tue p.m. o.o.s. Reservations requested*

'It combines the pretty atmosphere of an auberge with the grand cooking of a city restaurant, with a wine list to match.' – David Sweetman.

Well I'm not sure about grand cooking of a city restaurant because the Auberge has resolutely remained anything but grand in style, but the ingredients are prime and the cooking here is certainly more sophisticated than one would dream of finding in such a rustic situation. Menus from 95f. The ambiance and welcome are warm and I can guarantee a rewarding relaxing evening. An arrow for all this.

THE REGION AND THE MARKETS

For a visit to the old France travel inland to the mediaeval fortress town of Montreuil. Situated high on a hill Montreuil can trace its origins back to a 7th-century monastery. Though much of the architecture that remains is of houses built in the 17th and 18th century style, very little has changed in the last two hundred years. Its convenient position in the area makes it an ideal touring centre for either the coast or country.

The region's countryside offers the inquisitive traveller an opportunity to find areas of thick forests, calm lakes or the pretty towns and quiet villages of the Boulonnais so often missed by the Routes Nationales traffic.

Some of the prettiest places to visit nestle in the valleys next to the N1 road. Visit the Course Valley, running south from Desvres to Montreuil with its streams, lakes, good fishing, inns and cottages; the scenic Authie Valley, named after its river – the leafy tree-lined Canche

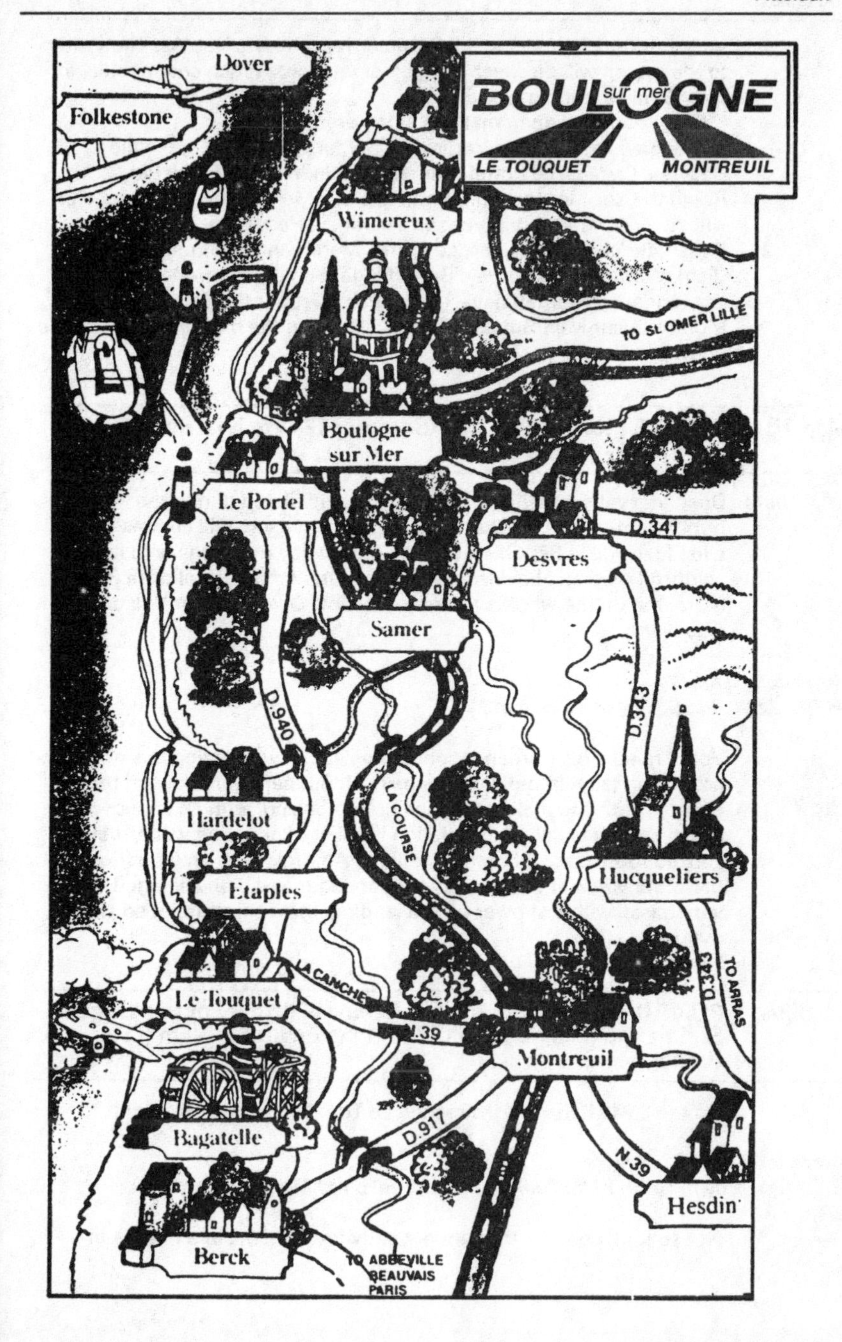
BOULOGNE
sur mer
LE TOUQUET
MONTREUIL
Dover
Folkestone
Wimereux
TO St. OMER LILLE
Boulogne sur Mer
Le Portel
D.341
Desvres
Samer
D.940
D.343
LA COURSE
Hardelot
Hucqueliers
Etaples
LA CANCHE
D.343
TO ARRAS
Le Touquet
N.39
Montreuil
Bagatelle
D.917
N.39
Hesdin
Berck
TO ABBEVILLE
BEAUVAIS
PARIS

Valley or the picturesque little-visited river valley of the Aa. The visitor to the region will discover a region of unspoilt French countryside, all just 30 miles from England.

Here Is a list of open markets in the area:

Monday: Le Touquet, Merlimont, Samer. Tuesday: Berck Ville, Desvres, Etaples, Le Portel, Wimereux. Wednesday: Berck Plage, Boulogne-sur-Mer (perish.), Boulogne-sur-Mer (all day – non-perish.), Hucqueliers, Merlimont (veget.). Thursday: Hesdin, Le Touquet. Friday: Berck Ville, Etaples, Le Portel, Merlimont, Montreuil-sur-Mer (fish), Wimereux. Saturday: Berck Plage, Boulogne-sur-Mer (perish.), Boulogne-sur-Mer (all day – non-perish.), Fruges, Le Touquet, Montreuil-sur-Mer. Sunday: Berck Ville. *All in the morning only, unless shown.*

Map 7B **POIX DE PICARDIE** 80290 (Somme) 124 km S of Boulogne; 28 km SW of Amiens

(M) *Thurs* Deep in a valley, the town of Poix was annihilated during the bombardment of 1940. Its reincarnation, however, still centres on the wide Place de la République, lively on Sunday mornings with its colourful market. I have some good reports on the **Hôtel de la Poste** there, but on the whole preferred to follow Diana McNair Wilson's discovery:

Hôtel de la Gare
(HR)S *22.90.00.36 Closed Mon. p.m.; V. P.*

NO NEWS

You'd need a recommendation to persist in investigating this not-very-promising tall thin building on the N29. But penetrate beyond the dusty façade and it all gets much better-looking, with an unexpected courtyard. As usual, with a station hotel, it offers good value, well-cooked food, on a 50f menu. Madame Ambroise is a smiling friendly patronne, and her bedrooms at 70f are light and high-ceilinged. All very basic, with a shower on the landing, but a recommended cheap overnight stop.

Map 2A **PONT DE BRIQUES**, near **ST. ETIENNE** 62360 Pont de Briques St. Etienne (Pas de Calais) Boulogne Environs; 5 km from Boulogne

On the D940 Paris road, direction Le Touquet, signposted right.

➔**Hostellerie de la Rivière**
(R)L(H)M *r. de la Gare 21.32.22.81. Closed Sun. p.m.; Mon. All Cards*

Not so long ago one thought of La Rivière in terms of a middle-of-the-road, solidly dependable suburban restaurant – a good bet for a *repas dominical en famille.* But not only the wooden spoons have been stirring in this little restaurant down by the modest river from which it takes its name. Nowadays there is little doubt that here is Boulogne's No. 1 restaurant.

Jean Martin's Norman origins have always meant a rich and generous cuisine. It still does but perhaps it is the advent of his Paris-trained son Dominique as his second that has resulted in the newly judicious blending of the modern with the traditional. Certainly the desserts are transformed by Dominique's pâtisserie skills. Each component of his tarte aux pêches – wispy feuilleté, crème anglaise, fanned lightly poached peaches with caramelised surface, raspberry coulis surround – was admirable individually and as an impressive ensemble.

Flavourings undreamt of in the classic Norman range surface in le filet de rascasse braisé au gingembre and les poissons de l'hostellerie au pur malt et au safran, but a straightforward turbot in herbed butter commendably still features.

M. Martin's particular delight is to be allowed to choose the menu himself: 'Do you like fish today? Leave it to me.' This abdication of responsibility produced a terrine de poissons, colourfully layered with salmon and sole, lobster chunks interspersed, in a wonderfully sharpened beurre blanc, dill-infused; then meaty bland monkfish in vivid saffron sauce contrasting with fluffy, earthy beetroot mousse. Then came the feuilleté aux poires and a bill for 250f. Note though that the 160f weekday menu is a bargain not to be slighted. It offers; adventurous amuse-gueules, petite salade tiède d'aiglefin au poivron doux, rôti de lotte aux coulis de langoustines or noisette d'agneau au thym frais, followed by le fondant aux deux chocolats.

M. Martin showed me round the new rooms he has furnished, all very comfortable and highly recommended at 260-340f a double.

The garden too has been recently upgraded, making La Rivière an altogether appealing summer escape from Boulogne's go-go.

Map 3B **PREURES** 62650 Hucqueliers (Pas de Calais) 32 km SE of Boulogne

13 km S of Desvres, by the D343 and the D150.

Heaven forbid that the valley of the Course, the little road that follows it and its restaurants and cafés should ever be too crowded and spoiled, but if that were the sad outcome of its popularity, there are plenty of villages a few kms either side that show absolutely no slgn of any traffic more disturbing than the hay carts or tractors that fill the narrow lanes at harvest time. Preures is one such.

→**Auberge de Preures**
(R)S *21.90.51.31. Open all year Lunch only*

NEW MANAGEMENT

Another of those wonderful restaurants seemingly indigenous to the valley of the Course, where the patronne dishes up, day after day, incredible value lunches. For 55f, Madame Violier-Vasseur produces four courses which change every day, but could offer as main ingredient chicken or pork or fish.

The fact that she's always busy with locals and full on Sundays when she offers a five-course menu for 70f, or 90f with more choice, even with a surprisingly spacious dining room behind the little bar, is indicative of the value here.

1993: Highly recommended. Menus now from 90f.

Map 4A **ROUTHIAUVILLE** (Somme) 55 km S of Boulogne

2 km S of Fort Mahon Plage on the D32. Big skies, sand dunes, marsh, canals surround the area between the Bay of the Authie and the Marquenterre ornithological park. Bizarre to find here:

Auberge du Fiacre
(R)M *22.23.47.30. Closed Mon. p.m.; Tue.; Wed., Feb. AE,EC, P*

Once an old Picard farm, now a sophisticated restaurant, with waiters in black jackets and a cocktail bar. Not the place to drop in, as we did, for a quick light lunch, nor yet for the bird-watchers with muddy boots and binoculars.

Chef-patron Jean-Pierre Masmonteil's food is as sophisticated as his place-settings – confit of goose, boned duck stuffed with foie gras, a salad of warm veal sweetbreads and bacon. The most interesting menu is 134f, but there is a perfectly good no-choice 90f mid-week version too which, considering the classiness, is excellent value.

Map 6D **SAILLY LAURETTE** 80800 Corbie (Somme) 129 km SE of Boulogne; 27 km W of Amiens

Follow the D233 on the north bank of the Somme through a watery wilderness, where the river often loses itself in lakes and marshes, reeds and bullrushes, willows dipping into a lush and vivid greenness, every vista punctuated with patient fishermen. A gentle, unsophisticated, damp, far-away region, with simple inns catering for outdoor appetites.

Two bridges cross river and canal here and, one each side, lie two rivals:

Auberge de l'Ecluse
(R)S *22.76.60.12. Closed Wed.; Tues. p.m.; Feb.*

From outside the scruffier of the pair, but preferred. The little bar is invariably occupied by stout red-faced fishermen and their families. Go past them to find an unexpectedly attractive dining room, where M. Nowak feeds his regulars on good home-cooking. There is a menu of four courses at 48.70f, but the one to go for, if time and appetite allow, is the 86.50f, which offers smoked salmon or home-made terrine, then stuffed and garlicky mussels or trout from the river cooked in cream, then duck with port wine sauce or quails or steak, then cheese, then fruit.

A rare find in these parts, well worth the drive.

Auberge des Pêcheurs
(R)S *22.76.64.20. Closed Sun. p.m.; Mon.*

Perhaps a little more soigné but still basically a fishermen's restaurant, this time with a pleasant rear garden. The 75f menu has four courses including, of course, the trout. The 120f *menu pêcheur* is all fish, with interesting dishes contrived from local ingredients, like grilled eels, pike quenelles, fish terrine. To include half a lobster is 15f more.

There are two more expensive menus, but I wouldn't bother, and the rooms, claimed to be *très confortables* are among the grottiest even I have ever encountered. Perhaps at 60f a double, one shouldn't mind, but you'd have to be pretty desperate.

Map 3A **ST AUBIN** 62170 Montreuil (Pas de Calais) 30 km S of Boulogne

---

The triangle west of Montreuil, enclosed by the busy N39 to the north and the D134 and D917 to south and west, is an unexpected delight. Prosperous local businessmen are wisely buying the more substantial houses set peacefully in the undiscovered flowery villages – St. Josse, Le Moulinel (see p. 135); so strategically near coast and port yet so far from summer hassle or industrial distress. No hardship to get lost here, but to find St. Aubin take the D144 south of Le Touquet and turn left on to the D144E.

Auberge du Conquelet
(HR)S *21.94.60.76. Closed Tue. p.m.; Wed.*

All black-and-white and geraniumed outside and very rustically pretty within this erstwhile forge. The only menu is 110f but it comprises six courses, of more than usual interest, claimed to be a mixture of traditional and modern. If you can't face this lavishness, the carte is an extensive one, with fish featuring strongly.

On the day I tried to look at the bedrooms the auberge was closed for one of those irritating *fermeture exceptionnel's* that always seem to occur when I have expressly made a particularly long detour, so all I can report is that they cost 130-180f, including breakfast, have no showers or bath attached, and whatever their condition, would make a tranquil and inexpensive base from which to explore the region.

1993: Rooms 208-278f. Menus now 85-115f.

Hôtel du Port et des Bains
(HR)S *22.60.80.09. 1 quai Blavet Closed Nov. P*

This must be the best value in FE6. 85f buys a double room overlooking the water, and please don't write and complain that the lino was cold. Others from 70-120f. All the locals agree that the food is the best in town, with lots of fresh fish on the menus, which start at 85f and include sole on their 110f version. Full pension is 180f per person, per day, with Madame Kappel smilingly presiding. The bedrooms are very basic, but at this price they must be in line for an arrow, as is the food, for good value, in an attractive town.

Map 8A **ST. GERMER-DE-FLY** 60850 (Oise) 168 km S of Boulogne; 30 km W of Beauvais

On the N31. Turn off on to the D129 to find this picture-book village on the Normandy border.

Like St. Riquier, St. Germer is completely dominated by an amazing abbey church. Otherwise it is but a handful of low shuttered cottages, a war memorial, two or three food shops, lots of flowerbeds and a popular restaurant.

Go through the 14th-century fortified gateway to enter the abbey. Linked to it by a vaulted passage from the apse, is the elegant Sainte Chapelle, modelled on the famous Paris original – the soft curves of the Romanesque abbey and the crisp pinnacles of the Gothic chapel as clear an exposition of what happened to church architecture in the two centuries between their building as any school teacher could wish. Both are quite lovely outside and within, though I do worry about all those distressing cracks and the ominous smell of damp. *Son et lumière* in summer.

Just opposite is another good reason for visiting the village:

L'Auberge de l'Abbaye
(R)M 44.82.50.73. *Closed 18/8-31/8; 5/1-25/1; Tues. p.m.; Wed.; Sun. p.m. All Cards*

Long and low and all covered in creeper, prone to attack by coach parties but otherwise commendable, especially for its mid-week 58f menu. Otherwise it's 142f and 150f. The dining room is pleasantly rustic and the view of the abbey from a table on the terrace, glass in hand, makes an excursion here worth a considerable détour.

Map 3A **ST. JOSSE/LE MOULINEL** 62170 Montreuil (Pas de Calais) 42 km S of Boulogne

By far the most agreeable way to get from Montreuil to Le Touquet is to forget the nasty N39 and stay south of the Canche on the D139. Glimpses of the river sparkle on the right as the little road winds past impressive manor houses, through the lush valley, to a mostly undiscovered area of delightful villages, each vying with its neighbour to cram most flowers into its window-boxes, tubs and parterres. **St Josse** must be the floweriest of all; petunias jostle geraniums, the nice old houses are called 'Les Roses', 'Les Jonquilles', 'Les Hortensias' and even the road signs are planted in beds of riotous colour. In the square is an unsophisticated restaurant/hotel, **Le Relais,** where you can still eat a very simple meal for 35f. Le Moulinel, next door, is even smaller, but boasts:

Auberge du Moulinel
(R)S *Hameau du Moulinel 21.94.79.03. Closed Wed.; Thurs.*

A real village inn with a few regional dishes like ficelle Picarde. Good fish and charcoal grills, menus from 70f.

Map 4C **ST. POL-SUR-TERNOISE** 62130 (Pas de Calais) 74 km SE of Boulogne

22 km E of Hesdin on the N39. Not my favourite town, not my favourite area, but perhaps a useful overnight stop if needs be.

Le Lion d'Or
(HR)M. *74 r. Hesdin 21.03.12.93. Closed Sun. p.m. o.o.s.*

M. Théret is a well-known and worthy local character. His restaurant in a busy approach road to the town centre is a few doors away from the hotel of the same name, run by his sister-in-law.

He really cares about carrying on the tradition of good regional cooking. Even his cocktail list is evidence:

Le Perlé de Groseilles is a pretty scarlet drink made nearby from red-currants and Poirette and Reinette de Picardie are made from local pears and apples respectively; L'Apéritif du Pas de Calais is a secret recipe.

The duck braised with rhubarb is described as his own *création* – an interesting and clever combination, the sharpness of the fruit cutting the richness of the bird, but it's his Jambon de Pays à l'Os, braisé aux deux bières du Pas de Calais that won him a 'Prix d'Excellence' in a gastronomic competition.

You can spend up to 164f on a menu lavish in quality and quantity, but there's no need – the 78f is splendid value. A gratin of mussels with leeks, followed by braised local rabbit and apple pie, washed down with a pichet of house wine for 24f, makes a stop here more than expedient.

The rooms at the moment cost 200-280f – OK-ish if a bit noisy.

Map 5B **ST. RIQUIER** 80100 (Somme) 71 km SE of Boulogne; 9 km NE of Abbeville

Wed

One of my favourite Picard halts. Just a square full of plane trees, dominated by the abbey, all the more marvellous because of the scale. That anything as impressive and strikingly beautiful as this should be the centre of what is now such a small town is truly miraculous.

Twelve centuries ago the abbey and the town, enclosed by fortified walls, was one of the most formidable strongholds in Picardy. The abbot of the time, brother-in-law of Charlemagne, ruled over a centre of scholarship which produced illuminated manuscripts of incomparable workmanship. In 881 the Vikings razed it to the ground and although it was sacked and rebuilt several times later it never regained its former importance.

Today's building is mostly 17th century, with traces of its 13th-century origins. The outside is under restoration still, but the interior was cleaned some twenty years ago and is upliftingly light and bright and altogether stunning. The local white stone has been delicately wrought into icicles of flowers and leaves and animals. Pass by the gruesome skull of St. Riquier – he of the ill-fitting dentures – and admire the statues of the saints and the glorious staircase. The size is big enough to be impressive, small enough to be appreciated as a whole.

The words *centre culturel* usually fill me with dread, but here in the monks' refectory and upstairs in their cells is the very model of a museum, again full of light and spaciousness. Well displayed are ancient cider presses, ploughs and harrows, Picard cottage reconstructions. In the barns outside, again sympathetically restored and exhibited, are venerable carts, waggons and carriages. Do visit.

The charming curator (who speaks good English) confirmed that there was no notable hotel or restaurant in the little town, but recommended the family-run **Café de la Place** for an honest three-course meal at 65f. It's certainly the hub of local activity and even to sit outside with a coffee and admire that intricate abbey façade alongside is a very rewarding way to pass the time.

ST OMER EN CHAUSSÉE Oise. 12 kms NW of Beauvais on the D901

Auberge de Monceaux
(HR)S *44.84.60.32. Closed Wed. p.m.; Thurs.*

Don't be put off by the outward appearance of this little restaurant on the main road – this is France. It could be a useful re-fuelling stop according to a reliable correspondent:

'We had an excellent meal and very good attention by M. and Mme Rouillard, in spite of their being extremely busy with French diners.' – Dennis Osborn.

Map 5A ST VALERY-SUR-SOMME (Somme) 67 km S of Boulogne; 18 km NW of Abbeville

Madame Sauvage
Chambre d'hôte 37 quai du Romerel 22.60.80.98.

Overlooking the bay is an eccentric tall and narrow gothicky house, which also has the *chambre d'hôte* sign up. I cannot help believing that the Château du Romerel will often be full and this might prove a welcome alternative. Although it cannot match the Château's elegance, it does have the advantage of sea views, and the two rooms are spacious, with high ceilings and big windows. They both have bathrooms and cost 270f which includes two breakfasts. For a family with children who might find the Château inhibiting, this might even prove the better choice.

Map 4B SAULCHOY 62870 Campagne Lès Hesdin (Pas de Calais) 48 km SE of Boulogne

Probably the largest village along the valley of the Authie, on the north bank, with bridge connection to Argoules. At one side of the plane-tree-lined village square is:

Val d'Authie
(R)S *21.90.30.20. Closed Thurs. o.o.s. All Cards*

Very pretty outside, with flowers and white tables and pots and tubs, very over-decorated within, with incredible embossed velvet curtains, all swags and bosses, bobbles and bows, plastic flowers and mauve flock wallpaper – probably in honour of its status as the only restaurant along the Authie mentioned by the great god Michelin.

But the row of French cars outside testifies to the quality of the food, and any place that doesn't turn away a lone female at 2 p.m., wanting only a one-dish lunch and a glass of wine (dinner at the Château de Montreuil the night before!) gets my vote.

For 75f you get an honest no-choice three courses – hors d'oeuvres, which included a substantial roll of home-cooked ham stuffed with good mayonnaise, the dish of the day (chicken in white wine-enriched sauce when I was there) and cheese or an excellent tarte aux mirabelles. *Cuvée de la patronne*, the beaming chef Madame Bridenne, is 45f. There are more ambitious menus, up to 150f, and some impressive *vieilles bouteilles*, up to 600f for a St Emilion, but it's an unusually reliable 'S' restaurant, in an extremely pretty area, and I rate it most highly.

Map 10D **SENLIS** 60300 (Oise) 227 km SE of Boulogne; 100 km S of Amiens, 50 km N of Paris

I am mortified to admit that on the several previous occasions that a route skirting Paris led me through Senlis I always saw it as an ugly traffic-ridden thoroughfare, to be driven through with as little pause as possible. We even made an enforced overnight stop there once, in a horrid noisy hotel, and left hastily first thing next morning, without bothering to explore behind the main road.

Had we done so, we would have found the most enchanting mediaeval town in the whole of this book's area. Dump the car in the *parking* by the ramparts and make for the Place du Parvis by the usual excellent method of following the signs to the cathedral. Pure delight whichever way you look, whichever steep cobbled street you climb, whichever ancient grey house or hotel or square you come across. No wonder it has been the setting for numerous 'period' films.

The cathedral, Notre Dame, begun ten years before its upstart namesake in Paris, in 1153, dominates the tranquil Place du Parvis, with a magnificent 13th-century spire surmounting the right tower. The arrangement of the statues round the great doorway dedicated to the virgin was subsequently imitated in the cathedrals of Chartres, Paris, Amiens and Reims. Maddeningly, the interior was under plastic sheets when I last tried to penetrate, in November '86, but the restoration had already uncovered much of the luminous yellow stone and the impression was already one of lightness and grace.

Senlis' history is impressive. First a Roman city, with traces of some of the towers that were built into the surrounding walls still remaining, then the residence of the very first Kings of France. Attracted by the abundance of game in the neighbouring forests, the two premier dynasties made their home here. Hunting was literally the downfall of Louis V, who was killed in an accident, bringing the Carolingian dynasty to an end. In 987 Hugues Capet, Duke of the Franks, was nominated as his successor, and also chose to live here.

As befits a town with such aristocratic connections, the shops in Senlis are decidedly upper-crust. The delightful rue du Chatel is lined with classy boutiques, for clothes, porcelain, presents, expensive chocolates, wonderful pastries. On a Tuesday morning one of the best markets I know spreads along its length. Contrive a visit then if you possibly can, and buy olives, herbs, local cheeses, charcuterie, country-fresh veg, glowing fruits, both fresh and glacé, and bars of soap with old-fashioned fragrances like vanilla and rosemary. Indulgent grans should look out for handsmocked and tucked dresses at a fraction of the price of their Liberty equivalent.

Ignoring the ugly through route, the r. de la République, Senlis is not a large town, and can be explored happily on foot (flat heels advisable on the cobbles). A longer stay might include a visit to another ancient church, 11th-century St. Pierre, or a walk round the ramparts, some transformed into encircling boulevards, good for parking, lined with trees, dotted with tubs cascading with flowers, and offering a good view of old Senlis. A visit to the Musée de la Vénerie (10 a.m.-12 noon, 4-6 p.m., closed Tues; Wed. a.m.) reveals the only museum in Europe devoted to game and hunting (it had to be in France).

I find it quite remarkable that in this situation – ideal for approaching or avoiding Paris, just off the autoroute, attractive enough in its own right to merit a visit – a town like Senlis should be so badly served for hotels. It makes up for this shortcoming, to some extent, by a wide choice of restaurants.

Hostellerie de la Porte Bellon
(HR)M *51 r. Bellon 44.53.03.05. 20/12-15/1.*

A nice old building set back from one of the boulevards, with a range of good rooms, from 190-390f, some in the annexe, some in the main building (one on the top floor, at 390f with bath, being particularly agreeable), this hotel could be the answer to most prayers. Alas, its obvious advantages have gone to its head and the management have a reputation, confirmed by my own experience, of being off-hand to the point of rudeness. They are nearly always full, even in winter, so don't have to try too hard. However, if you book well ahead, and don't mind the frostiness, the Hostellerie is a good idea; if you like to eat in your hotel (menus from 110-199f said to be not at all bad) it's the only idea.

La Rôtisserie de Formanoir
(R)M (R)L *17 r. du Chatel 44.53.04.39. Bistro closed Sun.; rest. always open*

NO NEWS

Another exceptionally attractive restaurant, sited in a 16th-century house in a steep cobbled street. You have to bang on the ancient oak door to gain admittance.

Here there are two alternatives – a luxury restaurant downstairs with the kind of lavish accoutrements, like porcelain place settings and out of season flowers, that send the bill soaring to around 250f. The cooking is reliable, if somewhat unexciting, in the traditional style, like roast beef, turbot with crayfish, salmon with blinis. Useful on the days when other restaurants are closed and solid comfort is a first requirement.

Upstairs the bistro is in an equally attractive setting, even if the napkins degenerate to paper, the cloths to vinyl and the flowers to plastic vines and grapes. But the striking elegance of the room is hardly affected and it is a great pleasure to sit beneath its high beams painted a surprisingly successful dark green. What appears to be an enormous four-sided mantelpiece dominates the room and was used in some film set, I gather.

Here there is a *suggestion du jour* menu at 46f – an entrée and the dish of the day. Otherwise the bill will work out at around 80f, for starters with regional overtones like a quiche aux poireaux, or a picodon – a kind of potato galette – meat or fish (the daurade en papillote was a good 34f worth) and rather boring puds. House wine is 52f.

Les Remparts
(R)M *37 pl. de la Halle 44.53.58.59.; 44.53.01.34. Closed Tues.*

I suspect the only reason Les Remparts hasn't got an arrow is because I failed to eat there, put off as no doubt readers might be by its outward appearance. While I had good reason to appreciate the busy bar in the market square which offered welcome refuge during the dark wet low time between tea and bath of the November research days, it never occurred to me that the restaurant upstairs (two flights) would be a pleasant surprise.

It needed a local assertion that the best meal in Picardy was to be found there to get me up those stairs, to find a delightfully airy and light room facing away from the square, windows opening on to a unique view of the cathedral. In summer you can sit here on the roof terrace, which must be very good news indeed, in the very heart of the town. The décor is an unlikely modern navy-blue and red, but it's the view that matters.

During the week there's a 85f menu. On Sundays it's 120f. For this you get a generous *nouvelle-cuisine*-influenced choice – say vinaigrette d'écrevisses et saumon sauvage, served with a coriander-spiced sauce, pigeon with a mousse of wild mushrooms and truffles,

or an assortment of poached fish of the day, then a good cheeseboard with nut-studded bread accompanying, and a super dessert trolley.
Will someone please tell me it's as good as I think?

Le Chatel
(R)S-M *12 r. du Chatel. 44.53.01.49. Closed Sun. p.m.; Mon.*

A tiny bar/bistro almost opposite the Formanoir. You turn the corner beyond the bar to find the little restaurant with six tables. 55f plus 15% service buys an entrée (a good hors d'oeuvre trolley perhaps) a main dish (carré de porc), cheese and pud. More exciting dishes carry a 10f supplement.

Le Scaramouche
(R)M *pl. Notre Dame 44.53.01.26. Closed Wed.*

A pretty little restaurant opposite the cathedral, all *fin-de-siècle* décor, with fringed lamps casting soft lights on pink tablecloths. Good for a romantic dinner *à deux*. The bill will set him back 95f each if he suggests sticking to the menu, or around 300f if you're celebrating.
Count on a good evening, both food and atmosphere-wise.

Somme Battlefields

I hesitate to write about the military cemeteries and memorials of the Somme, because it is a subject on which so many readers must be more expert than I, but no book on Picardy would be justifiable without at least an acknowledgement.
I can only say to those who, like myself, are fortunate enough not to have any personal reason for a visit, do not dismiss too lightly an opportunity to go there. I guarantee an informative and enlightening experience that can be gained in no other way. Unfortunately, on the day we chose, the November fog was so dense and driving so hazardous that our tour had to be curtailed; on good advice we limited it to two of what I believe must be the most stirring examples.
At the Newfoundland memorial in Auchonvillers the trenches have been left exactly as they were; the sheep that were introduced to crop their grassy slopes kept getting tangled in the authentic barbed wire, so that has had to go but, peering through the bitter-cold grim greyness towards the stark blackened stump that marks the so-near German front lines, we could gain just a glimpse of how it must have been.
Then on to the mighty Thiepval memorial, recording the names of 73,000 British soldiers with no known graves. Even the chattiest of visitors grow silent as the impact hits them and they pause to absorb the implications.

Everywhere is commendably neat and tidy, well cared for, well documented and 'Route des Souvenirs' is clearly marked. You can pick up a detailed map and description from any tourist office or hotel in the Albert region.

I wish I could wholeheartedly recommend a hotel in this much visited area. The **Victoria** (HR)M at Villers-Bretonneux (*22.48.02.00*) or **Madame Bellenge's Chambre d'Hôte** at Grandcourt are the best I found – clean and wholesome if not exciting – but Amiens is not far away.

Map 8B **TILLÉ** 60000 Beauvais (Oise) 4 km N of Beauvais

On the N1.

Auberge Le Pradou
(R)M *r. de l'île de France 44.45.66.14. Closed Sun. p.m.; Mon.; 1/3-16/3*

A useful stop on the main road, with a pleasantly verdant garden and flowery terrace to relax upon. Good fish dishes on 130f menu.

Map 3A **LE TOUQUET** 62520 (Pas de Calais) 32 km S of Boulogne

(M) Mon., Thurs., Sat. 1/7-15/9. Thurs., Sat. 16/ 9-30/6

I continue to be astounded at the number of letters I get saying, 'Le Touquet attractive? You cannot be serious.' But I am serious, and unrepentingly, conviction strengthened by every visit that it is an outstandingly attractive town, with a lot to offer at all times of the year. Conceding that nostalgia from many a successful family holiday could rose-colour my spectacles, that the prom is now a vast concrete jungle, that the beer-bottled coach-loads make me ashamed to be British, that the apartment blocks that have steamrollered our charmingly eccentric old holiday villa make me weep, that some of the prices are ripoffs, that at low tide it's a day's march to the water's edge and back, I still love the place with undiminished affection and am totally out of sympathy with those who don't. So there!

For the defence I would cite the following: the approach. What a lift to drive through pine-bordered avenues and arrive at the most impressive roundabout I know: over-the-top with flowers, Casino to the left, elephantine **Westminster Hôtel** (4 star; 21.05.48.48) to the right, evoking many a ghost. This is upmarket Le Touquet, named Paris Plage with justification. Elegant boutiques make for fine window-shopping, café tables on the lawns are more peaceful (but just as expensive) as those on the front; as likely as not Flavio will be chatting up the customers at his Club de la Forêt and greeting old friends as they promenade by.

If neither Flavio nor 20f for a cuppa is your scene, the woods opposite provide summer cool for picnics. Penetrate a little further behind them to discover a world of well-groomed villas, many with tell-tale English names. Hard to imagine that it was from one of these that P. G. Wodehouse was incongruously snatched away to a German jail.

Follow the main street, the r. St Jean, seawards and downtown Le Touquet takes over. O.K., it may not look its best on a grey February day or on a crowded August one, but for most of the year I'd rather be here than in any other resort in the North. The shops deteriorate and change hands more often the nearer you get to the prom, but there are still many old-time favourites like **Le Chat Bleu**, famous for hand-made chocolates for over seventy years. Other top chocs, gift-wrapped, always good for presents, can be found at **Diot, Léonidas** and **Le Lido**, where you can take tea and cakes too. Still in the r. St. Jean, stop at **Au Pré Fleuri** for impressive foodie presents like Fauchon pâtés or cherries in brandy. But the best recent news in Le Touquet is in a side street, the r. St Louis – the recently-opened **Au Frais St Louis**, where under one roof you can buy all picnic requirements – wonderful cheese choice, bread, fruit, vegs, charcuterie, pâtisserie, wine. Usefully open Sun. a.m. but closed Weds.

Press on to the front itself, and again it is with mixed feelings that I view the dominating new glass complex of the **Aqualud**, housing sophisticated swimming pools, restaurants, bars, shops. I liked it better when my children played on the very unsophisticated swings here. But there's no doubt that the project has been carried out stylishly and there were squeals of approval from the patrons of the mammoth, contorted slide in the mega-pool.

I tried **Le P'tit Boulonnais**, one of the new café/restaurants there because (a) it was at the end of my longish walk and I needed a sit-down, (b) it seemed a crime to eat indoors on a beautiful day and Le Touquet is strangely bereft of tables outdoors, and (c) a restaurant owned by a fish wholesaler bodes well – but I can only suppose M. Fourfroy's best fish gets diverted elsewhere because my crab was dry and tired; perhaps it had grown old waiting – the service was hopeless. However this was in the first week of opening and I hope matters may have improved.

Lots of interesting newcomers in the restaurant scene too:

➔Le Café des Arts

(R)M *80 r. de Paris 21.05.21.55. Closed Mon.; Tues. All Cards*

Jerome Panni graduated from the prestigious hotel school in Le Touquet and promptly opened up down the road. Anyone interested in food in the district is talking about his prowess with great respect.

There are two dining rooms, the downstairs in vaguely art deco style, with pierrot dolls, monstrous *percolateurs,* writhing gramophone horns and appallingly bad paintings. You don't go there for the décor, nor yet the simple place settings, but for the superb value, and probably the most interesting food in the neighbourhood.

Take the 135f menu: for starters a 'tartare de bar au cerfeuil et carpaccio de saumon', mini-strips of raw bass, marinated in lime, strewn with parsley, garnished with paper-thin, air-dried salmon, chopped avocado and melon garnish. Then try medallions of chicken in a tarragon cream sauce with home-made pasta. The cheeses are good and interesting – a range of goats cheeses from local Maringhem – but it would be a pity to forego the desserts. Hot orange and kiwi-fruit tart and the bavarois flavoured with melon, chocolate and crême de menthe were both inspiring. It all sounds a bit much, with ill-assorted flavours, but somehow it works. Go soon before others discover.

L'Escale
(R)M *21.05.23.22*

No resemblance to the usual airport café, Locals dine here regularly on good, honest French food at good honest prices. Worth the détour even if you're not meeting friends off 'Love Air's' 5-seater planes from Lydd airport.

Le Petit Village Suisse
(R)M *52 avenue St Jean 21.05.69.93*

A pretty little restaurant located in an old Le Touquet mansion, opposite the Westminster Hotel. More reports needed please.

La Flambée
(R)M *117 rue de Metz 21.05.21.82*

Specialises in seafood and in particular a cook-it-yourself seafood 'fondue'. Good on atmosphere (Swiss chalet style). More reports needed.

Le Picardy
(H)M *avenue du Maréchal Foch 21.06.85.85. Open all year*

The newest addition to Le Touquet's hotel scene, located in the woody suburbs, just 5 minutes from the centre. Ultra modern – an architect's paradise (I'm told), though I found the its 'celled' corridors (relieved by a plethora of plant life) a touch on the stark side. Not so the luxurious indoor swimming pool, sauna, jacuzzi and tennis court. Outsiders recommend the food at 'Le Touquet' restaurant (very fishy, very fresh and very good).

Le Bristol
(H)M *17 rue Jean Monnet 21.05.49.95. Open all year*

Well located in the centre of town with a comfortable bar area, but no restaurant (friendly staff happy to point you towards the best eateries). Rooms verge on the pokey side.

Le Red Fox
(H)S *rue St Jean/rue de Metz 21.05.27.58 Open all year*

Recently opened small, family hotel with friendly owners trying hard to please. Well located in central town on the corner of rue St Jean and rue de Metz. Rooms are small, functional and excellent value, from 200f.

Pérard
(R)M *67 r. de Metz 21.05.13.33. Closed never. No cards, No cheques.*

Far from new. Serge Pérard, well into his sixties, continues to run his lively brasserie-style fish restaurant with aplomb. His famous fish soup sells all over the world; buy a jar to bring home along with some rouille, and impress your guests.

The faint-hearted can settle for an assiette de fruits de mer (74f) leaving the mammouth grand plateau (135f) to the ravenous with a couple of hours to spare. A bouillabaisse du nord (99f) is obviously another favourite, but you can eat more modestly on the 84f menu, and the wine is affordable. Try Pinot Blanc at 47.80f.

Flavio, Club de la Forêt
(R)L *av. du Verger 21.05.10.22. Closed Wed. o.o.s. 1/11-1/3. AE, DC.*

Another Touquet institution, so well-known that he gets taken for granted. Flavio Cucco, a British subject himself, though with a Monégasque and Italian background, makes his trans-Channel guests – many of them old friends – especially welcome, and to sit at one of his tables is a sure invitation for a chat from the gregarious host. Alas, the Brits who used to overflow from the Westminster next door, or make Flavio's their natural rendezvous after a day on the golf course, are fading fast away, with the onslaught of prices that will add up to

Flavio's.

450f on the carte. But for a special occasion, the 180f menu is still well worth the money, even if it means foregoing the lobster for which Flavio is famous.

Chef Guy Delmotte serves only the freshest of fish. His panaché de trois poissons – sole, turbot, salmon served with an exemplary beurre blanc – is a model of how to present prime ingredients cooked simply, but he is no slouch with more demanding dishes like an exquisite feuilleté of wild mushrooms. Regulars insist on retaining the old favourite – his pigeon cooked in 'honey from a thousand flowers'.

La Dune aux Loups
(R)M *av. de la Dune aux Loups 21.05.42.54. Closed Wed.; Thurs. p.m. EC, DE*

Delve deeper into the forest, following the signs to centre *équestre* to find yet another welcome newcomer to the scene. At its best on a hot day, when it is most agreeable to drive through the deep shade of the pines and sit outside this little auberge under parasols on the lawns, far removed from the teeming town, but pleasant enough at any time.

Inside there is a log fire and a little bar, generating a warm atmosphere, and the cooking aims to use the best of local produce.

1993: Menus from 92f with wine.

Le Chalut
(R)M *7 bvd. Jules Pouget 21.05.22.55. Closed Tues. p.m.; Wed.; Jan.; Feb. CB*

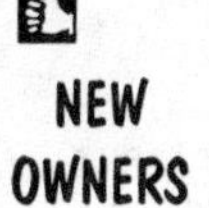

Not everyone agreed with me when I wrote in FE 4 that here was the best restaurant in town, and so, for the time being, the arrow must go, but I believe the discrepancy between my blissful experience here and that of some readers was a bad patch that has now passed.

This one is for serious eaters. Bernard Dupont was voted best sommelier in France last year. That doesn't come easily. One of his menus, 'oenologique' is food chosen round the superb wines rather than vice versa, so for wine buffs this is a must. Browsing through his bible of a wine list, representing 15,000 bottles, is an education, but there is no need for intimidation – excellent house wine is 45f.

The 96f menu is a winner, offering lots of fresh fish, like an escalope of bass cooked in cider, or brill with immaculate beurre blanc, or, for the fish-fatigued, a hefty lamb steak, pink and garlicked, served on a bed of artichoke hearts.

Sorry unlucky readers. Le Chalut still gets my vote if not my arrow.

Bistro de la Charlotte
(R)S *36 r. St. Jean 21.05.32.11. Closed Sun. p.m.; Mon. All Cards*

Small, pretty, cheap and interesting; good at lunchtime for individual dishes, but the 78f menu is good value – seafood terrine, with a shrimp sauce, a fish curry, mild and creamy, with redcurrants in the sauce, and a fresh fruit charlotte and raspberry sauce. They now have a separate take-away shop where you can buy the products prepared on the premises.

1993: New décor – now you eat in a boat!

Le Jardin
(R)M *21.05.16.34. pl. de l'Hermitage*

The old l'Orée du Bois at the entrance to the town, opposite the Casino, has been taken over by eager-to-please new proprietors. It's still as pretty as ever, with the charcoal grill functioning in the big fireplace, and a light and airy glassed-in terrace. Locals speak well of it, but I have not tried it yet, and so reports would be specially welcome.

Specialities are the charcoal-grilled steaks and fish, with a cuisine that is claimed to be a mixture of *nouvelle* and *traditionnelle*. Menus start at 99f.

There is a famous hotel school in Le Touquet – one of a surprisingly small number in the whole of France – and I am told that some of the best food in the town can be sampled here, cooked by the students. I should love to experience this experiment myself and intend to do so at the first opportunity, but for readers who get there before I do, the address is Lycée Technique Hôtelier, Avenue du Château (near the Casino de la Forêt). (21) 05.04.00. Open every day except during school holidays.

Hotels in Le Touquet are not an easy proposition. I suspect they have it too easy. **Le Manoir** is very comfortable, pleasantly old-fashioned, but the rooms vary considerably and it does pay to go for the best, which costs a hefty 650f; as demi-pension is obligatory in season and the food is nothing special, I think it can only be wholeheartedly recommended for the golfers.

La Côte d'Opale has met with approval from several readers and has a good sea-view, but they also insist on demi-p., so it's no good for those who like to benefit from the local restaurants.

The best bets are probably:

La Régence et Le Chalet
(H)M *15 r. de la Paix 21.05.12.44. All Cards*

New management in this little back-street hotel means a smartening up and special desire to please. There are some cheap rooms across the courtyard, which would be fine for children and some comfortable doubles with showers in the main hotel at 270f.

Pension Armide
(HR)S *56 r. Leon Garet 21.05.21.76.*

Le Touquet is a wonderful resort for children and it seemed a necessary challenge to find a not-too-smart affordable base for a family. This is it. In a quiet side street, central, not far from the beach, an old-fashioned pension.

1993: Demi-pension 175-180f per person. Menu 58f.

Hôtel Moderne
(H)S *41 Grande Rue 21.05.15.33.*

A totally misleading address. The Grande Rue is not very 'grande' just here, by the covered market, and the hotel is not very 'moderne'. Rather old-fashioned in fact, but with a pleasant French ambiance, and good-value, simple rooms at 84-180f.

Map 9D **VERNEUIL-EN-HALATTE** 60550 (Oise) 216 km from Boulogne; 6 km N E of Creil

---

(M) *Fri pm* Creil is a dismal industrial town, but difficult to avoid on a cross country route. If hunger pangs threaten, stop here, just outside, especially if you fancy fish.

Auberge des Sablons
(R)M *74 rte de Pont St. Maxence 44.25.09.07 Closed Sun. p.m.; Mon.; 24/12-3/1; Aug.*

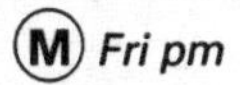

Exclusively fish in fact, with good reason since the patronne's father is the best fishmonger in Creil. Her husband, M. Colten, chooses the best of father-in-law's display and cooks them superbly, simply or with perfect sauces. But make no mistake, eating at Les Sablons is a serious business. The marine décor (nets, fish tank) is as banal as possible, the covers are basic and the atmosphere lacks warmth. You should only consider a meal here if you can accept all this and a bill for 140f for the menu (weekdays only) and 250f otherwise; but then you will eat like Neptune – pearly turbot with a mousseline sauce, rougets cooked 'en papillotte' with fresh tomatoes, salmon with thyme, and a vast choice of shellfish. The portions are generous enough to make one course feasible (75f-ish), but the hot fruit tarts are worth leaving room for. Well-chosen wines from the Loire.

Map 4A **VERTON/LE BAHOT** (Pas de Calais) 44 km S of Boulogne; 7 km E of Berck-Plage

---

Turn E of the D143 on to the D142E, or W at Wailly Beaucamp on the D142 and 142E.

This is the flat, dull countryside approaching the coastal marshes. In the middle of nowhere is:

Auberge du Bahot
21.84.24. 10. Diners only Closed Mon.

I would never have located this one without the advice of a charming local lady whom I met in the Darnétal at Montreuil. 'I only eat at two restaurants around here,' she said. 'The Darnétal is the best and the Bahot is the cheapest.'

Inside is a bar presided over by the rubicund M. Moinard. He seemed amazed at seeing a G.B. car draw up and even more amazed to meet me at the bar, but as I couldn't understand a word of his patois I had to pass on to Madame Moinard, who showed me the attractive and surprisingly big restaurant behind the modest façade.

The food on offer is absolutely basic – côte du porc, beefsteak, chicken, sauté de veau, fish. It changes every day and you take what Madame cooks, which is the way I like it. With a bill of 65f for four courses and wine at 30f, it might well prove to be a winner in this desolate area. Reports most welcome.

Map 10D **VILLENEUVE-SUR-VERBERIE** 60410 (Oise) 214 km SE of Boulogne; 20 km NE of Senlis

Just west of the autoroute between exits 8 and 9.

Auberge du Clocher
(R)S *30 r. des Flandres 44.54.70.13. Closed Tues.*

This is a hearty local recommendation, still to be checked. I include it because I am told it offers a cheap meal in an area short of good modest eateries (around 75f) and that M. and Madame Daniel Georges make their customers welcome. Reports please.

Map 10D **VINEUIL-ST FIRMIN** 60830 (Oise) 224 km SE of Boulogne; 3 km E of Chantilly

Between Chantilly and Senlis, signposted to the south off the D44.

Les Grands Prés
(R)M *rte. d'Avilly 44.57.71.97. Closed Sun. p.m.; Mon.*

A pretty green-and-white latticed restaurant and *salon de thé*, with cane chairs and a nice garden, useful for a cuppa stop in green fields away from the traffic, and particularly popular with families; there are always lots of kids making full use of the swings and slides and open spaces.

The range is versatile, from a one-course light lunch to the full works, so it's hard to estimate a cost, but menus start at 85f, except Sundays.

Map 2B **LE WAST** 62142 Colombert (Pas de Calais) 19 km E of Boulogne

Well marked from the N 42, turn north on the D 127, driving in an attractive rural area between the two *nationales.*

Château des Tourelles
(RH)M *21.33.34.78.*

The Château des Tourelles has caused me more headaches than any other entry in any book and I find it hard now to be dispassionate about its virtues and shortcomings. The fact is that I got my timing wrong. I found it very early, before its fame spread, believed the promises made about instant improvements in the facilities and took the risk of praising it very highly, in view of its obvious potential. The position and Madame Feutry are both charming, and M. Feutry cooked me one or two very good meals.

I subsequently came to dread any letter headed 'Château des Tourelles', knowing before I read it that it would be a catalogue of disappointments. I could only apologise to my poor frustrated travellers and rebuke the Feutrys; it seemed I had backed a complete loser, until very recently. Now, as I was about to write 'Stay away', the tone of readers' letters has suddenly changed to one of approval, and P and O, who followed my recommendation, had no complaints at all. So, for new readers, prepared to take a chance: this is a large house, rather than 'château', strategically placed near Boulogne, with a patronne who aims to please. My room was spacious and comfortable, others have been less so. 230f a double. Menus from 85-250f.

WIERRE-EFFROY 62720 Rinxent. 15 kms NE of Boulogne. 5 kms SE of Marquise

The Michelin map colours several of the minor roads around Wierre-Effroy in green. Rightly so – it is lovely unspoiled farming territory, a pleasure to explore and exclaim over.

The hamlet is in the middle of nowhere. I usually seem to approach it by turning off the main road at Marquise and following the signs but

Hostellerie du Château des Tourelles

it is equidistant from the N421 via the pretty D234, or from the yellow 127 via the D232. It doesn't matter if you get lost – you're bound to – it's all so pretty and free from hassle that the experience will be a beneficial one.

➔**Ferme-Auberge de la Raterie**
(HR)S *21.92.80.90 cl. Sun p.m. and Mon*

The Auberge is outside the hamlet but clearly signed, down a dirt track. The Cocquerelle family and their ménage could well be a model for how to run a rustic hostelry. Draw in your mind's eye a picture of your ideal rustic hideaway and I guarantee that the reality will not differ greatly.

It still looks like a farm – low and rambling, rough stone walls, wooden shutters, courtyard, set among pastures – but a sanitised postcard version – fresh white paint, geraniums in pots or baskets, troughs and more white benches around to admire the view than your average farmer would have much use for. Inside the happy marriage of authenticity and comfort continues. There are beams, flagged floors, log fires, pine panelling, but the swinging lamps have electric bulbs and the case of the old grandfather's clock gleams with polish and everything is pristine. There is no sign of muddy boots nor any farmhouse clutter.

So far so very good but it is the family welcome that is outstanding about La Raterie. Père Jérome Cocquerelle will escort you round his province – the farm – from which will come most of the ingredients prepared for your dinner by his wife, Marie-Josée. Sophie, their eldest daughter, combines the roles of deputy hostess, maître d'hôtel, and head waiter with a smile and the two younger siblings, Anne and Christopher, are in willing attendance.

It is rare to see such a well-coordinated farm concern in any business and it is a pleasure to see them thriving. Five new bedrooms have been recently added to the original farm. Again the taste is irreproachable. They are all decorated in fresh and simple country-style fabrics and wallpapers, with white frilly curtains and lace bedspreads. The older ones at 220-260f have painted washbasins, the newer ones have bathrooms, for 310f – both prices inclusive of farm breakfasts.

Marie-Josée sees to it that every meal continues the theme – simple country food with copious home grown vegetables, well prepared and served. Five courses cost from 90-125f.

Who could carp at this one? An arrow for excellence on all counts.

Ferme Auberge du Vert

(HR)S-M *21.87.67.00. Closed 15/1-28/2.; Mon. AE, DC, V, P All Cards*

The charming M. Jo Bernard has transformed part of his farm into a *gîte d'étape*, with fifteen simple bedrooms contrived into one arm of the low stone buildings that surround the courtyard. They are starkly whitewashed, furnished with only bare essentials, almost monastic, but still well equipped with telephone, electric heating and individual bathrooms, shower and loo. The farm provides many of the ingredients for the evening meal, which is eaten in the farm kitchen.

It all looked extremly promising when I first discovered it for *FE4*, but prices are creeping up and although the utter peacefulness is a bonus, the value-for-money is not what it was. Rooms are 290-500f, menu 130-190f, and demi-pension from 520f for 2 people. Bicycles can be hired for a ride along the river.

'A charming host, exellent rooms, true quiet, but this is now an hotel rather than a farm, notwithstanding that the menu offers no choice. Nor is the food outstanding despite the honey for breakfast. Spoiled I guess by the influx of the British, it has become expensive at 1011f for two nights.' – Mr. and Mrs. J. H. Shofield.

'We called in to see Madame Bernard. We have been there several times for one night and enjoy the simple supper and excellent breakfast. Three new rooms across the yard should be finished soon and I believe will have bathrooms. The large salle in that block is to be a dining room, with a young chef to cook the dinner. Breakfast will be in the usual small room and served by Madame Bernard. They are evidently doing well and she is relieved not to have to cope with an evening meal.' – Cynthia Price.

Map 2A **WIMEREUX** 62930 (Pas de Calais) 6.5 km N of Boulogne

A good choice to stay, with easy access to Boulogne, without big-town hassle. It is most agreeable to explore the quiet residential back streets, stroll along the *digue*, take a swim, perhaps, all within ten minutes drive from the port. In fact this approach to Boulogne along the coast is easily the best, avoiding the suburbs.

The little resort has always been a favourite with the British; nowadays most of its stylishness has gone, but signs of former elegance remain in a few substantial white villas tucked away in flowery gardens. Unfortunately the main street suffers from a surfeit of through traffic and can be too unpleasantly fumed and noisy in summer to make shopping there a pleasure; more tranquil is the little Tuesday morning market by the river from which the town gets its name. Best shopping is fish bought there or direct from the fishermen's houses.

Hôtel du Centre
(HR)S *78 r. Carnot 21.32.41.08. Closed 2/6-16/6; 21/12-15/1; Rest. closed Mon.*

On the busy main road; light sleepers should avoid front rooms, but those at the rear are fine and now overlook a pretty flower-filled courtyard where an aperitif can be taken in the summer. The seven new rooms are the ones to go for, good value at 290f with bath. Others are 170f.

There is a new comfortable lounge, full of English watching Wimbledon telly on a blazing June day.

The Boulanger family are friendly, efficient hosts, and welcome back their loyal and regular visitors who appreciate the unusually good food. Here is one hotel whose restaurant stands up in its own right. Menus at 85f and 150f. Altogether a reliable choice, arrowed for consistent good value.

Hotel du Centre

Paul et Virginie

(HR)M *19 r. Général de Gaulle 21.32.42.12. Closed 14/12-19/1 Rest. closed Sun.; Mon. o.o.s. AE, DC ,EC, V*

The most impressive house in Wimereux, Les Mauriciens, built in 1850, used to have a stable block alongside. This is now the Hôtel Paul et Virginie, with cobbled yard making a pleasant setting for fresh-air eating and drinking. Inside it remains a typical old-fashioned French hotel, with corresponding virtues and detractions. The bad news is that the furniture is pretty basic (but wood, not plastic), the good that the family who runs it are just about the friendliest hosts one could hope for. The efficient Madame, who speaks perfect English, inherited the shabby old hotel, failed to sell and in desperation ended up running it herself, with the out-of-university-term help of her charming son and daughter.

Some of the rooms have been renovated and there is one family suite with bath, but most have only showers and are not cheap at 350f a double or 178f at attic level, but the position is peaceful and not far from the beach, the food not bad (the haddock with tarragon on the 90f menu was excellent, the tarte au citron thin and dry) and you get real jam and butter for breakfast. It's a question of priorities really – top marks for atmosphere, *accueil* and position, but a booby prize for room value.

Le Charolais
(R)M *25 r. Napoléon 21.83.59.28 Closed Sun. p.m.; and Mon. o.o.s.*

A new little restaurant in a side street parallel to the prom, chic-ly black and white, with a few tables outside, specialising, as its name suggests, in meat dishes – an antidote to the prevailing fishiness of the region. Some interesting starters include Crottin de Chavignol (grilled goats' cheese) 25f, salade aux foies de volaille at 30f; excellent meat comes grilled as steaks or brochettes on a sensibly short menu, between 50f and 60f. Côtes du Rhône 53f.

L'Atlantic
(H)M(R)L *Digue de Mer 21.32.40.15 Closed 1/12-1/3; Sun. p.m.; Mon. o.o.s. All Cards*

NEW OWNERS

Between the wars the Atlantic hotel used to be a good reason for crossing the Channel, and until a few years ago the restaurant boasted the region's only two Michelin stars. First one, then t'other was removed, and reputation and prestige sagged as father Hamiot handed over to his sons. Now I hear that it has changed hands again, and hope very much to learn that its former glory has returned. Meanwhile the most I can report is that the rooms, at 370f, mostly overlook the sea; readers' experiences would be most helpful.

1993: Menus from 140f.

Map 2A **WIMILLE** 62126 (Pas de Calais) 3 km N of Boulogne, Environs de Boulogne

A hamlet between the coast road and N 1.

➔**Relais de la Brocante**
2 r. de Ledinghen 21.83.19.31 Closed Sun. p.m.; Mon.; Feb.; 1st week Sept.

An old presbytery next to the church has been converted by chef J-F Laurent and *sommelier* Claude Janszen, both ex-Atlantique, into the prettiest restaurant in the district. Three rooms, stone-walled, beamed, have elegant couverts and service to match. They are aiming

high and whether the food will match the standard of the décor is not yet definitely established, but the potential is great and the French *hommes d'affaires* love it; so far it's otherwise undiscovered .

There is a tendency to try too hard – the sole would have tasted even fresher had it come to plate straight from pan rather than be tortured into a *tresse*, and every accompanying veg had been persuaded into a shape – basket, nest, filigree – other than its own. Radish roses, tomato petals may be *passé* but the same objection should apply to a faggot of asparagus tips tied up with a leek thread.

However, on the credit side is an enthusiasm for local recipes and ingredients, like marinade de poulette de Licques à la paysanne. Fish is straight from the boats – try Arlequin de poisson, sauce vierge and the cheeses are by Olivier. Gâteau au chocolat des aéronautes shows a witty acknowledgement to the local cross-Channel pioneer balloonists. Menus 145, 180f; à la carte allow 200f. Well-chosen well-presented but pricey wines – Claude Janszen is a *Sommelier du Nord.*

Agreeably and usefully situated, this is a most welcome newcomer to the district and, after a few more reports, a potential arrow.

Le Relais de la Brocant

Map 3B **ZERABLES** – see BEUSSENT p. 60

Map 1B **ZOUAFQUES** 62890 Tournehem sur la Hem (Pas-de-Calais)
33 km NE of Boulogne

On the N43.

Cheval Noir
(R)S *21.35.60.29.*

The best lorry-drivers' pull-up in the district. Need I say more.

'It was good to see the number of lorries parked outside the Cheval Noir and the welcoming carafe of plonk on the table. Once again an excellent lunch with the platter of the French equivalent of braised brisket and roast potatoes, enough for four people rather than just the two of us. The bill was 48.50f each, which included a café calva at the end of the meal.' – David Dunham.

DUTY UNBOUND – Buying Duty Free

Since January 1st 1993 there has been yet another incentive to go to France, and particularly the Channel ports on a short trip – the chance to buy at bargain prices the wine, spirits and tobacco that have been freed from British duty.

The Treasury has agreed to the abandonment of excise duty on 'reasonable' quantities of goods, provided they are for the buyers' own consumption and that duty has been paid in the French shop or warehouse. What exactly is reasonable the conscientious traveller might well ask. The guideline given to Customs officers at British Channel ports is reasonable enough to fill a hefty car boot with 10 litres of spirits, 20 litres of sherry or port, 90 litres of wine, of which 60 can be sparkling, and a formidable 110 litres of beer, 800 cigarettes and a kilo of tobacco are also considered generally justifiable, if not to the health-conscious.

Anyone taking full advantage of these new allowances – for his own consumption of course – will be able to pop across for a weekend, pay for his crossing and hotel bill and come home showing a profit (so long as the chassis doesn't fall off).

A little homework before setting off will reap dividends for the crafty shopper. The exchange rate is critical of course – the following comparisons have been made on the basis of around 8.40 francs to the pound.

For example: 800 Benson and Hedges in the UK would cost £84.80 but £56.40 in France; if, when in France you do as the French do and buy Gauloises, you could pocket a clear £1.60 profit on every packet (£2.35 here, 75p there – but note that French tobacco prices are due for a 30% rise). On brands of French and Belgian beer the saving will be significant: Kronenburg (£2.70 a litre here) costs 84p there; 33 Export (£2.36 here) 79p there.

Spirits need careful checking of comparative brands and sources as prices vary considerably between supermarket and duty-free outlets. A litre of Gordon's gin in the UK costs £10.49; its equivalent in a French supermarket will save nearly £4 a bottle – £40 on the 10 litre allowance. Own-brand cheap gin in a hypermarché costs £5.85 as against £8.10 in the UK. A 70 cl. bottle of Cointreau costs £11.64 in France, against £14.89 UK price; Rémy Martin V.S.O.P. – a luxury at home at £26.89 – costs a mere £19.50 at Auchan.

Most popular buy of all is wine but here personal preferences and careful comparisons of like with like must enter the equation. If you are of the never-mind-the quality-feel-the-width school of thought you can really make a killing (literally perhaps). Auchan's plonk retails at around 70p a litre! The general rule of thumb is that the higher the quality the lower the differential will be because the taxes are the same on all bottles regardless of price (over 90p in the UK, around 9p in France). But there is plenty of perfectly drinkable wine around on which to make a substantial saving. Vins du Pays are about half the price (£1) of the same quality in the High Street, so that the full 90 litre allowance would save a very worthwhile £120.

At home it's hard to find a drinkable sparkling wine for less than £4. Its French equivalent would be half that price. A good sparkling Saumur costs £3.29 at Le Chais warehouse (over £5 here). If you like the kick but don't care too much about the taste, the cheapest possible fizz is a mere 79p at Auchan (£3.69 here).

Brides' fathers are likely to receive gratifyingly sympathetic treatment from Customs officers, provided they can satisfy him that the cases of champagne are for a special private function. Any party will do. He could 'reasonably' expect to get away with 100 bottles. The officer will base his judgement on what the individual might need for a one-off, while always on the look-out for the fast-talking wholesaler who plans to sell the lot when he gets home. (Excise duty is still payable on goods imported for re-sale. Auchan's cheapest champagne costs 45f and is often better quality than the British cheapos at £4 more a bottle.

Generally unpretentious French country red wines will save between £1.50 and £2 a bottle. Look for wines from the Rhône, like Côtes du Rhône at 90p (£2 more in UK) at Auchan, Beaujolais at £1 or petits châteaux from Bordeaux at £1.10. Don't bother with the most popular Bordeaux brand, Mouton Cadet – it's cheaper at home.

White wines are more difficult to assess – personally I would stick to red for the really cheap buys and pay a bit more for whites. You could still save £3 on Sancerre and Pouilly Fumé. Muscadet is always a popular choice with the Brits but don't make the mistake of economising on a cheap brand (either at home or abroad). A single-estate bottle 'sur lie' will save £2 bought in France.

To recap on where to buy these bargains in Boulogne:

Le Chais: open Tue-Sat 10-7, is a vast warehouse with easy parking and loading. To find it drive up the Bvd Danou and turn sharp left immediately after the railway bridge into the rue des Deux Ponts. In normal times the owner, Guy Vanikout, is exceptionally friendly and informative and encourages tastings. How he is coping with the recent bonanza I cannot say. He has an excellent range of wines in all price brackets.

Auchan is the nearest hypermarché, at St. Martin, 8 kms out on the RN42. Open Mon-Sat 8.30-10 p.m.

The nearest to our idea of a wine merchant is **Vins de France** near the town centre, 4, rue de Lille, open Tue-Sat. 8.30-12.30 and Tues-Sat 3-7.15.

I can't help adding that my choice for Hotel of the Year for FE7 was the Château de Cocove at Recques-sur-Hem, near Calais, which is now being lionized as the best independent wine merchant in the area. If you prefer to taste your wines in comfort and buy assured hand-picked quality wines from all over France, I suggest a drive in that direction.

Enterprising British wine merchants aren't going to take all this potential loss to home sales lying down. A Battersea wine specialist, **the Grape Shop**, has been the first to stake a claim in Boulogne. The Grape Shop opened up in the rue Victor Hugo in early January, aiming to give better service to British customers than they might expect in the hypermarkets and to sell wines from the New World as well as from France. The Manager estimates that savings on UK prices will be between £1.50 and £3 a bottle on still and sparkling wines and £4 on malt whisky. Call him on 010.33.21.92.30 for more information. The Battersea number is 071.924.3638

NEW RECOMMENDATIONS

These are discoveries by readers or by myself that arrived too late for inclusion in the main text of the guide. They are a Lucky Dip assortment, without the usual checking, so any new reports based on personal experiences would be particularly welcome.

Amiens. *Aux As du Don* (R)M (Sue Robinson).
Restaurant Josephine (R)M
Arras *Ostel des 3 Luppars* (HR)M
La Rapière (HR)M (Glennis and John Weir)
Beauvais. Hotel Chenal (HR)M) (Ann and David Sutton)
Belle-Houllefort. *Mme de Montigny.* Ch.d'h. (Ann and David Sutton)
Beussent. *Regnis Lignier* (R)S (Roger Combs)
Blendecques.*Le St. Sébastien* (HR)S (P. Fenn)
Boulogne. *Le Fats Domino* (R)M-S (P. Fenn)
Chez Jules (R)M-S (P. Fenn)
Brimeux. *Les Trois Aigles* (HR)S (Dr. N. Kendall)
Le Crotoy. *Chez Gérard* (R)M (A. van Rose)
Équihen-Plage *Rest. Bouquet* (R)S (P. Fenn)
Fruges. *Cheval Noir* (R)S
Café du Centre (R)S
Hôtel Moderne (R)S
Houlle (nr. St. Omer). *Mme Poupart* (R)S
Lottinghen. *Auberge de la Mangerie* (R)S (P. Fenn)
Montreuil. *Hôtel des Remparts* (HR)M (Jane Pickering)
Les Hauts de Montreuil (R)M
Pas-en-Artois. *Hotel Poste* (HR)S
Picquigny (nr. Amiens). *Auberge de Picquigny* (HR)S
Pittefaux. *Auberge le Souverain Moulin* (R)S (P. Fenn)
Rue. *Le Lion d'Or* (HR)S (Several readers)
St. Josse. *Le Relais de St. Josse* (Dennis Osborn)
St Omer-en-Chaussée. *Auberge de Monceau* (R)S (Dennis Osborn)
St. Riquier. *Mme Thurotte* (Ch.d'h) (A. G. Mann)
St. Valéry-sur-Somme. *Guillaume le Conquérant* (R)M (Bob Smyth)
La Colonne de Bronze (HR)M
Le Touquet. *Les Deux Moineaux* (R)M (Charlotte Fenn)
Le Village Suisse R)M (Charlotte Fenn)
Hotel Red Fox (HR)M(Charlotte Fenn)
Tournehem-sur-Hem *Café de la Voute* (R)S (P.Fenn)
Wierre-Effroy. *Auberge de la Raterie* (HR)S (P. Fenn)

Wine Hints from Jancis Robinson and on Spirits from John Doxat

HOW TO READ A WINE LIST

Wine lists in France, just like their counterparts in British restaurants, can be confusing – and sometimes even terrifying, with the only affordable bottles hidden below a stack of great names at even greater prices. There are certain ground rules in their layout, however.

The most basic of wines made in France are called *vins de table*, and may well be listed under this heading, to differentiate them from wines with some sort of geographical designation, either *Appellation Contrôlée* (AC) or, slightly more lowly, *Vins de Qualité Supérieur* (VDQS). The 'house wine' in many French restaurants is of the simpler *vin de table* sort and may be described as Vin de la Maison, or Vin du Patron meaning 'our wine'. There are many branded table wines too, the sort that carry a brand name, and these should be listed under a special heading, *Vins de Marque*. There is also a newish breed of rather superior *vin de table* which is worth looking out for, and which may be listed under the heading *Vins de Table*, or the region where it was made, or under the general heading *Vins de Pays*. These are superior quality *vins de table* which are good enough to tag their provenance onto their name.

All other wines will usually be grouped under the heading of the region where they were made and, usually, split according to red wines (rouges) and whites (blancs). The following are the main wine regions of France, in the order in which they *usually* appear on a smart wine list (though there is, exasperatingly, no standard convention):

Champagne

Almost all champagne is dry, white and sparkling, and only the wines of the Champagne region in northern France may call their wines champagne. Other sparkling wines are Vins Mousseux, though they may boast on their label that they were made by the rigorous *méthode champenoise*.

Bordeaux

France's biggest and best-known region for top-quality dryish reds, wines that we call claret. Most of such wines are called Château This or Château That, which will vary from about 60 francs a bottle to the earth and then some. Bordeaux's great white wines are sweet (doux) dessert wines from Sauternes, though there are now some good value dry (sec) wines too.

Bourgogne

We call this small, highly-priced region Burgundy. Its dry whites such as Montrachet are the greatest in the world; its reds can be lovely scented, smooth liquids, though there are some highly-priced disappointments.

Beaujolais/Mâconnais

This is the region just south of Burgundy proper that can offer some less expensive versions of Burgundy's white wines from the vineyards round Mâcon and some easy-drinking, gulpable reds from the vineyards of the Beaujolais area. Drink all these wines young.

Rhône

Mainly red wines and generally very good value. The whites can be quirky and heavy, but there has been a run of extremely good vintages of the meaty or spicy reds.

Loire

France's other great river is best-known, rather neatly, for its white wines – all with lots of acidity and great with food. Most Loire wines are designed for early consumption.

Alsace

France's most overlooked wine region, perhaps because it is almost in Germany. Fragrant, dry whites named after the Germanic grape varieties from which they are made. (This practice, varietal naming, is still uncommon in France though it is gaining ground elsewhere throughout the wine world.)

Since French Entrée territory is so far from France's vine land, the visitor is offered a much more catholic selection of (French) wines than in wine regions further south. The French take chauvinism seriously and on a local scale. Remember that most dry white wines do not improve with age, so don't begrudge being asked to drink a very young vintage. Merely feel grateful that you can enjoy the wine while it's young and fresh. As for matching specific wines with food, I subscribe to the view that you should start by deciding what colour and weight you feel like drinking rather than following the choice dictated by the 'white with fish and red with meat' rule. If you want white with a rich meat dish, it makes sense to choose a full-bodied one such as white burgundy, while light-bodied, fairly tart reds like Beaujolais and Bourgueil make better fish partners than a rich Rhône would.

COMMON WINE TERMS – AN ALPHABETICAL GUIDE

The following are the words most likely to be encountered on labels and wine lists, with brief notes to help you towards the clues they give to what's inside the bottle.

Alsace – Wine region, see above.
Anjou – Loire source of lots of medium rosé and a bit of safe, unexciting dry white.
Appellation Contrôlée – France's top 20 per cent of wine, named after the area where it is made.
Barsac – Sweet white bordeaux. Part of Sauternes so all Barsac is Sauternes but not all Sauternes is Barsac.
Beaujolais – Light, juicy reds.
Beaune – Southern town in the Burgundy heartland. Any wine carrying this name alone will be expensive.
Blanc de Blancs – Sounds fancy but means very little. Literally, a white wine made of white grapes, unusual in a champagne but obvious in a still white.
Bordeaux – Wine region, see above.
Bourgogne – 'Burgundy', a wine region, see above.
Bourgueil (Pronounce 'Boor-gurr-yeh') – Light red from the middle Loire.
Brut – Extremely dry; applies particularly to sparkling wines.
Chablis – A much traduced name. True chablis (and the only sort of chablis you're likely to encounter in France) is steely-dry white burgundy from a village of the same name in the far north of the Burgundy region.
Champagne – Wine region, see above.
Château – Principally refers to Bordeaux wine estate, not necessarily possessing an actual château. Because of the prestige of "château", the title has become abused by dubious "phantom châteaux" labels for very ordinary wines: caveat emptor!
Châteauneuf-du-Pape – Full-bodied spicy red from the southern Rhône.
Chenin (Blanc) – The white grape of the Middle Loire, medium dry usually.
Corbières – Straiahtforward southern red.
Côte(s) de – 'Côte(s) de X' is usually better than a wine named simply 'X', as it means it comes from the (superior) hillsides above the lower ground of the X vineyards.
Coteaux de – Similar to 'Côte(s) de'.
Coteaux d'Ancenis – North Loire VDQS varietal whites. All dry except for Malvoisie.
Coteaux du Languedoc – Lightish southern red.
Coteaux du Layon – Small Middle Loire area producing some excellent but many unexciting medium dry whites.
Coteaux du Tricastin – Lightish version of Côtes-du-Rhône.

Côtes de Provence – Appellation for the dry white, herby red and, principally, dry pink wines of Provence in south-east France.
Côtes-du-Rhône – This big appellation with some new-style dry whites but mainly lightish spicy reds like Châteauneuf is usually good value.
Crozes-Hermitage – Convenient, earlier-maturing but still quite concentrated version of (almost always red) Hermitage.
Cru – Means 'growth' literally, Grand cru means 'great growth' and really rather good. *Cru classé* means that the growth has been officially classified as up to some definite scratch, and most of the world's best clarets are *crus classés.*
Demi-Sec – Literally, medium dry; more likely to mean sweet.
Domaine – Wine estate in Burgundy.
Doux – Sweet.
Entre-Deux Mers – Dry, and rarely exciting, white from Bordeaux.
Fleurie – Single-village beaujolais; superior.
Frappé – Served on crushed ice; e.g. *crème de menthe frappé.*
Gaillac – Inexpensive white and sometimes red from southwest France.
Glacé – Chilled; not the same as *frappé.*
Graves – Red and usually-dry white from a good-value area of Bordeaux.
Gewürztraminer – Perfumed grape grown in Alsace to produce France's most easily-recognisable white wine.
Haut – High or upper; topographical term. It happens that Haut-Médoc produces finer wine than the region's lower vineyards.
Hautes-Côtes de Beaune or Nuits – Affordable red and white burgundy from the slopes, high in altitude but not, for once, necessarily quality.
Hermitage – Long lived tannic red from the northern Rhône.
Juliénas – Single-village beaujolais; superior.
Kir – Chilled dry white wine poured on to a little *crème de cassis* (q.v.). Splendid aperitif. Also Kir *royale* – made with champagne!
Loire – Wine region, see above.
Mâcon – Southern end of Burgundy, source of good-value whites and some unexciting reds.
Margaux – Médoc village producing scented clarets.
méthode champenoise – The Champagne region's way of putting bubbles into wine and usually the sign of a good one.
Meursault – Very respectable burgundy, almost all white.
Minervois – Better-than-average southern red.
mis(e) en bouteilles au château – Bottled at the Château (as opposed to in some merchant's cellars) and usually a sign of quality.
Moelleux – Medium sweet.
Monbazillac – Good-value country cousin to Sauternes.
Montrachet – Very great white burgundy.
Moulin-à-Vent – Single-village beaujolais which, unusually, can be kept.

Mousseux – Sparkling.

Mouton-Cadet – Not a special property, but a commercial blend of claret.

Muscadet – Lean, dry white from the mouth of the Loire. Very tart.

Muscat – The grape whose wines, unusually, taste and smell grapey. Dry in Alsace; very sweet and strong from places like Rivesaltes, Frontignan and Beaumes de Venise.

Nouveau – "New" wine; see *primeur* (the more technical term) – popularised by Beaujolais shippers. Other regions have copied what some experts consider overrated fad.

Nuits-St-Georges – Burgundy's second wine town. Bottles carrying this name are often expensive.

Pauillac – Bordeaux's most famous village, containing three of the five top châteaux. Very aristocratic claret.

Pétillant – Slightly sparkling wine.

Pineau – Unfermented grape juice fortified with grape alcohol: chilled, an interesting aperitif drink. *Pineau des Charentes* best-known.

Pomerol – Soft, fruity claret. Similar to St Emilion.

Pommard – Soft, fruity red burgundy.

Pouilly-Fuissé – Famous appellation in the Mâcon region. Dry, white and sometimes overpriced.

Pouilly-Fumé – Much tarter than Pouilly-Fuissé, made from the Sauvignon grape (see below) in Loire.

Premières Côtes de Bordeaux – Inexpensive red and sweet white bordeaux.

Primeur – Wine designed to be drunk within months of the vintage e.g. from November till Easter. Beaujolais Nouveau is a 'Primeur'.

*Puligny-Montrache*t – Steely white burgundy and often very good.

Riesling – Germany's famous grape produces great dry wine in Alsace.

Ste-Croix-du-Mont – Inexpensive sweet white bordeaux.

St Emilion – Soft, early-maturing claret from many little properties, most of which seem to be allowed to call themselves *crus classés.*

St Estèphe – Sometimes rather hard but noble claret.

St Julien – Another Médoc village housing many great châteaux.

Sancerre – Twin village to the Pouilly of Pouilly Fumé, and producing very similar wines.

Santenay – Light red burgundy.

Saumur – Town in the middle Loire giving its name to wines of all colours, degrees of sweetness and some very good sparkling wine too.

Sauvignon – Grape producing dry whites with lots of 'bite'.

Savigny-lés-Beaune – Village just outside Beaune responsible for some good-value 'proper' red burgundy.

Sec – Literally "dry", but don't be fooled – usually a sweetish wine.

Supérieur(e) – as Haut (above), and not a qualitative term, an exception being in VDQS (q.v.).

Sylvaner – Alsace's 'everyday' light, dry white. Often the best wine you can buy by the glass in a French bar.
Touraine – An area in the middle Loire producing inexpensive Sauvignon and other wines.
VDQS – Vin Delimite de Qualite Supérieure (see above) between AC and Vins de Pays.
Vin de Pays – Quality level at the top end of table wine. Many good-value inexpensive reds and some whites stating their region of origin on the label.
Vin de Pays des Marches de Bretagne – The only wine with an obviously Breton name. Light, tartish, usually white.
Vin de Table – The most basic sort of wine made in France. Very few excitements in this category. The blends with the name of a Burgundy merchant on the label are usually the most expensive.
Volnay – Soft red burgundy.
Xérès – ("ereth"): *vin de Xérès* = sherry.

HINTS ON SPIRITS FROM JOHN DOXAT

The great French spirit is brandy. Cognac, commercially the leader, must come from the closely controlled region of that name. Of various quality designations, the commonest is VSOP (very special old pale): it will be a cognac worth drinking neat. Remember, *champagne* in a cognac connotation has absolutely no connection with the wine. It is a topographical term, *grande champagne* being the most prestigious cognac area: fine champagne is a blend of brandy from the two top cognac sub-divisions.

Armagnac has become better known lately outside France, and rightly so. As a brandy it has a much longer history than cognac: some connoisseurs rate old armagnac (the quality designations are roughly similar) above cognac.

Be cautious of French brandy without a cognac or armagnac title, regardless of how many meaningless "stars" the label carries or even the magic word "Napoleon" (which has no legal significance).

Little appreciated in Britain is the splendid "apple brandy", Calvados, mainly associated with Normandy but also made in Brittany and the Marne. The best is Calvados *du Pays d'Auge*. Do taste well aged Calvados, but avoid any suspiciously cheap.

Contrary to popular belief, true Calvados is not distilled from cider- but an inferior imitation is: French cider (*cidre*) is excellent.

Though most French proprietary aperitifs, like Dubonnet, are fairly low in alcohol, the extremely popular Pernod/ Ricard *pastis*-style brands are highly spirituous. *Eau-de-vie* is the generic term for all spirits, but colloquially tends to refer to, often rough, local distillates. An exception are the better *alcools blancs* (white spirits), which are not inexpensive, made from fresh fruits and not sweetened as *crèmes* are.

Liqueurs

Numerous travellers deem it worth allocating their allowance to bring back some of the famous French liqueurs (Bénédictine, Chartreuse, Cointreau, and so on) which are so costly in Britain. Compare "duty free" prices with those in stores, which can vary markedly. There is a plethora of regional liqueurs, and numerous sickly *crèmes*, interesting to taste locally. The only *crème* generally meriting serious consideration as a liqueur is *crème de menthe* (preferably Cusenier), though the newish *crème de Grand Marnier* has been successful . *Crème de cassis* has a special function: see Kir in alphabetical list.

Glossary of cooking terms and dishes

(It would take another book to list comprehensively French cooking terms and dishes, but here are the ones most likely to be encountered.)

Aigre-doux	bittersweet
Aiguillette	thin slice (*aiguille* – needle)
Aile	wing
Aiolli	garlic mayonnaise
Allemande (à l')	German style, i.e.: with sausages and sauerkraut
Amuse-gueules	appetisers
Anglaise (à l')	plain boiled. *Crème Anglaise* – egg and cream sauce
Andouille	large uncooked sausage, served cold after boiling
Andouillettes	ditto but made from smaller intestines, usually served hot after grilling
Anis	aniseed
Argenteuil	with asparagus
Assiette Anglaise	plate of cold meats
Baba au rhum	yeast-based sponge macerated in rum
Baguette	long, thin loaf
Ballotine	boned, stuffed and rolled meat or poultry, usually cold
Béarnaise	sauce made from egg yolks, butter, tarragon, wine, shallots
Beurre blanc	sauce from Nantes, with butter, reduction of shallot-flavoured vinegar or wine
Béchamel	white sauce flavoured with infusion of herbs
Beignets	fritters
Bercy	sauce with white wine and shallots
Beurre noir	browned butter
Bigarade	with oranges
Billy By	mussel soup
Bisque	creamy shellfish soup
Blanquette	stew with thick, white creamy sauce, usually veal
Boeuf à la mode	braised beef
Bombe	ice-cream mould
Bonne femme	with root vegetables
Bordelais	Bordeaux-style, with red or white wine, marrowbone fat
Bouchée	mouthful, e.g. vol-au-vent
Boudin	sausage, white or black
Bourride	thick fish-soup
Braisé	braised
Court-bouillon	aromatic liquor for cooking meat, fish, vegetables
Couscous	N. African dish with millet, chicken, vegetable variations
Brandade (de morue	dried salt-cod pounded into a mousse
Broche	spit
Brochette	skewer
Brouillade	stew, using oil
Brouillé	scrambled
Brûlé	burnt, e.g. *crême brûlée*
Campagne	country style
Cannelle	cinnamon
Carbonnade	braised in beer
Cardinal	red-coloured sauce, e.g. with lobster, or in *pâtisserie* with redcurrant
Cassolette or *cassoulette*	small pan
Cassoulet	rich stew with goose, pork and haricot beans
Cervelas	pork garlic sausage
Cervelles	brains
Chantilly	whipped sweetened cream
Charcuterie	cold pork-butcher's meats
Charlotte	mould, as dessert lined with sponge-fingers, as savoury lined with vegetable
Chasseur	with mushrooms, shallots, wine
Chausson	pastry turnover
Chemise	covering, i.e. pastry
Chiffonade	thinly-cut, e.g. lettuce
Choron	tomato Béarnaise
Choucroute	Alsatian stew with sauerkraut and sausages
Civet	stew
Clafoutis	batter dessert, usually with cherries
Clamart	with peas
Cocotte	covered casserole
Cocque (à la)	e.g. *oeufs* – boiled eggs
Compôte	cooked fruit
Concassé	e.g. *tomates concassées* – skinned, chopped, juice extracted
Confit	preserved
Confiture	jam
Consommé	clear soup
Cou	neck
Coulis	juice, purée (of vegetables or fruit)
Galette	Breton pancake, flat cake
Garbure	thick country soup
Garni	garnished, usually with vegetables

Crapaudine	involving fowl, particularly pigeon, trussed
Crécy	with carrots
Crème pâtissière	thick custard filling
Crêpe	pancake
Crépinette	little flat sausage, encased in caul
Croque-Monsieur	toasted cheese-and-ham sandwich
Croustade	pastry or baked bread shell
Croûte	pastry crust
Croûton	cube of fried or toasted bread
Cru	raw
Crudités	raw vegetables
Demi-glâce	basic brown sauce
Doria	with cucumber
Émincé	thinly sliced
Étuvé	stewed, e.g. vegetables in butter
Entremets	sweets
Farci	stuffed
Fines herbes	parsley, thyme, bayleaf
Feuilleté	leaves of flaky pastry
Flamande	Flemish style, with beer
Flambé	flamed in spirit
Flamiche	flan
Florentine	with spinach
Flûte	thinnest bread loaf
Foie gras	goose liver
Fondu	melted
Fond (d'artichaut)	heart (of artichoke)
Forestière	with mushrooms, bacon and potatoes
Four (au)	baked in the oven
Fourré	stuffed, usually sweets
Fricandeau	veal, usually topside
Frais, fraîche	fresh and cool
Frangipane	almond-cream *pâtisserie*
Fricadelle	Swedish meat ball
Fricassé	(usually of veal) in creamy sauce
Frit	fried
Frites	chips
Friture	assorted small fish, fried in batter
Froid	cold
Fumé	smoked
Galantine	loaf-shaped chopped meat, fish or vegetable, set in natural jelly
Gaufre	waffle
Gelée	aspic
Gésier	gizzard
Gibier	game
Gigot	leg
Glacé	iced
Gougère	choux pastry, large base
Goujons	fried strips, usually of fish
Graine	seed
Gratin	baked dish of vegetables cooked in cream and eggs
Gratinée	browned under grill
Grecque (à la)	cold vegetables served in oil
Grenadin	nugget of meat, usually of veal
Grenouilles	frogs; *cuisses de grenouille* – frogs' legs
Grillé	grilled
Gros sel	coarse salt
Hachis	minced or chopped
Haricot	slow cooked stew
Hochepot	hotpot
Hollandaise	sauce with egg, butter, lemon
Hongroise	Hungarian, i.e. spiced with paprika
Hors-d'oeuvre	assorted starters
Huile	oil
Île flottante	floating island – soft meringue on egg-custard sauce
Indienne	Indian, i.e. with hot spices
Jambon	ham
Jardinière	from the garden, i.e. with vegetables
Jarret	shin, e.g. *jarret de veau*
Julienne	matchstick vegetables
Jus	natural juice
Lait	milk
Langue	tongue
Lard	bacon
Longe	loin
Macédoine	diced fruits or vegetables
Madeleine	small sponge cake
Magret	breast (of duck)
Maïs	sweetcorn
Maître d'hôtel	sauce with butter, lemon, parsley
Marchand de vin	sauce with red wine, shallots
Marengo	sauce with tomatoes, olive oil, white wine
Marinière	seamens' style e.g. *moules marinière* (mussels in white wine)
Marmite	deep casserole
Matelote	fish stew, e.g. of eel
Pot-au-four	broth with meat and vegetables
Potée	country soup with cabbage
Pralines	caramelised almonds
Primeurs	young veg

Médaillon	round slice
Melange	mixture
Meunière	sauce with butter, lemon
Miel	honey
Mille-feuille	flaky pastry, (lit. 1,000 leaves)
Mirepoix	cubed carrot, onion etc. used for sauces
Moëlle	beef marrow
Mornay	cheese sauce
Mouclade	mussel stew
Mousseline	Hollandaise sauce, lightened with egg whites
Moutarde	mustard
Nage (à la)	poached in flavoured liquor (fish)
Nature	plain
Navarin (d'agneau)	stew of lamb with spring vegetables
Noisette	nut-brown, burned butter
Noix de veau	nut (leg) of veal
Normande	Normandy style, i.e. with cream, apple, cider, Calvados
Nouilles	noodles
Onglet	beef cut from flank
Os	bone
Paillettes	straws (of pastry)
Panaché	mixed
Panade	flour crust
Papillote (en)	cooked in paper case
Parmentier	with potatoes
Pâté	paste, of meat or fish
Pâte	pastry
Pâté brisée	rich short-crust pastry
Pâtisserie	pastries
Paupiettes	paper-thinslice
Pavé	thick slice
Paysan	country style
Périgueux	with truffles
Persillade	chopped parsley and garlic topping
Petits fours	tiny cakes, sweetmeats
Petit pain	bread roll
Piperade	peppers, onions, tomatoes in scrambled egg
Poché	poached
Poêlé	fried
Poitrine	breast
Poivre	pepper
Pommade	paste
Potage	thick soup
Saucisse	fresh sausage
Saucisson	dried sausage
Sauté	cooked in fat in open pan
Sauvage	wild
Savarin	ring of yeast-sponge, soaked in syrup and liquor
Sel	salt
Printanier (printanière)	garnished with early vegetables
Profiteroles	choux paslry balls
Provençale	with garlic, tomatoes, olive oil, peppers
Pureé	mashed and sieved
Quenelle	pounded fish or meat bound with egg, poached
Queue	tail
Quiche	pastry flan, e.g. *quiche Lorraine* – egg, bacon, cream
Râble	saddle, e.g. *râble de lièvre*
Ragoût	stew
Ramequin	little pot
Râpé	grated
Ratatouille	Provençale stew of onions, garlic, peppers, tomatoes
Ravigote	highly seasoned white sauce
Rémoulade	mayonnaise with gherkins, capers, herbs and shallots
Rillettes	potted shredded meat, usually fat pork or goose
Riz	rice
Robert	sauce with mustard, vinegar, onion
Roquefort	ewe's milk blue cheese
Rossini	garnished with foie gras and truffle
Rôti	roast
Rouelle	nugget
Rouille	hot garlicky sauce for *soupe* de *poisson*
Roulade	roll
Roux	sauce base – flour and butter
Sabayon	sweet fluffy sauce, with eggs and wine
Safran	saffron
Sagou	sago
St-Germain	with peas
Salade niçoise	with tunny, anchovies, tomatoes, beans, black olives
Salé	salted
Salmis	dish of game or fowl, with red wine
Sang	blood
Santé	lit. healthy, i.e. with spinach and potato
Salpicon	meat, fowl, vegetables, chopped fine, bound with sauce and used as fillings
Thé	tea
Tiède	luke warm
Timbale	steamed mould
Tisane	infusion
Tourte	pie
Tranche	thick slice
Truffes	truffles

Selle	saddle	*Tuile*	tile, i.e. thin biscuit
Selon	according to, e.g. *selon grosseur* (according to size)	*Vacherin*	meringue confection
Smitane	with sour cream, white wine, onion	*Vallée d'Auge*	with cream, apple, Calvados
		Vapeur (au)	steamed
Soissons	with dried white beans	*Velouté*	white sauce, bouillon-flavoured
Sorbet	water ice		
Soubise	with creamed onions	*Véronique*	with grapes
Soufflé	puffed, i.e. mixed with egg white and baked	*Vert(e)*	green, e.g. *sauce verte*, with herbs
Sucre	sugar (*sucré* – sugared)	*Vessie*	pig's bladder
Suprême	fillet of poultry breast or fish	*Vichysoise*	chilled creamy leek and potato soup
Tartare	raw minced beef, flavoured with onions etc. and bound with raw egg	*Vierge*	prime olive oil
		Vinaigre	vinegar (lit. bitter wine)
		Vinaigrette	wine vinegar and oil dressing
Tartare (sauce)	mayonnaise with capers, herbs, onions	*Volaille*	poultry
		Vol-au-vent	puff-pastry case
Tarte Tatin	upside down apple pie		
Terrine	pottery dish/baked minced, chopped meat, veg., chicken, fish or fruit	*Xérès*	sherry
		Yaourt	yoghurt

FISH – Les Poissons, SHELLFISH – Les Coquillages

Alose	shad	*Daurade*	sea bream
Anchois	anchovy	*Écrevisse*	crayfish
Anguille	eel	*Éperlan*	smelt
Araignée de mer	spider crab	*Espadon*	swordfish
		Étrille	baby crab
Bar	sea bass	*Favouille*	spider crab
Barbue	brill	*Flétan*	halibut
Baudroie	monkfish, anglerfish	*Fruits de mer*	seafood
Belon	oyster – flat shelled	*Grondin*	red gurnet
Bigorneau	winkle	*Hareng*	herring
Blanchaille	whitebait	*Homard*	lobster
Brochet	pike	*Huître*	oyster
Cabillaud	cod	*Julienne*	ling
Calamar	squid	*Laitance*	soft herring-roe
Carpe	carp	*Lamproie*	lamprey
Carrelet	plaice	*Langouste*	spring lobster, or crawfish
Chapon de mer	scorpion fish	*Langoustine*	Dublin Bay prawn
Claire	oyster	*Lieu*	ling
Coquille St-Jacques	scallop	*Limand*	lemon sole
		Lotte de mer	monkfish
Crabe	crab	*Loup de mer*	sea bass
Crevette grise	shrimp	*Maquereau*	mackerel
Crevette rose	prawn	*Merlan*	whiting
Morue	salt cod	*St-Pierre*	John Dory
Moule	mussel	*Sandre*	zander
Mulet	grey mullet	*Saumon*	salmon
Ombre	grayling	*Saumonette*	rock salmon
Oursin	sea urchin	*Seiche*	squid
Palourde	clam	*Sole*	sole
Pétoncle	small scallop	*Soupion*	inkfish
Plie	plaice	*Thon*	tunny
Portugaise	oyster	*Tortue*	turtle

Poulpe	octopus
Praire	oyster
Raie	skate
Rascasse	scorpion-fish
Rouget	red mullet
Torteau	large crab
Truite	trout
Turbot	turbot
Turbotin	chicken turbot

FRUITS – Les Fruits, VEGETABLES – Les Légumes, NUTS – Les Noix

HERBS – Les Herbes, SPICES – Les Épices

Ail	garlic
Algue	seaweed
Amande	almond
Ananas	pineapple
Aneth	dill
Abricot	apricot
Arachide	peanut
Artichaut	globe artichoke
Asperge	asparagus
Avocat	avocado
Banane	banana
Basilic	basil
Betterave	beetroot
Blette	Swiss chard
Brugnon	nectarine
Cassis	blackcurrant
Céléri	celery
Céléri-rave	celeriac
Cêpe	edible fungus
Cerfeuil	chervil
Cerise	cherry
Champignon	mushroom
Chanterelle	edible fungus
Châtaigne	chestnut
Chicorée	endive
Chou	cabbage
Chou-fleur	cauliflower
Choux de Bruxelles	Brussels sprouts
Ciboulette	chive
Citron	lemon
Citron vert	lime
Coing	quince
Concombre	cucumber
Coriandre	coriander
Cornichon	gherkin
Courge	pumpkin
Oseille	sorrel
Palmier	palm
Pamplemousse	grapefruit
Panais	parsnip
Passe-Pierre	seaweed
Pastèque	water melon
Peche	peach
Persil	parsley
Petit pois	pea
Piment doux	sweet pepper
Courgette	courgette
Cresson	watercress
Échalote	shallot
Endive	chicory
Épinard	spinach
Escarole	salad leaves
Estragon	tarragon
Fenouil	fennel
Fève	broad bean
Flageolet	dried bean
Fraise	strawberry
Framboise	raspberry
Genièvre	juniper
Gingembre	ginger
Girofle	clove
Girolle	edible fungus
Grenade	pomegranate
Griotte	bitter red cherry
Groseille	gooseberry
Groseille noire	blackcurrant
Groseille rouge	redcurrant
Haricot	dried white bean
Haricot vert	French bean
Laitue	lettuce
Mandarine	tangerine, mandarin
Mangetout	sugar pea
Marron	chestnut
Menthe	mint
Mirabelle	tiny gold plum
Morille	dark brown crinkly edioble fungus
Mûre	blackberry
Muscade	nutmeg
Myrtille	bilberry, blueberry
Navet	turnip
Noisette	hazelnut
Oignon	onion
Pomme	apple
Pomme de terre	potato
Prune	plum
Pruneau	prune
Quetsch	small dark plum
Radis	radish
Raifort	horseradish
Raisin	grape
Reine Claude	greengage
Romarin	rosemary

Pissenlit	dandelion	*Safran*	saffron
Pistache	pistachio	*Salsifis*	salsify
Pleurote	edible fungi	*Thym*	thyme
Poire	pear	*Tilleul*	lime blossom
Poireau	leek	*Tomate*	tomato
Poivre	pepper	*Topinambour*	Jerusalem artichoke
Poivron	green, red and yellow peppers	*Truffe*	truffle

MEAT – Les Viandes

Le Boeuf	Beef	*Le Porc*	Pork
Charolais	is the best	*Jambon*	ham
Chateaubriand	double fillet steak	*Jambon cru*	raw smoked ham
Contrefilet	sirloin	*Porcelet*	suckling pig
Entrecôte	rib steak		
Faux Filet	sirloin steak	*Le Veau*	Veal
Filet	fillet	*Escalope*	thin slice cut from fillet
L'Agneau	Lamb	*Les Abats*	Offal
Pré-Salé	is the best	*Foie*	liver
Carré	neck cutlets	*Foie gras*	goose liver
Côte	chump chop	*Cervelles*	brains
Epaule	shoulder	*Langue*	tongue
Gigot	leg	*Ris*	sweetbreads
		Rognons	kidneys
		Tripes	tripe

POULTRY – Volaille, GAME – Gibier

Abatis	giblets	*Lièvre*	hare
Bécasse	woodcock	*Oie*	goose
Bécassine	snipe	*Perdreau*	partridge
Caille	quail	*Pigeon*	pigeon
Canard	duck	*Pintade*	guineafowl
Caneton	duckling	*Pluvier*	plover
Chapon	capon	*Poularde*	chicken (boiling)
Chevreuil	roe deer	*Poulet*	chicken (roasting)
Dinde	young hen turkey	*Poussin*	spring chicken
Dindon	turkey	*Sanglier*	wild boar
Dindonneau	young turkey	*Sarcelle*	teal
Faisan	pheasant	*Venaison*	venison
Grive	thrush		

Other Entrée Guides

French Entrée 5	Brittany	£6.95
French Entrée 6	Coast to Capital – Boulogne, Pays d'Opal, Picardy	£6.95
French Entrée 8	The Loire	£6.95
French Entrée 9	Normandy Encore	£6.95
French Entrée 10	South of France	£6.95
French Entrée 11	Paris	£6.95
French Entrée 13	Provence	£6.95
Entrée to Malta		£6.95
Entrée to Mallorca		£6.95
Coming		
French Entrée 12	The North of France	£6.95
Entrée to the Algarve		£6.95

'She doesn't care what she says.' *Observer*

'Well worth looking through for anyone wonderlng where to spend the first (or last) nlght of a holiday in France.' *Country Life*

'Makes you want to drive down to Dover and onto a cross-Channel ferry right away.' *Sunday Telegraph*

'An excellent, evocative but crisp little guide to the neglected North of France.' *Good Book Guide*

'...a very objective and highly readable book for visitors to the three ports of Calais Le Havre, Cherbourg and their environs.' *Autosport*

'Can there be an auberge or dockside café that Ms Fenn has failed to report on?' *Books and Bookmen*

'Patricia Fenn's immensely reliable guides to the places to eat and sleep need no recommendation to anyone who has used them.' *Evening Standard*

'Time and again she has got to good places and chefs before the news reached Michelin or Gault-et-Millau.' *Guardian*

'Lively, humorous and above all immensely readable.' *Country Life*

'Makes you want to dash across on the ferry immediately.' *Good housekeeping*

In preparation:
FRENCH ENTRÉE 14 Dordogne
ENTRÉE TO TUSCANY and many others

Also published by Quiller Press

– two companions to French Entrée to help you enjoy your holiday more.

LEGAL BEAGLE GOES TO FRANCE
Bill Thomas £3.95
All you need to deal with problems involving the law in France – accidents, houses, travel – even births and deaths. Includes: legal and customs formalities; daily life in France; eating, sleeping and drinking; en route; getting around without a car; renting a gîlte and buying a house.

SPAIN BY CAR
Norman Renouf £7.95
The essential guide to food and accommodation for all motorists in Spain. Objective information and photographs of over 650 hotels, guest houses, motels and hostels along the main roads.

WALES – A GOOD EATING GUIDE
Roger Thomas £5.95
A guide for tourists and locals alike, to nearly 300 restaurants and shops recommended for typically Welsh food. Inside information on where to eat in Wales, with a map and 40 line drawings.

INVITATION TO DEVON
Joy David £6.95
Places to visit, eat and sleep throughout the county, by a devoted Devonian. With over 100 line drawings.

EVERYBODY'S HISTORIC LONDON
Jonathan Kiek £6.95
Historian and teacher Jonathan Kiek's award-winning guide to London is now in its fourth edition. 60 photographs, maps and plans complement background history and up-to-date practical information.

EVERYBODY'S HISTORIC ENGLAND
Jonathan Kiek £6.95
Much-praised combination of popular history and carefully thought-out tours of the whole of England – required reading for all travellers who enjoy our national heritage.

Please order from your bookshop or, in case of difficulty, write with payment to:
Quiller Press, 46 Lillie Road, London SW6 1TN.

Notes